PRAISE FOR

How To Manage Your
DICK*

*Destructive Impulses with Cyber-Kinetics

Redirect Sexual Energy and Discover Your
More Spiritually Enlightened, Evolved Self

"It's bold, it's brazen, it's provocative. And that is just the title."
—*Publishers Weekly*

"…more than just a quirky title; it's a heartfelt and remarkably comprehensive manifesto, drawing on wisdoms from East and West, about how not to behave like an absolute jerk."
—Anneli Rufus, author of *Magnificent Corpses*

"Destined to be a classic…you need to read this book."
—David Rothenberg, author, *Is It Painful to Think?*
editor, *Terra Nova*

"If a few hundred guys throughout history would have had the benefit of Dick Management, the world would be a much better place."
—Thom Elkjer, author and playwright

"Magnificent!"
—David Yeadon, author of *The Way of the Wanderer*

"Sigmund Freud was wrong on a lot of things, but he was right on this one—genitalia are at the root of the most important passions. Sexuality is the indispensable home plate of the human soul."
—Howard Bloom, author of *The Lucifer Principle: A Scientific Expedition into the Forces of History,* and *Global Brain: The Evolution of Mass Mind from the Big Bang to the 21st Century*

How To Manage Your

DICK*

*Destructive Impulses with Cyber-Kinetics

Redirect Sexual Energy and Discover Your More Spiritually Enlightened, Evolved Self

How To Manage Your
DICK*

*Destructive Impulses with Cyber-Kinetics

Redirect Sexual Energy and Discover Your
More Spiritually Enlightened, Evolved Self

BY
SEAN JOSEPH O'REILLY

The Auriga Publishing Group
Maryland

Published by The Auriga Publishing Group
An imprint of Auriga Limited
A Maryland Corporation
www.dickmanagement.com

Distributed by Ten Speed Press
P.O. Box 7123
Berkeley CA 94707
510-559-1600
Toll Free Ordering 1-800-841-2665

Cover image by Mark Matcho
Cover design by Archer-Ellison
Interior design and page composition by Cynthia Lamb

ISBN: 1580083501

Non Fiction
Category: New Age, Self Help

Printed in the Canada by Webcom Limited
1-800-665-9322

For Beatrice and Bert Hernady, who died on the Way.

TABLE OF CONTENTS

PART III
CIVILIZATION: PUBLIC VERSUS PUBIC POLICY

B . A . B O O N E

INTRODUCTION

How to Manage Your Dick is one of the most unusual books you will ever read. It is also one of the most important. It is a book about self-discovery, and what it means to be a man—a serious book that deals humorously, and with a unique and brutal honesty, about a subject desperately in need of critical attention, but all too often left in the backwaters of the human mind. Sean O'Reilly has discovered the Holy Grail of philosophers, saints, sociologists and world leaders, a behavioral Theory of Everything which physicists have sought for generations, which psychologists and psychiatrists have tried to articulate since the days of Freud and Jung, and which philosophers have struggled to outline for millennia.

Politicians drone on about the decay of civilization and weak leadership; preachers wail about sin and moral decline; talk show hosts gibber salaciously about celebrity affairs, divorce, wife-beating and graffiti; concerned parents mutter about lewd TV shows, pornography on the Internet, guns and drugs in schools, and assaults on teachers; world leaders mutter, "we must do something" about violence in the Balkans, Africa, Sri Lanka, and the Middle East; op-ed writers snarl about sodomy in the prisons and road rage, but O'Reilly, a former seminarian and prison instructor, tells us what all these problems have in common. He tells us how they relate to Aristotle and Thomas Aquinas, Einstein and Stephen Hawking, Jesus and the Dalai Lama. And in this marvelous book, with an extraordinary talent for fusing filth with metaphysics, marrying obscenity with virtue, O'Reilly articulates their common solution: Dick Management.

You will learn how the angle of your dangle is connected to collapsed quantum waves, how your dog nature can be turned to moral advantage, how your basest desires can be surfed without corroding you or those around you, how the veneration of women, children, and the natural world is the highest purpose of your Dick, which you will learn has more than one meaning.

Your Dick is the elephant in the room which everyone denies, the Emperor with no clothes, the Dog with no Master. Can anyone pretend that the world's chronic problems, from murder and rape, pillage and war, assault and insult, graffiti and torture, child molesting and domestic abuse, are not in the main caused by men? Only a fool will deny that men are the scourge of the world, they fill the world's prisons, they are the Beast waiting to tear apart your world, rip you limb from limb, set your house on fire, and shit on the ashes. They are Stalin and Hitler, Charles Manson and Saddam Hussein, Jeffrey Dahmer and Pol Pot, Ted Bundy, Idi Amin, and ten thousand nameless demons. They are you and they are I.

But your Dick, as Sean O'Reilly tells us, can also be your baton of bounty, your dowsing-rod to the waters of life, your pointer to true happiness, your Obi-Wan Kenobi who will outlive the Darth Vader lurking in your underwear. In *How to Manage Your DICK*, you will learn that "Your ASS Is Behind Your Dick," you will see how "Ancient Dick Technologies Meet Modern Physics," and learn how to "Negotiate with Your Johnson." You will take the PECER test and you will see where you place on the "Gandhi-Hitler Index." You will cringe as you see yourself in "Portrait of a Creep" but you will also be inspired as you read "How a Real Man Behaves" and the "Management Tips" that follow the chapters. You will quickly come to agree that the cultivation of cyber-kinetic knowledge, or what has traditionally been called virtue is the missing link between the destructive impulses of evolutionary biology and the achievement of excellence as a human being. You will rediscover the ancient wheel of common sense as you read about the rewards of virtue and continence as they apply to everyday activities such as driving and putting up toilet seats.

You will want all the women in your life to read this book because "Every Woman Is a Dick Manager." You will want the young men and teenage boys you know to possess this gift of truth, and the young women and teenage girls to fully understand the power that is theirs not only to bring life into the world but to encourage the men in their lives to be the heroes they secretly yearn to become.

So my friends, come with me and explore the world of your Dick, and become the Manager—the Man—you have always wanted to be.

B.A. Boone is a writer who lives in Northern California with his family.

Both art and virtue are concerned with what is harder.

—ARISTOTLE

PART I

THE THING BEHIND YOUR DICK

CHAPTER 1

THE WORLD NEEDS DICK MANAGEMENT

Art, like morality, consists in drawing the line somewhere.

–G.K. Chesterton

EACH MAN WHO HAS A DICK AND EVERY WOMAN WHO LOVES HIM AND must deal with him, think they know enough to use the equipment properly, without an instruction manual. The dick appears to be user friendly—no need to learn how it works, what it should be doing or what it should not be doing. You assume that your dick will find its own way in the world. It is, after all, not a shy organ, nor an overly complicated one, and it certainly seems to have a simple enough agenda. you just use it whenever and wherever the urge takes you. What could be simpler?

Now, imagine getting into a new car that didn't have a steering wheel, brakes or a fuel gauge. If a sales person presented this to you as a complete automobile, you would think he or she was insane. Your dick is just like that—it comes without steering, brakes or a fuel gauge. These are accessories that you must personally add to your rod in order to increase its usefulness. If you don't learn how to steer and stop, and monitor your rod's fuel consumption, you won't be able to take much of a quality trip down this road we call life.

Let us step outside of the car and driver analogy and look at your dick more closely. Your dick has a dark side, a serious history that has, give or take a few millennia, three million years of evolution behind it. Yes, Mr. Dick and his girlfriends got us here, but he is also part of a biological survival system that has been associated with a history of looting, pillage, rape, torture, assault, and every form of socially destructive behavior imaginable. I'm going to make the case that these are the inevitable results of untutored, testosterone-laden dicks going about their business—cars running amok if you will—without drivers. You don't need to look very far to see the evidence. Perhaps you saw it on the bus this morning, as a teenager surreptitiously spat on a senior citizen, or in artless graffiti tagging on fences and walls, or in a newspaper report about spousal abuse, or when someone gave you the finger on the freeway because you didn't get out of the way quickly enough.

Your dick might also be thought of as a heat-seeking missile, and it has one simple target: a warm place to explode. But like all missiles, it needs a well-trained fire control officer. Properly guided, your dick can lead the way to love, happiness, family and fulfillment. Unguided, it can lead you to depression, divorce, illness, violence and even death. An untutored dick is a dangerous dick—ask any woman—but there are countless men who have mastered their organs and led inspirational lives. This book presents ideas about energy, moral development, and sexual management from many different cultures and philosophies that will help you become such a man. These ideas, put into practice, will enhance your moral and social consciousness and show you how to have more energy to become who you really are.

WHAT IS DICK MANAGEMENT?

In our society we appreciate and teach concepts such as time management, resource management, cash flow management, personnel management and information management systems, but for the most part we ignore the most important kind of management of all—Dick Management.

Dick Management is an ecology of personal energy use that studies destructive impulses from the perspective of philosophy and science. It is a new discipline that integrates the metaphysical wisdom of the ancients, from Socrates to Lao Tzu, from Christ to Gandhi, with the discoveries and implications of post-quantum physics for meaning in our lives, and applies it to our most primitive biological urges.

Dick Management is about discovering what truly works for you and your dick: discovering your own personal life ethic. It is not about simply saying "no" or strictly controlling your desires, but rather, about saying "yes" to something larger than the tunnel vision of the Cyclops in your pants. Managing your dick is about making good choices about how you use your energy, about making compromises between what you want in the short term, and what you really desire in the long run. More importantly, it is about discovering who you really are and finding your place in the universe. Managing your dick is the beginning of a long journey toward your own future, and ultimately, an encounter with your soul.

One day the Lord came to Adam to pass on some news. "I've got some good news and some bad news," the Lord said. Adam looked at the Lord and said, "Well, give me the good news first." Smiling, the Lord explained, "I've got two new organs for you, one is called a brain. It will allow you to be very intelligent, create new things, and have intelligent conversations with Eve. The other organ I have for you is called a penis. It will allow you to reproduce your now intelligent life form and populate this planet. Eve will be very happy that you now have this organ to give her Children." Adam, very excited, exclaimed, "These are great gifts you have given to me. What could possibly be bad news after such great tidings?" The good Lord looked upon Adam and said with great sorrow, "The bad news is that when I created you, I only gave you enough blood to operate one of these organs at a time."

—Anonymous

"Good Lord, Professor! There it goes—the theory of everything!"

MANAGEMENT TIPS

- Your will, your mind and your dick are part of an energy system that requires conservation.

- Your dick uses energy. You need to have a mental gauge or schematic to measure this energy use, otherwise, you won't know when you need to stop or refuel.

- Saying no to bad impulses is never enough. You must have good reasons to say no, and then you must have the tools to implement your wishes.

- Your will is a muscle. You have to work it to build it up.

- Sexuality is one of our most powerful drives. By learning to manage your sexual impulses, you will be better able to manage other problem impulses such as overeating, and tendencies towards fear and laziness.

CHAPTER 2

YOUR ASS IS BEHIND YOUR DICK

Men are qualified for civil liberty in exact proportion to their disposition to put moral chains upon their own appetites...It is ordained in the Eternal constitution of things, that men of intemperate minds cannot be free.

—Edmund Burke

"NOW HOLD ON A MINUTE!" YOU MAY BE SAYING, "I'M NOT EVEN SURE I want to manage my dick, let alone do I believe I have a soul." Well, bear with me a while as I share some basic thoughts about this mysterious thing called life. I think we can all agree that your dick has an awful lot of energy and your dick is connected to your body, which has even more energy, and there is something about your body that is present when you are alive, and not present when you are dead.

Have you ever seen someone die, literally take their last breath? If you have, no doubt you will have been impressed with the absence of what was there a moment before. Let's call it the *life force.* Your life force is connected with the rest of the universe, just as your dick is connected to your body. But just as your dick is not your body, your life force is not the universe. And just as you are not your dick, you (as in your personality) are not your soul. The thing you saw leave the dying body was the life force, an expression of that person's soul as it animated physical tissue. Your soul, sometimes called the *oversoul,* is the larger "you" that exists simultaneously in the now and beyond time, outside of the physical universe.

In other words, the life energy of this soul, that basic force that is expressing you through the unique packet of matter that constitutes your body, is a link to energy beyond your comprehension. Say that to yourself: *beyond my comprehension.* Who or what is running the chemical and biological activities of your body in such a way that you would not be able to fully describe its activity with 100 or 1,000 or 10,000 scientific books? This life force is engaged in extraordinary activities, whether you believe in a higher reality or not.

Do you remember when you were conceived? Most of us have no memory of this event, but what do you think was going on with that tiny speck of tissue shortly after your parents had a roll in the hay? How did all those billions of neurons and cells get hooked up and working in unison? When did you last calculate the sodium exchange rate between the main axons of your nervous system, or the semen production schedule of your testicles? Did you supervise the construction of your nose, arrange the color of your eyes, or design the shape of your backside? Clearly, there is a force or an innate intelligence at work that we have little conscious contact with.

To say that God or some evolutionary process is doing it is the easy way out. We have enormous energy and potential—possibly even before conception, and who or what is controlling that energy may hold the key to understanding the meaning of life. You want to be in touch with this mysterious source so that you can live life to the fullest.

TAKING A PEEK AT MORALITY

Every organism, according to the tenets of ecology, exists in a complex web of energy relationships. Ecology is the branch of science concerned with the interrelationship of organisms and their environment. Your instincts and urges are part of a hidden, interactive network that spans culture and biology. The purpose of Dick Management is to provide a road map of this network for the individual and for society; it is also an ecological ethic that helps provide a safety zone from the instinctive impulses and destructive actions that seem to be associated with male sexuality.

Unfortunately, there seems to be a blind spot in our society regarding the relationship between impulse management, sexuality and an entire gamut of potentially related social problems. Indeed, moral ethics, which concerns itself with such questions is thrown into the same relativist dustbin as religion. Whose morality, or whose religion will you use for standards of behavior? This question is used by many individuals to prematurely close the discussion. But morality of course is not religion, so it is important to have a definition that will return it to realm of public discourse.

Morality consists of making good or positive choices regarding your appetites.

Many of us have different ideas of what constitutes "good" but an analysis of how our appetites and urges work, in relation to this thing we are calling life force, goes a long way towards clarifying the many levels of what might be meant by the term "good choices."

Appetite is the first stage of an urge and represents a primordial expression of your life force. You could say that what you have an appetite for is the same as "desire" or "impulse" but "appetite" is a much better word. Appetite is how you begin to experience your desires, and in general is thought of in a positive way; for instance, we speak of a baby as having a good appetite.

Whatever we call them—appetites, urges, hungers, wants, needs, drives—they are the things that run us as biological creatures. Your personality is a filter for these appetites, which like actors at an audition, are constantly looking for a role in the theater of your life. You, the personnel director, must learn to screen them properly. In order to do this well, you need to learn more about these chameleons, which are constantly parading in front of you and begging for your undivided attention. The worst of these appetitive characters would have you believe that the show cannot go on without them. They are experts at overriding your common sense by appealing to your basic instincts, which are the lowest common denominator of your life force.

THE 4-F CLUB

You may be familiar with the 4H Club (health, hearth, happiness and home) but your strongest instincts are members of what is known as the 4F Club. These are life force instincts, which we share with other animals and they are part of our common biological inheritance for survival.

- Fighting
- Fucking
- Feeding
- Fleeing

The four F's comprise your life force's *Appetite Survival System*, or *ASS*, which is made up of your will and evolutionary layers of instincts and essential survival reflexes that are often at odds with the conventions of modern society. Your ASS's survival instincts are a reptilian legacy from millions of years of evolution. Fight, fuck, eat and run—that is what it does best. It seldom wants to do anything else. Freud called this irascible nightmare the "Id," while Nietzsche referred to it in a more elemental way, as the "will-to-power." Modern thinkers such as Howard Bloom have described it as the "Lucifer Principle," Ken Wilber as the "Fuck It/Kill It" urge and others describe it as the limbic or primitive ancestral brain. Your life force's ASS is a member of this primeval 4F Club!

YOUR LIFE FORCE HAS AN ASS

Let's sketch your ASS in some simple ways: You have just had some very satisfying sex with your spouse, and yet an hour later you find yourself eyeing the backside of a shapely female who is not your wife. Maybe you saw some strapping young men misbehaving recently—perhaps vandalizing property—and your impulse was to walk the other way. How much thinking have you done in these or similar circumstances? You haven't had to think—your ASS has simply acted for you, without the mediation of thinking, feeling or reflecting. It goes almost without saying that under the right circumstances, these can be welcome attributes of your Appetite Survival System, but you have to be on guard against this automatic piloting feature lest you end up acting like an animal.

Think about the last time you felt the urge to strike someone. Wouldn't it have been wonderful if your fist could have connected with a smirking face or your foot with the backside of an unhelpful bureaucrat, an insufferable salesperson or a rude waiter? If you'd had a gun, wouldn't it have been fun to shoot out the tires of the guy who cut you off in traffic and flipped you off when you honked your horn? Many have fantasized about such things.

Your Appetite Survival System is also your best defender. Recall, if you will, the last time you had to jump out of the way of a speeding car or truck. You might have been walking slowly across the street when suddenly, you saw out of your peripheral vision a hurtling object. Do you remember how quickly you leapt out of the way—without having to think? Offensively and defensively, your life force's Appetite Survival System is always on duty, instinctively reacting to danger, urging you to use your genitals at every opportunity, fill your stomach to ward off lean times, escape, and in general, scramble to the top of the heap.

There is, of course, a time and a place for everything. There are times when one must fight, there is a time and a place for sex, there is a time to "pig out" and sometimes it is necessary to flee a bad situation. The 4F instincts only become a problem when they take over rational thought processes. Those who have not been trained to manage their instinctive appetites can sometimes lead truly decayed lives. A mastery of the 4F's, a training program for managing the impulses to fight, fuck, feed and flee is simply a requirement for modern civilization. These impulsive instincts and appetites—when unmanaged—can result in high murder rates, rampant teenage birthrates, flotillas of overweight human beings, and a vast increase in those who flee from every problem and effort without seeking either reasonable solutions or making a sufficient effort. Dick Management is based, in part, on the simple proposition that if you do not learn to manage your 4F instincts, they will manage you!

A positive feature of your Appetite Survival System is that it incorporates the 4F's and your will into a combination package that is very powerful. Together, your will and your ASS can help you to be a superb provider and succeed at business. You may invoke this dynamic duo when others need to be corrected or you need to discipline yourself. Are you being threatened or presented with a life-threatening situation? Your life force's Appetite Survival System is there to help you. An ASS that is managed by your will can be powerful protector, but an unmanaged ASS can be a thing of nightmares. This is because your Appetite Survival System has software problems associated with its on-off switch! Unfortunately the 4F Club does not provide either a manual or technical assistance when you find yourself unable to shut it off.

YOUR ASS HAS AN ORIGINAL FACTORY DEFECT

Much like your brain or your backside, your ASS has two parts or functions. It has instinctive appetites and it has a will. Human beings, unfortunately, come with an original factory defect, a *life force malfunction* if you will. Your appetites and your will are always on—they never shut off. They run like hidden software programs that may not be visible on your computer screen, but are running constantly in the background. These two programs are evolutionary survival mechanisms. Once you understand the two functions of your ASS, and this original factory defect, you will understand the difficulty that most human beings face every day. The constant background desire to engage the 4Fs takes on many different forms. Men may engage in hand-to-hand combat over trivialities, women may engage in aggressive social backstabbing, and others have to struggle with the desire for multiple sexual partners, the desire to overeat, and the inclination to avoid anything that is unpleasant. What part of laziness, for example, belongs to the desire to flee? One might also pose the same question in regards to overeating or what used to be called gluttony.

> Sex is the point of contact between man and nature, where morality and good intentions fall to primitive urges.
>
> ◆
>
> —Camille Paglia

Let's say, for example, that you are in a fast food restaurant. You have already eaten the Half Pounder and are feeling pleasantly full—suddenly you start to slobber at the thought of those fat-loaded fries. You find your hand reaching for your wallet almost as if it has a mind of its own and before you know it, you are stuffing your face with yet more food! The Appetite Survival System, just like your average carnivore, only knows that it may not eat tomorrow, so it must instinctively stuff itself today. You, on the other hand are not your ASS and can note this reaction taking place in the amphitheater of your senses. Send the animal back into its cage and put your wallet away. You may need to identify with your appetites when they serve you but only you can determine that. Do not allow your ASS to be the only speaker in the parliament of your thoughts.

Another example of this life force malfunction can involve the 4F instinct to flee, or the flight response, as it is sometimes called. This instinct seems to be enjoying a new vogue in the human populace. Casual divorce, post-suburban migration, indifference to crime, and abandonment of responsibility is, apparently, attractive to many of us. It is often easier and perhaps more natural to run away from a problem than it is to face it. Your ASS subscribes to the view that nothing is ever its fault. The important thing is that *you* make the decision and not let your instinctive nature make it for you. Your ASS wants to be in charge but your ASS does not think; it only reacts to pleasure and pain.

Anything that is annoying, unpleasant or difficult is perceived by your ASS as a threat, and your ASS instinctively reacts to all threats by seeking to avoid, dismiss or remove them by violent force. Short-tempered adults are not referred to as assholes or snakes without reason. You will no doubt have noted that your ASS has a reptilian sort of cunning, as it positions you to satisfy all urges. The only thing that registers positively on its radar is pleasure, and there is nothing too vile or gross for your ASS in this regard.

The root of all irrationality is your reptilian brain stem's primitive interpretation of all unfavorable stimuli as a threat. Your life force's ASS interprets reality on its terms, not yours. Instead of using reason, which is a function of the higher brain, (this is called the cortex and it is wrapped around your more primitive brain stem) your Appetite Survival System operates on a herd wavelength that corresponds to the instincts of the 4F Club. This vibration uses social viruses, known as *memes*, to communicate. Memes, much like computer viruses, are ideas and impulses that replicate in the collective mind of humanity and seek to survive in *your* brain. They are socially transmitted bugs that your Appetite Survival System can suck up without critical evaluation.

There are, of course, good memes such as the concepts of citizenship, democracy, and public service but these are quieter memes. Memes that relate to the 4Fs are the ones that generally get the immediate attention of your ASS. Who could describe, for example, the mass insanity of sports fans or politicians willing to kill members of the opposing side as anything but 4F related? You must learn to manage this meme absorption reaction of your ASS, or the meme collective of the 4F Club will turn your mind into mush. In this respect, you may find it helpful to think of your ASS as the Appetite Suction System or a vacuum cleaner that sucks up whatever comes near its hose.

Advertising tosses suggestive material towards the vacuum cleaner of your desires and presto—you've got a brand new need. This is why many products associate themselves with pictures of gorgeous men and women. The association is one of sexual acquisition and likeness. Buy this product and you will get the pretty girl or the handsome guy—or you will be just like them. Your ASS falls for this every time—even if you know and momentarily observe the reaction in yourself. This is why advertising patronizes your ASS ad nauseam. Advertisers know they will get a predictable reaction—even if you don't buy the product!

WHERE IS YOUR ASS?

Has your ASS taken up residence on your shoulders? Are your appetites getting bigger or smaller? Do they obey you or do they tell you what to do? What does it mean when someone calls you an asshole or a butthead? Our language holds a host of hidden meanings in insults and name-calling that directly relates to our affiliation with the 4F Club. These are not of course the only negative 4F behaviors we have to deal with. Territoriality, inhospitality to strangers, tribalism (think herd instinct!) and its sorry cousin racism are problems that do not simply disappear with the awareness that they exist. Instincts and their emotional derivatives—the appetites—operate whether we are aware of them or not. The issue is what we do with them once we become aware of their presence and influence in our lives. Do we ignore them or pretend that instincts don't apply to us humans, or do we try to find some way of managing our instinctive appetites that takes into account their socially unacceptable and destructive capabilities?

Road rage, vandalism, gratuitous cursing, assault, and overall rudeness have become an increasing part of our daily lives, as are the results of worshipping the god of immediate gratification. Mad at your wife? Divorce her. Girlfriend gets pregnant? Not my problem. She looks at another guy? Beat her up. The shocking statistics of crime and violence in America illustrate the problem: one murder every 27 minutes, one forcible rape every 6 minutes, one robbery every 59 seconds, one aggravated assault every 31 seconds, one burglary every 13 seconds, one larceny-theft every 4 seconds and one vehicle theft every 23 seconds (all figures from the US Department of Justice).

Our life force's Appetite Survival System can help us deal with these problems but often not in a rational, civilized or loving manner. Defensively speaking, we can flee the consequences of bad behavior by ignoring a country's woes or a neighbor's plight. Offensively, your ASS might want to drop nuclear weapons or pack a handgun. Neither of these reactions on the part of the ASS are guaranteed to produce an improved situation—they are not for the situation or anyone else—they are for your survival, your comfort. The ASS can be selfish and destructive in the most absolute sense. Identify with your life force's ASS and you may be on the road to becoming an asshole.

A NEW SOCIAL PROBLEM

The Appetite Survival System can swallow minds. ASS-modified individuals may look and talk like normal people but they are not really human. Think about some of the true stories you may have heard about child molesters who everyone thought seemed so normal, the mobster who may have donated large sums of money to his local church, or the mass-murder who was such a polite neighbor. Among such corroded individuals are those lesser buttheads, who with heads buried deeply in their backsides, think that social disorder is not on the increase and that it is only our excellent reporting and ability to keep statistics that makes it appear to be so. These are the same people who think concentration camps are for producing orange juice. What all this means is that somewhere along the way, we let the Appetite Survival System out of the social containment system that was carefully, though roughly constructed by generations of philosophers, theologians and statesmen.

We are now facing an ASS infestation whereby human beings are being academically and culturally returned to their natural butthead state through the deliberate intervention of the social sciences, under the guise of liberation from material, psychological and spiritual oppression. Unfortunately, all the animals that are being released under this program are not going peacefully into the woods. They are returning to society under the auspices of the 4F Club "to roam, to hunt and to slay," in the immortal words of Zane Grey.

I don't mean to suggest that those who brought us the Inquisition or World War II were better people than we are, but that every generation must take responsibility for the flowering of its own culture, and the consequences of its decay. In the twentieth century, we let the ASS out of the bag in many harmful ways, creating a society in which the satisfaction of the appetites is more important than the growth of the spirit. I'm not just talking about the terrible manifestations of war or insanity, from Hitler's ovens or Stalin and Mao's vast butcheries or genocide in Rwanda or Cambodia, I'm talking about a weakening of the social structures that bind communities, families, and civilization.

And the only way to tame the worldwide and local manifestations of the ASS is to start with you and your urges. Whenever and wherever you find your ASS, you will note that your dick is very close by.

The normal male ejaculates enough semen (over a lifetime) to generate one trillion human lives. Within a single man's loins sits the capacity to sire more than two hundred times the present population of four billion on the planet! In a very real sense every man can create a stockpile of sex energy literally more potent than the atomic bomb. If this immense reservoir of psychic energy were to be redirected towards love and spiritual harmony, the possibilities for peaceful existence seem unlimited. Some Western scientists may scoff at the idea that semen is an immensely powerful substance. Yet no one can deny the prodigious life-potential in the seed of a single man. By gathering this life-generating force within oneself, one collects tremendous energy.

—Mantak Chia and Michael Winn, *Taoist Secrets of Love:*
Cultivating Male Sexual Energy

MANAGEMENT TIPS

- When you hear a good advertising jingle, remember that it is speaking to your ASS.

- If you walk into a room of angry people, you will become angry. If you visit with a group of happy people you will feel happiness. Be wary when you hear ASS spoken. The best slogans are designed to appeal to the immediacy of your appetites.

- Your Appetite Survival System is the one-track guidance system that controls your dick. Understanding how it operates can help you manage that trouser snake.

- What your life force's ASS tells you is "good" may not be what actually is "good."

- Becoming aware of a problem is nine-tenths of the solution.

CHAPTER 3

TESTOSTERONE—THE FUCK IT/KILL IT BIOHAZARD

The empiricist…thinks he believes only what he sees, but he is
much better at believing than at seeing.

—George Santayana, *Skepticism and Animal Faith*

MAN IS NO LONGER THE ONLY ANIMAL DOCUMENTED TO HUNT AND KILL its own kind. Over the past twenty years, chimpanzees have been observed hunting and killing other chimpanzees and monkeys with savage gusto[1]. The common denominator between man and chimp appears to be the male hormone testosterone, with its similar effect on the genetically comparable human and simian nervous systems.

One has only to reflect on the calming effect of castration on both the male sex drive and violence to understand the role that testosterone plays in both sex and violence. Richard Wrangham, professor of biological anthropology at Harvard University, and his co-author, Dale Peterson note in *Demonic Males* that the shoulders and biceps of male humans, much like the canines of many primates, appear to be a result of natural selection for sex and the violence associated with both hunting and defending territory.[2] Bodybuilders who use testosterone to make their muscles grow have been known to go berserk on occasion. This violent behavior is commonly thought to be due to the presence of too much testosterone.

In his groundbreaking book, *A Brief History of Everything*, Ken Wilbur describes testosterone as an evolutionary "fuck it/kill it tool." He notes that when women have been administered testosterone injections they will often tell researchers that they can't stop thinking about sex and request that the experiment be terminated. Wilber also notes that men can unconsciously fuse the appetite for sex with the appetite for violence.

If you will take a moment to think about this, you will realize how our colorful use of invective expresses this fusion of meaning very clearly. You have no doubt heard the common expression, "We fucked them over good," to indicate death and destruction, or at the very least, violence inflicted upon an enemy.

> If you find FIKI too strong a description, you might want to think of it as DIKI or Do It/Kill It.

These two activities—fucking and killing—and the appetites associated with them—sexual desire and violence—may be abbreviated with the acronym FIKI (Fuck It—Kill It) and will be referred to throughout this book. FIKI is an extreme product of the energy of the Appetite Survival System as it merges with some of the bio-chemical impulses of testosterone. Even if you are a soldier or fighter in frequent combat, it is important to be very aware of the negative consequences of FIKI. You must be careful not to lose your humanity with casual violence. It is amusing to note, however, that men may spend the first half of their lives fighting the negative effects of testosterone and the second half trying to recover some of the vitality that waning testosterone levels no longer provide.

At the same time, it is important to emphasize that violence and desire are frequently on the same energy spectrum, despite the presence or absence of testosterone. This is as true for moderate individuals in loving relationships as it is for the depraved and the perverted who abuse others—it is all a question of degree and where you draw what might be called the "Shadow Line." Intense sexual activity or connections change our pain-pleasure thresholds, so that some measure of sado-masochistic activity is simply natural to arousal. "Rough sex," bondage, exploration of fantasies, all come with the biological territory but not all of these impulsive activities can be attributed solely to the presence of testosterone. Testosterone is simply a biological tool that your life force uses to express and protect itself. There are, however, many negative ways your life force's ASS can seek to manifest its basic energy, if it is not properly directed. The intemperate cross the Shadow Line and dwell there; healthy individuals may flirt with it in moments of sheer fun in concert with their partners. You will explore this in Chapter 17, "Flirting with FIKI."

FIKI evolved as an instinct to protect the species, but it also can constitute a threat to the life force itself. It is possible for the life energy of the individual to get so connected to the negative aspects of the

Appetite Survival System and its off-spring FIKI that very little social progress is possible. We see this is in many parts of the world (the Balkans, Northern Ireland, Cambodia, the Middle East, America's inner cities, and parts of Africa come to mind) where armed groups of young men fueled by testosterone and socially unregulated appetites hunt each other like rabid dogs in mini-wars over drugs, territory, and women. The life force is in danger in these places because a transformation has occurred whereby its energy is diverted from productive activity, and instead becomes high-octane fuel for the ASS. Men become ASSES or Appetite Survival System Errors. The ASS is a major source of human demons when FIKI is involved.

Excessive indulgence affects different people in different ways. The consumption of too much alcohol, for instance, makes some people happy, some sad and others, violent. An unmonitored ASS can make you lazy, thickheaded or violent. Observe yourself after episodes of excess, and work hard to overcome the problems that may have been generated.

General Butt Naked was one of the most feared warriors in the Liberia of the 1990s. He and his cohorts went to battle wearing only their boots, hence the moniker, General Butt Naked. Spears, clubs and machetes were used with great effectiveness. Opposition victims' heads were sometimes put on spears. It is unlikely any of these characters were practicing Dick Management, but very likely that all of Butt Naked's "troops" were sticking their dongs into every hole they could find—willing or unwilling. Interestingly enough, Butt Naked is now reformed and preaching the gospel. He claims he had been in the grip of demons, but whether you believe that or not, it is certain that he had a full-blown case of the ASS gone wild. Biological possession by the Appetite Survival System is simply an advanced case of FIKI characteristic of the Non Dick Manager, about whom you will read more in Chapter 26.

ADDICTION AND HABIT

Those who have not been swallowed up by the Appetite Survival System may suffer from lesser variations on the theme of FIKI, which are basically bad or misdirected appetites. Addiction, for example, is the negative image of good habits. Addiction is "the devotion and surrender to something habitually or obsessively." Addiction is, in a sense, the kind of flattery that bad behavior pays to good habits. It imitates the root activity of excellence by choosing the repetition associated with good habits, but the repetition is rooted not in what is best, but in what is most immediate in terms of gratification. The root of the word addiction comes from the Latin *addicere*, which means, "to favor." Favor what? It means that you favor what your ASS wants. If you allow your ASS to do your thinking for you, addictive behavior can be the result. Your life force's ASS prefers well-worn paths and solid, predictable results for its pleasure seeking. Your ASS will convince you that you have no choice because it is not in the interest of your ASS that you have a choice! Mass murder and modern day cannibal, Jeffrey Dahmer, and others like him have lost sight of where their appetites might be taking them. Your ASS will not tell you where it is going—that is up to you to observe and determine.

We must discover and question aberrant habits the life force may have established in its quest for balance. The ASS does what you let it do! If your life energy cannot have what it needs for development, it will spill over into channels where it does not belong. If you do not cultivate good habits, your ASS will cultivate bad habits! Your ASS wants something to do. If you do not find something useful for it to do, it will find something useless to do. Your life force's ASS is the motor force behind all habits. It will work for you like a donkey if you train it but if you fail to discipline it with good habits, your ASS will be your adversary.

THE PLEASURES OF SELF-RESTRAINT

As Sigmund Freud notes, the search for pleasure is basic to all human endeavors. We automatically and subconsciously ascribe a value to whatever we do. Unfortunately, Freud failed to emphasize that there is also a pleasure to be found in exercising self-control or seeking what might be described in moral terms as good. The Greek philosopher Epicurus noted this two hundred years before the birth of Christ. He insisted that the performance of moral duties could bring the highest sort of pleasure because they brought the greatest possible good into an individual's life.

How can self-restraint bring as much, or more pleasure than plunging your bone into a quivering moist receptacle or stuffing yourself with lip-smacking food? The pleasure of self-restraint may be more subtle but its effects are often more profound and satisfying than immediate physical gratification. For instance, when you exercise, there is an initial difficulty in overcoming the natural resistance of the body to self-inflicted pain, but after a while, the deep satisfaction of both the physical discipline and the results of a more powerful and contented body more than compensate for the initial discomfort.

What is "good," in this instance, is really a kind of psychic currency, whereby we become richer in the energies necessary to lead a productive life. What is "bad" might be likened to a currency deficit, whereby the energy of the life force is constantly being released but not replenished. Evil is deficit spending of psychic currency. The moral checkbook requires psychic currency. Have you checked your balance lately?

VIRTUE AND BUTT-CRACK IDEOLOGY

There are basically two kinds of pleasure. One is short-term such as eating and drinking, sleeping, emoting, evacuating your bowels, urinating, farting, belching, talking with friends, picking your nose, scratching an itch, drug taking, ejaculating, playing sports and games of chance, and so on. The other is long-term and involves pleasures that take time to cultivate, such as the crafting of buildings and careers, attending school or even preparing and planning a gourmet meal. These are pleasures that may require effort to attain. The Greeks called this kind of effort *virtue* as it involved acting in accordance with what they called *right reason*. Right reason is another way of talking about what really works for you, as opposed to what doesn't work. It means that what you are thinking or planning is in conformity with the highest rational levels of who you really are. When this is done consistently and over time, it becomes a good habit or a virtue. Today, we might also describe virtue as habitual excellence, or *right action that gets right results*.[3] It is life force management that puts money or capital energy into your psychic bank—and it feels very wholesome. Vice is exactly the opposite; it takes money out of your psychic bank. It is a set of bad habits and actions *that delivers the wrong results*.

Psychologists, often refer to virtue as delayed gratification, which is a term that lacks any sort of moral connotation and leads to the unfortunate conclusion that delayed gratification is purely relative to whatever other appetites you happen to be having. This is known as *moral relativism*, and is based on the idea that there are no objectively valid standards of behavior that can deliver good results for human beings. From the perspective of moral relativism, nothing can or should supercede whatever it is that you subjectively decide you want. This is an ideology your ASS is comfortable with. Moral relativism is butt-crack ideology and no matter what color your ASS is, this ideology has the moral depth of toilet paper.

There are three kinds of virtue or habitual excellence that oppose the subjective ideology of your ASS and can help you to manage your dick.

> For I do nothing but go about persuading you all, old and young alike, not to take thought for your persons and your properties, but first and chiefly to care about the greatest improvement of the soul. I tell you that virtue is not given by money, but that from virtue come money and every other good of man, public as well as private.
>
> ◆
>
> —Plato,
> *The Apology of Socrates*

There are intellectual habits, such as wisdom, which come from cultivating the power of the intellect; moral habits, such as courage and patience, which come from developing the power of the will; and spiritual habits that come from accepting the dictates of spirit. Spiritual virtues such as faith, hope and love are beyond the scope of this book, but you should remember that all the virtues or habitual excellences of life energy management are on a continuum—one will lead sooner or later, conceptually to the other—unless discouraged by the spiritually confused. (We will talk more about these virtues in Chapter Seven.)

YOUR ASS AND DEATH

The relationship of *Thanatos,* the Freudian death instinct, to pleasure and sexuality is murky but subjectively measurable. Are there not many things we might do in a moment of anger or excitement that could result in both our deaths and the deaths of others? The man who kills his spouse when he finds her cheating with another man may be overwhelmed with the desire to seek vengeance. The satisfaction of this thirst for vengeance and the need to slake his anger could hardly be described as painful. On the other side of the coin, outdoor enthusiasts who climb dangerous mountains or race car drivers competing in high speed road tournaments take pleasure in their accomplishments, despite the fact that they may be flirting with death. The closer we examine the matter, the more it appears that the relationship of pain to pleasure, and excitement to death is on a very curious continuum. There is a kind of flirtation with death that can be very exciting for some of us.

We frequently enjoy painful things even though we may regret them later. Competitive sports and contests can be very painful to participate in but that does not stop us from going all out. The greater the danger, the greater the thrill of victory. Does this sort of compulsive seeking of victory at almost any price remind you of FIKI?

Your life force's testosterone-driven ASS connects with FIKI as a potential solution in the presence of any obstacle or threat—almost before you can stop it. The expression, "fuck it, let's do it," is indicative of this kind of frontal assault on reality. Your ancient reptilian Appetite Survival System, however, is untroubled by any associated moral questions; to it, a solution is a solution, and its solutions are very, very simple. Your ASS wants whatever is in its way or bothering it, to get out of the way, or simply stop being there. This is why some individuals do irrational things when they are threatened. The irrational reptilian response to ALL threats is to fight, fuck, eat or run from them; there is no middle ground. Therefore, you must be extremely careful about letting your ASS go to the House of his good friend FIKI. If you let your ASS go into this house too often, you will become a very bad human being indeed. Do not go there; the House of Death and Destruction is full of misery and unhappiness.

We might also suggest that this fusion[4] of the death instinct and Eros in FIKI that modern philosopher Ken Wilbur points to, isolates and enhances the energy available to your ASS by *excluding* ASS-reducing activity such as *sublimation*. Sublimation is a volitional act (sometimes conscious, sometimes not) that converts the expression of an instinctual desire or impulse into other forms of satisfaction. The sublimation of anger and annoyance, for example, can transform these emotions into patience and self-restraint. Sublimation is not just about sex, it is learning how to shift the gears of the appetites and the will in a productive and even fun way. Without the natural buffering activity of sublimation, the Appetite Survival System can reign supreme and intellectual development can be left, so to speak, at the door of the 4F Club. Welcome to the world of mindless impulses. Was there another drive by shooting in your neighborhood, or the senseless murder of a neighbor or friend? You do not have to look very far for the culprits. The intellectual parents of all criminals are those who pretend that what you do with your dick and impulses is morally neutral.

What kind of moral values, for example, would allow the international community to stand by while the

> Evil is the absence of a good, which could and should be present.
>
> ◆
>
> —Old scholastic saying

Nazis butchered Jews and other innocents during World War II—or when Stalin and Mao butchered their millions for the sake of an insane ideology?

What kind of moral compass was at work in 1994 when the United States ignored over 800,000 killings that took place over 100 days in Rwanda? The United States is a signatory to the Genocide Treaty, which stipulates that in the event of genocide, force must be used by the treaty members to restore order. Rwanda had no oil and so they could not expect the royal treatment accorded Kuwait in the Gulf War, but what did the United States do? The State Department deliberately and coldly dithered over the *meaning* of genocide, so they would not be required to send in the troops. Those in power knew full well what was happening, and will no doubt go to their graves with a secret shame—that is, if they wake up to their humanity.

What is the link between what you do with your dick and the toleration of evils such as these? What is the relationship between your life energy and the ability to make sound moral decisions? Can your ASS and your dick consume moral capital? If energy is like money think carefully about those actions that might take you into moral bankruptcy. It will vary for each one of us, but rest assured that both virtue and vice are growth industries in the hinterland of your being.

Do unmanaged, testosterone laden dicks in positions of political or economic power reason or care anymore than your dick does when it's hard? No. So think carefully about the meaning of the words "dickhead" and "butthead" when they are applied to presidents and politicians. What they do with their dicks does indeed matter very much. Someone's life may depend on it.

Konrad Lorenz [in his book, *On Aggression*] agreed with earlier ethologists [scientists who do objective studies of animal behavior] that animals used aggression to optimize population density, accumulate and defend resources, and protect themselves and their young. But Lorenz emphasized that aggression was not simply a response to an instinct but was itself an innate, driving force... "it is the spontaneity of the instinct that makes it so dangerous." In Lorenz's eyes, aggression was not an aversion but an appetite—and a ravenous one at that. Humans were not only born bad, but born helpless, at the mercy of a killer instinct that bubbled up from a dark corner of the mind like oil and that needed only the match of some trivial insult to ignite. Contained for too long, it would combust spontaneously. The fragile defenses of ritual, culture, and morality were barely a match for this seething flood of instinctive rage.

—Debra Niehoff, Ph.D., *The Biology of Violence:
How Understanding the Brain, Behavior, and Environment
Can Break the Vicious Circle of Aggression*

MANAGEMENT TIPS

• Managing your Appetite Survival System requires leverage. Think of virtue as a crowbar for your ASS.

• Testosterone declines by one percent a year, once males reach their peak of sexual maturity sometime in their twenties. The cooler heads commonly attributed to older men is not based just on experience, but on more manageable levels of testosterone.

• Testosterone levels peak in men sometime between midnight and the early morning hours. That is one reason you may wake up with an erection, and it is a good reason to have sex at night, if you find sexual activity depletes your mental energy. Your juices are restored overnight.

• The next time you feel yourself becoming angry for no good reason, think of yourself as "assuming the reptile."

• Sublimation is something that you actually have to do. You cannot covert instinctual energy into other forms of satisfaction without resisting the impulse to begin with.

And Cain rose up against Abel
and violated his civil rights.

CHAPTER 4

HER YIN
AND YOUR YANG

To conquer oneself is a greater task than conquering others.

—Buddha

YOU ARE CONNECTED TO A LARGER ECOLOGY OF ENERGY AND INFORmation than you may be aware of. Your urges are only the most obvious part of this system. Your life force's Appetite Survival System is connected to the energy and information services of Mother Nature. Mother is not a big thinker, but she does have an agenda that is sometimes at odds with your own. Remember that she is the founder of the 4F Club; she is not at all interested in you personally, as she only thinks in terms of species! You may, for example, be at work and attempting to have an intelligent conversation with an attractive co-worker, when Mother calls—suddenly your trousers cannot quite contain the telephone pole she needs for all-channel communications. It is sometimes difficult to carry on an intelligent discussion with a hard-on tapping into your mind. Think of Mother Nature as a much-loved but troublesome in-law who is constantly trying to get you to have children, but without settling down. There will be a time and place to accept her calls and listen to what she says, but there will also be times when you may need to disconnect her, so that you won't be disturbed. In order to learn how to do this you must learn some basic metaphysics and physics so that you might understand how morals and energy work in relation to your appetites and urges.

THE GLUE OF THE UNIVERSE

Physicists tell us that the entire universe is composed of energy and information. The energy part we can readily accept, but the information part is a little harder to grasp. If you believe that a stone is composed of energy then clearly something is making that energy behave in a certain way. There is some coded information along with the energy that makes the stone be a stone rather than a tree. The ancient Chinese described this energized information as *Chi*, whereas Plato and Aristotle referred to it as *idea* or *form*. Plato used to refer to the idea of horse as being the universal template of all horses. Aristotle referred to such an idea as a form, which in his metaphysics had a very different meaning from Plato's idea. For Plato, an idea was in the mind of God or in some state of being far removed from earthly affairs. Aristotle's form was specific to a thing; a thing was what it was because of its form, and each form was unique to the piece of matter that it was in-forming. The question of how forms can affect matter has a very long and convoluted philosophical history. The Chinese concept of Chi might be thought of as being both like Plato's idea and Aristotle's form, but more fluid, and collapsed into the process of reality as a whole, rather than being a principle outside of matter.

The great Indian philosopher Sri Aurobindo maintained that wherever there was force, there was consciousness, and vice versa. This is a polarity that runs through much of Eastern metaphysical speculation about nature and matter. *Consciousness-Force*, even though Indian in conceptual origin, is an incredibly useful way of thinking about Chi. It is a paradigm that helps us think about the polarity of the life force in the larger context of nature and God. Consciousness-Force may be the glue that holds the universe together.

YOUR IMPULSES CAN MOVE FASTER THAN YOU CAN

Energy has the capability of movement and change. How fast does it move? Light, which is one form of electromagnetic radiation, moves at 186,000 miles per second. How fast is the energy moving that is contained in our stone? This is an unknown. Clearly, the energy is not moving at 186,000 miles per second—at least not to our unaided vision. So what is the energy of a stone doing? Well, it is *being* a stone, which involves an indeterminate amount of energy. If we take this idea of things being slowed-down energy (which is simple physics) and turn it upside down, we could say that when energy is moving very fast, it does not present much information to the naked eye. Likewise, your urges are slowed down energy but the faster they move, the less information they present. Similarly, if you can slow down your urges, the more information about them becomes visible. Think about the last time you did anything foolish. Did you take the time to slow down or did you just jump in? Think about it. This principle of interrogating energy and its emotional equivalent, the impulse—to examine and make visible what is hidden, is at the heart of all rational behavior.

Appetite, from the perspective of a branch of philosophy known as metaphysics, is what we might call a *quickening*, or movement of life force energy that gets filtered through other energy information systems such as your ideas, beliefs, layers of social instruction and your body. The more layers your appetites have to go through, the more slowly they will move and the clearer their principles of operation will become. Your Appetite Survival System can really "haul ASS," so the first step in dealing with it is to slow it down.

THE TWO FORCES THAT MAKE UP THE WORLD

Your life force, which in conjunction with bodily hormones gives momentum to your impulses, is made up of a female energy and information principle that the Chinese call *Yin* and a male energy and information principle known as *Yang*. Yang is considered a positive force and Yin a negative (but not a bad) force. Together, like day and night, hot and cold, love and hate, drive and thought, life and death—and matter and anti-matter these two forces are in opposition and generate power ful energy when they come into contact with each other. The battle of the sexes, for example, is rooted in something far greater than physical differences; male and female represent two sides of an energy generating system. It is for this reason that men and women ultimately work better together than apart. Men need the Yin energy of women as desperately as women need the Yang energy of men. The energy of each compliments and balances the other.

Yin and Yang, much like the particles of modern physics, exchange energy and information in an eternal conflagration and balancing of opposite charges. Chi is a manifestation of this energy exchange.

Some physicists think that leptons (electrons are leptons[5]) and quarks (particles with a fractional charge) which are 100 million times smaller than individual atoms, are the fundamental particles that make up all existing things. It is also thought that encounters between particles and anti-particles may produce energy. Positrons are anti-particles and when quarks and anti-quarks collide, energy is released. Whether you use the

Yin and Yang model, the consciousness-force paradigm or the quark—
anti-quark analogy for your thinking, the idea that there are two fundamental and yet hidden principles at work in our everyday world is useful.

> The Standard Model is a theoretical construct that governs a set of axioms regarding modern physics. It states that all matter is com-posed of six leptons and six quarks. The best known of these particles is the lepton particle we know as the electron.

Analogies, as the theologians say,
"limp" but our minds are naturally
comfortable with opposites such as "on
and off," "darkness and light," "yes and
no," "in and out," and male and female
being used to mirror the structure of
the universe. We must learn to interrogate the operations behind these analogies whenever possible and gaze back
into the mirrors that the universe holds
up for us to see ourselves in.

The mating process that we see throughout the animal kingdom (yes
that includes you) is one example of the information exchange that
occurs between male and female energy systems. We dress up this biological event with medical and genetic analysis but the reality is that data
is exchanged between two apparently different energy states—however
we choose to describe them, and new life is the result of this exchange.
Sex simply mirrors the deeper processes of Yin and Yang.

WAYS OF THINKING ABOUT CHI

The flow of electrical current between the positive and negative pole of
a battery is created by a flow of electrons moving between positive and
negative poles. Likewise, if we interpret the energy information model of
Yin and Yang in electrical terms, energy flows through your body with
the positive pole at the top of your head, and the negative pole running
from between your legs to your feet. (This is why "up" is considered positive and negative is associated with "down.") Have you ever held a bar
magnet under a piece of paper covered with iron powder and watched
the curved lines form along the pattern of energy flow from north to
south pole of the magnet? Chi, just like the energy of the magnet, flows
along lines of electromagnetic force called flux. Chinese medicine refers
to these lines as meridians.

In the Chinese system, this same information principle applies to the
earth and Mother Nature. Energy is exchanged between the North and
South Poles of the Earth along meridians called Dragon Lines, also known

in New Age circles as Ley Lines. Feng Shui is the Chinese art that enables architects and city planners to build so as to take advantage of the heavy duty Chi that flows along the Dragon Lines. Many Chinese buildings and homes are designed so that the energy of the Dragon Lines does not harm the occupants or interfere negatively with their life styles. Likewise, there is an art to managing the information and energy flow of Chi in your personal life!

Let us designate the higher than average levels of this current of Chi, as it flows along meridians and through the body as an urge, so that we have a handy reference for the energy used by our appetites. Urges are like the tip of an iceberg—they are what we notice first in life because they have a certain amount of force that can overwhelm our less energetic and slower moving thinking processes.

YOUR APPETITES ARE ALWAYS ON

The life force energy generated by the opposing forces of Yin and Yang is always seeking expression. Remember that it has a lot of power, and anywhere that it can find an outlet, that is where it will push. This brings us to one obvious outlet—your dick! The life force loves genitals because they are such an easy gateway to energy release. Look at the giddy abandon with which life is generated through all species! The life force loves to propagate and that stiff or wet thing between your legs, like a lightning rod, attracts all sorts of energy.

There is a problem with this lightning rod however. The life force can cause you to act a bit like the famous monkeys who were wired for pleasure in an experiment[6] at a brain research facility. Researchers hooked electrodes directly to monkeys' pleasure centers, and those monkeys that were so wired had only to push a button to experience waves of pleasure. Most of the monkeys pleasured themselves to death. The life force channeled by your ASS is a little like this; it will push the pleasure button until you tell it to stop. Does this also remind you of your dick?

Your life force has the Chi energy of Mother Nature behind it, and this consciousness-force is always pushing for a greater expression of itself. The life force may be the driving energy behind evolution and has one direction—outwards. Scientists generally dismiss this kind of theory as *vitalism*[7] and speculate that the forces of evolution are driven simply by the genetic directive to reproduce at all costs, and the mutations that support this effort.

The idea that Mother Nature exerts a push on matter through the life force or some other unknown mechanism might be dismissed as neo-vitalism, but it does logically account for a far greater diversity of species than the random mutations and genetic imperative to survive that evolutionary theory stubbornly clings to. Howard Bloom, in his book *Global Brain: The Evolution of Mass Mind from the Big Bang to the 21st Century,* argues that evolution is the product of a collective earthly intelligence, which comprises a vast multi-cellular network of organisms, linked together, much like computers in parallel processing.

Unfortunately, the program of this network has some bugs in it. Little things like disease indicate that this global organism can also develop structures that are sometimes at odds with each other. For instance, through the process of evolution, the energy of this global brain may have pushed matter into configurations that ultimately resulted in your taste buds. (Funnily enough, not everyone has the same number of taste buds. Some people have hundreds of them, others as few as five or six.) Now, who doesn't particularly care for a lot of flavoring in their food? Probably those people with the fewest taste buds, while those with more may be counted among the gourmands. Anyway, one problem that the evolutionary energy of the global brain may have created goes like this: you just ate a full meal and you know that you ate enough of everything. Your friend brings in an apple tart

> The notion of a global brain, as put forward by Howard Bloom, is essentially a new and improved version of Mother Nature. As a concept, the global brain looks to evolutionary biology for its origins, whereas the notion of the Appetite Survival System looks to the life force for its origins. One might say that the global brain has its head in the ground, while the life force—at least as a concept—is gazing heavenwards.

with ice cream. You don't really want it but your appetite says, "yeah, go ahead" because the taste buds can still enjoy the caress of one more bite, even though your stomach may be swollen.

The energy of the instinctive appetites, in this example, is constantly operative. The "yes to appetite" button is always on. Only you can decide to turn this button off or ignore it. The same is true of power, sex, sports, violence, or whatever it is that you might have an appetite for. What is a creep or a dickhead but a monkey who does not know how to turn the switch to off? In this way, your life force and indeed the global brain, if there is such a thing, contends with itself.

The Appetite Survival System generates a lot of urges and this energy rubs up against the Chi of some of the energy information systems of your mind! When this happens, you may experience some confusion as the fast moving energy of urges mingles with the slower moving energy patterns of deliberation. The irrational and culturally retarded individual allow urges to dominate their thinking patterns, whereas the wise person interrogates all urges. Interrogating your ASS is the beginning of Dick Management.

Dick Management is based on the simple proposition that your genitals are connected to your life force and that sexual activity consumes some of this life force energy.

Fortunately, the Chi energy used by sexuality is a renewable resource, but too much of it consumed at any one time can lead to unfortunate system glitches in your mental operating system. Your brain and the requirements of daily living need this life energy to run properly, so you must learn to manage, and particularly, use your sexual energy wisely. Many reputable scientists believe that the brain consumes roughly twenty-five percent[8] of all the energy used by your body, so you always need to make sure you've got enough psychic fuel (think Chi) to make it through the day with grace.

Your ASS, which is frequently driven by testosterone is not concerned with either gracefulness or squandering energy, and will frequently insist on genital load reduction whether or not you think it wise or unwise. Your ASS seldom looks at the gas gauge! You, however, are the driver and must learn to pace yourself. You know when you are running low on energy, or feel overextended with too many things to do and not enough time to do them. This may not be the best time for you to get your rocks off. There is always a time and a place for you to use your equipment and you—not your ASS—must be in charge of the process.

It is important, however, that you not think of your ASS as a completely separate entity from your "mind" or your overall consciousness. The life force that generates both your intellect and Appetite Survival System forms a continuous whole that most of us would refer to as, "mind" or "our state of being." This state, which is more or less continuous, produces a mentality that has elements of your intellect and your appetites fused together, in such a way, that it functions largely on the basis of immediate reaction. This reactive state[9] has two modalities that cycle back and forth—much like Yin and Yang. When these two modalities of *thought* and *drive* are in harmony, you have a human being. When they get out of cycle, or when one or the other cycle gets the upper hand, you get inhuman extremes ranging from savage inhumanity to over-intellectualization of what should not be endlessly thought about, but what should be done without further ado. The balancing of thought and drive can be achieved by any sensible person. The first step is realizing that the two need to be balanced, and that there should be some accounting of energy spent well, or thoughtlessly dissipated. Morals are ultimately a kind of energy grid, whereby we plot the excess and deficit conditions that our appetites and fears generate. The ideas of too much and too little, developed and undeveloped, are mental footholds that we can use to climb the cliffs of our impulsive nature.

Yin and Yang can symbolize a safe balance of thought and drive, inasmuch as negative and positive elements must always be balanced in the heart and mind of anyone who would be fully human. Just as you need sleep and exercise, you need balance in your moral and intellectual life. It is nearly as easy to become intellectually unbalanced, as it is to become morally unbalanced. Occasionally you may have to take a stick to both your ASS and your intellect. Sometimes neither of them will shut up.

The undisciplined mind is like an elephant. If left to blunder around out of control, it will wreak havoc. But the harm and suffering we encounter as a result of failing to restrain the negative impulses of mind far exceed the damage a rampaging elephant can cause. Not only are these impulses capable of bringing about the destruction of things, they can also be the cause of lasting pain to others and to ourselves. By this I do not mean to suggest that the mind is inherently destructive. Under the influence of a strongly negative thought or emotion, the mind may seem to be characterized by a single quality. But if, for instance, hatefulness were an unchangeable characteristic of consciousness, then consciousness must always be hateful. Clearly this is not the case. There is an important distinction to be made between consciousness as such and thoughts and emotions it experiences.

—The Dalai Lama, *Ethics for the New Millennium*

MANAGEMENT TIPS

* Drive and thought or energy and information take many forms. Understanding the origin of these forms can give you enormous clarity on how to behave.

* Pleasure is a powerful motivator. Make sure that you are motivated by something that is good rather than something that is darkness in disguise.

* You might find it helpful to think of Yin and Yang as energy and information. There is always energy associated with information and always information associated with energy. This is your key to discovering the secrets of the universe.

* Energy flows on the subatomic level are known to exist and for metaphysical purposes it can be helpful to think of these flows in terms of Chi.

* Get up at dawn once in a while; it might change your life.

CHAPTER 5

DRAINING THE LIZARD

The man who masters himself is delivered from the force
that binds all creatures.

–Goethe

WHAT SEXUAL ACTS DO YOU NOT WANT TO BE KNOWN FOR ENGAGING IN?
If you are married, you generally don't want your spouse to find out that
you were doing it with someone else. If you are a single man you might
boast of your conquests but seldom, if ever, of your masturbatory style.
Why is that?

Who among us boasts of jerking off—excluding exhibitionists and
some immature young men? Yet many people of all ages, races and sex
masturbate on a regular basis, unless of course they have a religious or
moral prohibition against it. What is it about masturbation that is so universally problematic? Is it a sign of some kind of inability to get the real
thing or is there something deeper at work? I suspect the latter.

Masturbation is on the frontier of moral consciousness. It is the flash-
point between the objective moral values that your intellect might
subscribe to and the subjective values of your ASS. Modern Situation
Ethics (everything is relative) limits itself to a party mentality—with
objective values being an unwelcome guest. Ethics can only be completely relative in a subjective universe but that is not the limit of your
consciousness or your universe. Your consciousness will always have one
foot in objectivity and the other foot in subjectivity—much in the same
way that your being is dually rooted in consciousness-force.

What you do with your sexual organs does make a difference—not
only to you but also to everyone else around you. Your genitals want to
get off without qualification or scruple, but a deeper part of you realizes
that there is more to the picture than shooting off a load. There is no need

to feel overly conflicted about this. The struggle between the subjective values of your immediate biology and the objective values of your higher nature will continue until you die. The key is figuring out how to engage subjective and objective values, and in such a way that biological necessity is not compromised, and objective values are not violated. You will often feel that you are caught between a rock and a hard place in this regard, but this is the sort of struggle that when engaged, produces moral heroes, and when carelessly relinquished, produces monsters.

THE PRIME DIRECTIVE AND PSYCHIC RAPE

What is your dick's biological agenda? Your dick follows the biological prime directive, which is to *get off*. Remember, the sexual appetite is always on, so your dick is always in the *on* position. This is the very reason masturbation is problematic. The difference between masturbation and rape might only be a hop, skip and a jump for some morally confused individuals. Men who masturbate are not generally counting sheep. They are more than likely thinking about the most sexually attractive partner that they can think of while flogging the dog. If masturbation is a substitute for sex, then we can pose a very simple question: Do the men who imagine themselves having sex with an attractive male or female generally ask permission to have imaginative sex with the person in question?

Of course not. *One conclusion that can be drawn from this is that on many occasions, masturbation may involve a kind of psychic rape.*

Engaging your higher values is the first step towards dealing with masturbation and psychic rape. The sense of unease that evolved individuals may have about masturbation has less to do with culture and more to do with a deep inner knowledge. There is a feeling that ideally, one would be better off having sexual relations with a soul mate or someone that you care deeply about. There is also the suspicion that in some unspecified way, incessant jerking off can rob an individual of the character needed for this kind of ideal relationship. This deep inner knowledge (which in some circles is called conscience) is not merely an accumulation of cultural debris gathered up by the subconscious mind, but originates in the core of your personality, which like the tip of an iceberg has structures not apparent to the conscious mind. The life force energy conversion that takes place in sublimation, for example, is subtle but the effects are powerful and noticeable. At the core of your being, you know that sublimation has power, even if you don't use it.

The Tibetans have a marvelous concept, difficult to translate exactly into English that fingers the dynamic and yet subtle relationship between subjectivity and higher values in human consciousness. *Kun long*, according to the present Dalai Lama, is a participle (an "ing" word) that means to thoroughly awaken or to make stand up from the depths, a person's whole heart and mind. It is the act of standing up; of taking the moral high road and taking a stick to one's own ASS or the collective ASSES of others. *Kun long* is the voice of the prophets in the desert and of all reformers whose actions spring from a pure heart.

PREDATOR AND PREY CONSCIOUSNESS

There are, of course, those who when queried on the pros and cons of masturbation will gaze at you incredulously, as if masturbation were something entirely positive like the right to vote. What the average meat beater doesn't understand is that masturbation is *predator-prey sexuality*. Remember that your ASS is a survival mechanism and that reproduction is very high on your ASS's to do list. In order to make sure that reproduction occurs, your ASS enlists the help of his right hand man FIKI to make sure the job gets done. If there are no females available to impregnate, brother FIKI will see to it that Madam Thumb and her four daughters are pressed into immediate service. This ensures a fresh supply of itchy semen and trigger-happy dongs. This doesn't mean that every time you wax your dolphin, moral destruction occurs, but what it does mean is that a healthy life is on a continuum with healthy sexuality, which involves self-restraint, and masturbation is on a continuum with destruction, or something tending towards FIKI, which if you recall, stands for Fuck It/Kill IT.

> Step not beyond the center of the balance.
>
> ◆
>
> —Pythagorean Maxim

How might we characterize female masturbation? If men, in general, fantasize about *sexual taking*, when they masturbate, women fantasize about being *sexually taken*. Female masturbation, in this context, might be thought of as *prey sexuality*. Anyone who doubts this has only to look at the covers of Romance novels to see what the women who read these books are actually buying. Note the torn bodices and the muscular males on these covers. The women are clearly sexual prey for the handsome males on these covers, albeit willing prey. If we were to begin to attempt to delineate the problem of masturbation for women, we would have to start with the notion of prey and what thinking of oneself, as prey, does to a woman's sense of self-worth and integrity. Why do you think that so many women stay with abusive boy friends, lovers and spouses? They have allowed and consigned themselves to be prey for men who, in turn, have allowed themselves to be controlled by the biological prime directive of "getting off!" It is not without reason that a woman's sexual purity has been referred to as her virtue. A woman's safeguarding of her sexuality is the lock that must only be opened with the key of commitment. All other attempts to open this lock are acts of moral and spiritual vandalism. This is not to say that all men are vandals but that men and women both need to reflect on the meaning of sexuality in the direction of their lives as a whole, rather than simply as means of "getting off."

Look at the following list closely and reflect on the meaning of FIKI. Note the violence and sexual mockery implicit in many of these phrases:

- flogging the dog
- waxing the dolphin
- spanking the monkey
- jerking off
- moving a load
- stroking the dog
- jacking off
- floating the boat
- talking to Mr. Goodbar
- helping Harry
- visiting madam thumb and her four daughters
- whipping José
- wrangling the dangler
- beating off
- flicking your mickey
- stroking the snake
- clocking your Clinton
- whacking off
- thumping the donkey
- slapping Mr. Happy

- strangling the turkey
- working the Johnson

So I ask you: after looking at this list, how much of a leap do you think it is—from thinking about doing it—to actually doing it? How many times have you undressed someone in your mind as a prelude to the real thing? This is the rape continuum. "If a man looks upon a woman with lust in his heart, he has committed adultery," said Jesus, seconded by Jimmy Carter. (This same principle applies of course to the ladies even if their desires appear less blatant.) Note that Jesus uses the word adultery, which is normally indicative of having sex with someone else's spouse. Does this mean that thinking about sex with someone who is not married is okay? No, Jesus is addressing the issue of having sex with someone's future husband or wife. Casual sex may rob someone else's future!

Given our culture's commercial celebration of adultery and the gratification of almost all impulses on television and the big screen, why are we surprised that rape and violent crime is on the increase among adolescents (even though it is declining for adults)? FIKI, FIKI, FIKI. This is why self-restraint is so critically important. Given the *on* position of the sexual appetites, unless we put our dicks on a short leash, they will take over. What are soldiers who are raping and pillaging but a bunch of hoodlums running wild?

The deeper issue here is energy usage. Every human being has a daily energy quotient. There is only so much Chi available every 24 hours for the left brain and the right brain. If most of this energy is consumed by excessive sex, little may be left over for other more constructive activities.

Freud, insisted that sublimation (utilization of instinctual energy by other activities) was critical to human development[10]. This is a view that some professional anthropologists also maintain, i.e., that sublimation represents an advance in a civilization rather than a form of psychopathology, as is sometimes maintained by developmentally retarded schools of psychology. It is no accident that many professional athletes refrain from sex altogether or are advised to do so at least three or four days before a game or a meet, so that they will have more energy. This is not an old wives' tale and don't let anyone tell you otherwise. The life force energy that is so necessary for competition can in fact be drained by your lizard.

Kun long! Stand up and look reality in the face.

We are not damned for doing wrong, but for not doing right; Christ would never hear of negative morality; thou shalt was ever his word, with which he superseded thou shalt not. To make our idea of morality center on forbidden acts is to defile the imagination and to introduce into our judgments of our fellow-men a secret element of gusto. If a thing is wrong for us, we should not dwell upon the thought of it; or we shall soon dwell on it with inverted pleasure. If we cannot drive it from our minds—one thing of two: either our creed is in the wrong and we must more indulgently remodel I [ourselves]; or else, if our morality be in the right, we are criminal lunatics and should place our persons in restraint.

—Robert Louis Stevenson, *A Christmas Sermon* (1900)

MANAGEMENT TIPS

- Treat your dick like a valuable resource or a bank account; make withdrawals only when necessary.

- Courage is fear saying its prayers.

- The hardest thing in the world is patience and it is the thing that makes the biggest difference.

- Sex can become a dead habit, particularly jerking off.

- Fasting is part of any great diet program and it is good for your body. Put your dick on periodic fast. You might be amazed at how energetic you feel.

CHAPTER 6

PORTRAIT OF A CREEP

Why is it that every woman has to go out with fifty creeps before
meeting a nice guy? Shouldn't it be the other way around?
—The Shepherd

WHAT IS A CREEP? A CIRCULAR ANSWER TO THIS QUESTION MIGHT BE someone who makes us feel creepy. There is great wisdom in this observation, even though it does not answer the question. If creepy people make you feel creepy, how do good individuals make you feel? How we are does affect others. If our private lives are creepy, that creepiness may leak out in our dealings with others. But back to creepiness. What is it? Creepiness is a state of consciousness that results from an ASS that is manipulating an immature mind. Creepiness might be thought of as a kind of mental and moral imbalance caused by poor life force energy management. Let's look at a list of creepy activities and attributes and see if we can't get a clearer idea of something that we all know deep down is a problem. Some of these things are of course creepier than others but the notion of activities that we can generally be repelled by because they are "creepy" is an almost universal reaction when we encounter someone who makes our skin crawl.

- Talking loudly about sexual activity without regard for who might be present
- Peeking through holes and watching people shitting or having sex
- Sniffing other peoples' underwear
- Picking noses in public
- Never knowing when to be quiet
- Unable to take turns in conversation, i.e., not knowing how to listen in a big way
- Playing with the genitals of animals

- Molesting children
- Urinating on toilet seats and failing to clean up
- Deliberately not bathing or brushing teeth
- Farting loudly at meals
- Eating like a pig thrown a bucket of slop
- Enjoying inflicting pain
- Giving themselves over to any impulse
- Beating women, children, and pets
- Given to vandalism and graffiti
- Yelling obscenities out of car windows
- Gazing at women as collections of parts with no regard for their individual personalities
- Do not wipe their asses properly, or attempt to clean under their nails
- Loud, often inappropriate laughter
- Enjoying being rude to old people
- Would rather jerk off than find an acceptable partner (Motto: A dick in hand is worth two in the bush.)

We feel uncomfortable around creeps because they have no respect for themselves or others. Creeps are almost invariably shallow because they have little or no sense of self- worth or, on the other side of the coin, they have an excessive self-worth based on inordinate pride. (We've all met adults who are unable to lose gracefully or feel like they have to boss everyone around.) Teenage creeps, for example, need to cruise around in cars looking for cheap thrills or someone to bother. They frequently do not have the interiority, or sense of self to want to be alone, or to be engaged in constructive activity. This is not always their fault, for they have never been taught otherwise.

> One of the most destructive forces is unused creative power. If a man out of laziness does not use his creative energy, his psychic energy turns to sheer poison.
>
> ◆
>
> —Carl Jung

Creeps also serve a useful purpose on occasion. They remind us of how easy it is to become forgetful of higher values. The continuum between the creep and the criminal is almost seamless. The creep is on a slippery slope that is almost always going downhill.

A creep is a fake man, a man lacking moral balance and self-conquest. If you have a few of these qualities, do not worry. There is a little bit of the creep in all of us. Remember that the truly creepy person is not interested in improvement—they have lost faith in having anything to improve.

In classical Athens, whether the struggle was between you and the world's pleasures, or between you and your body, this state of conflict was normal and natural. What was abnormal was to put up no resistance, to be continually and instantly overwhelmed. Such feeble characters threw in the towel without a fight. They were defeated and enslaved by their desires. They were known as the *akolastoi*, the uncorrected, the unchecked, the unbridled, or the *akrateis*, the powerless, the impotent, the incontinent.

—James N. Davidson, *Courtesans and Fishcakes*

MANAGEMENT TIPS

◆ Animals are the wrong way to go. Stay with your species.

◆ Assholes are for shitting. Stirring beans with your dick is unhygienic.

◆ Go to a monastery for a retreat.

◆ Go camping by yourself in the wilderness. Learn outdoor skills.

◆ Don't wear tight underwear to bed.

CHAPTER 7

ENTROPY AND YOUR DONG

It is essential that we reach a consensus in respect to what constitutes positive conduct and what constitutes negative conduct, what is right and what is wrong, what is appropriate and what is inappropriate. In the past, the respect people had for religion meant that ethical practice was maintained through a majority following one religion or another. But this is no longer the case. We must therefore find some other way of establishing basic ethical principles.

—The Dalai Lama

MAKING GOOD CHOICES REGARDING YOUR URGES AND ACTING accordingly is more commonly referred to as morality. Without arguing over what constitutes "good," morality might simply be described as responsible urge and information management. Urges use energy, so if we are going to understand how urges work, we must also understand how energy works. Some of the same rules that apply to energy also apply to that friend who lives between your legs.

Energy (with its information component hidden) is typically defined as the ability to do work, but this kind of energy doesn't always actually do work. Energy can be either potential or actual, which is a way of saying that it can either loaf or actually be in use. Energy, like water, also seeks equilibrium and balance. If you heat water, for example, it turns into steam but the most stable state for it to be, under moderate temperature conditions, is in a liquid state. If we use this as a scientific metaphor, rather than as a scientific fact (I can see physicists jumping up and down), we could say that water, in general on this planet, has a tendency to seek the equilibrium or balance of this liquid state. The same metaphor can be applied to frozen water. You can sculpt it into many fantastic shapes, but unless freezing temperatures are maintained, it melts and returns to a state of equilibrium in the form of liquid water. Note that it requires extra energy in all cases to move it out of a state of equilibrium, if we assume for argument's sake that the equilibrium state is room temperature. Now think about this in terms of a skating rink. Energy is required to maintain the water in a frozen state through the use of compressors and ice making machines. But what does water really want to do at room temperature? It wants to rest and it rests best as a liquid. Maintaining water in any state other than a liquid (at room temperature) requires energy, and if energy is not available to move it into another state, water will go to its default position, which is—you guessed it—liquid. What is your default position? Do we not refer to someone who does nothing as a lazy ass or a lump of shit? A state of equilibrium is not necessarily a good thing. It is frequently a state of lower energy or a less formed state of being.

The rules that govern the peculiar way that energy (with its information component hidden) operates are known in physics as the Laws of Thermodynamics.

1. The First Law: Energy is neither created nor destroyed, only changed from one form to another. This is commonly known as the Law of Conservation of energy from one form to another.

2. The Second Law is the *tendency* of all things towards a lower energy equilibrium, rather than a higher state of energy and order. All atoms and molecules tend towards randomness rather than order and this randomness increases over time. This is commonly known as the Law of Entropy.

3. The Third Law is the law of Absolute Zero, which states that as temperature decreases the change in energy loss attributed to entropy also decreases.

How does this apply to you? Your natural state is one of equilibrium, where needs for food, fuel, shelter, thought and sex are met. It requires energy to move beyond this sometimes restful, and primitive state of satisfaction and physical equilibrium. Where does the energy come from that you use to get beyond simply dozing in the sun, using your dong indiscriminately, stuffing yourself, or defecating whenever and wherever you please? What is it you draw upon to rise from a state of nature to go out into the world and make yourself into more than just a collection of appetites to be sated? Do you not cast your thoughts into the well of your being and search for energy and information? Where does this "juice" come from—if it comes? Where indeed even does life come from, as it is clearly opposed to the death march of entropy? Life temporarily violates physics. Clearly there is an anti-entropic principle that we are linked to, whether we like it or not. This is known as *negentropy* and while it is not officially one of the Laws of Thermodynamics, it is one of the principles that make the universe tick. I like to think of Negentropy as the Fourth Unofficial Law of Thermodynamics. There is something disturbing, however, about the separation of entropy from negentropy in science (with the exception possibly of the biological sciences) but the ostensible reason is very simple: negentropy cannot be measured, it can only be observed—but the *interest* in randomness and disorder on the part of the scientific establishment in general is itself suspect. One would think that scientists would put more energy into discovering the principles of negentropy rather than those of entropy but that is perhaps, the domain of biology and metaphysics rather than physics. You will discover that theories regarding Dick Management are rooted in negentropic ideas such as Chi, the life force and the soul.

Entropy, the Second Law of Thermodynamics, might be thought of as the tendency of matter towards inertia and decay. It is easier in one sense to be nothing rather than to be something. To *be* something requires energy and energy has to come from somewhere. The energy for something *to be* must be maintained or it will slowly decay. This is the origin of the thermodynamic expression "heat death." Energy is used up during every single minute that an object exists and unless renewed in some fashion, the overall energy of the package declines over time. This is entropy in action. Think about a new car: even if you maintain your vehicle from day one, wear and tear from use and the environment will sooner or later grind it into the entropic equilibrium of the junk yard and ultimately into rust and dust.

The science of Dick Management is based both on the problem of entropy and the mystery of negentropy. The extraordinary negentropic activity, for example, that occurs throughout the animal kingdom with conception—the upgrading of complex genetic material into something living—is an almost incomprehensibly negentropic activity. The life force is constantly challenging the Law of Entropy but your dong is much more comfortable with the randomness of the Second Law. Dick Management, as you will see, will help you to challenge the Law of Entropy in a positive and creative way.

WHAT CHILLING OUT REALLY MEANS

If we think carefully about these concepts, we will begin to understand that much like Yin and Yang, there appear to be two major evolutionary principles at work in the universe: entropy which might be described as the tendency of energy towards winding down and negentropy, the information principle that allows things to wind-up.

The expression "chilling out," for example, points to a profound truth. When we "chill" our passions, we decrease entropy and increase information. The Third Law of Thermodynamics shows how this could be possible. By slowing entropy, less energy is dissipated. What is patience but an application of the Third Law of Thermodynamics? Do we not also refer to bad behavior as dissipation? The Second Law of Thermodynamics or Entropy is the basis of all natural disorder including biological and intellectual dysfunctions. Disease is frequently a result of biological entropy, and psychological dysfunctions, from cruelty to mental illness, can similarly be related to entropic conditions of moral decay and malfunction. Some of these malfunctions are genetically based but we must be careful to distinguish these from intellectual and moral dysfunctions. What do you think laziness is but entropy at work?

Laziness isn't the only problem that can be attributed to entropy. Consider cruelty. Is it not easier to be cruel than kind to someone who insults you? And what about your sexuality? Isn't it easier to drop your pants and have madam thumb and her four daughters help you with your load whenever the urge strikes? Unfortunately, the lowest and most stable state for your urges may be down the drainpipe of your genitals. This is where anti-entropic activity is needed to direct your energy to "higher" and more internally balanced states. The good habit of sexual self discipline, for example, is one of the conceptual pillars of Dick Management.

There is no set of words in the English language that can get at all the concepts we are going to need to understand why impulse management is important, so let's jump backwards, from physics to metaphysics, from the present to the time of Socrates. Some of the answers to the questions that are being raised require links to the past, and there are some things that the ancients understood better than modern man.

VIRTUE AND VICE: THE QUEST FOR EXCELLENCE

Socrates (470-399 BC) and his disciples Plato (428-348 BC) and Aristotle (384-322 BC) used the term virtue,[11] as we discussed earlier, to describe responsible urge management, and vice to describe irresponsible urge management. For example, we describe overeating and drunkenness as vices. If we eat or drink too much, we are allowing an urge to control our actions. This might be thought of as the beginning of vice—when we allow our urges to decide what we do. Drinking or eating moderately might be thought of as being virtuous, to the extent that we allow the urge for pleasure to be tempered by self-control. This is the virtue or good habit that Aristotle described as *temperance*. Finding the balance between excess and deficiency, between doing something too much and doing something too little is known as the "Golden Mean." The moderate person can usually find a balance between indulging and tempering possibly dangerous urges with reasonable limitations. This is a way of managing the energy of your life force's Appetite Survival System and is also anti-entropic activity of a high order.

Another way of thinking about virtue is to think about how the practicing of any sport or job can make you better at it. The more you do it, the more likely you are to improve at what you are doing. Likewise, the more you practice being truthful, or being fair to others, the easier it becomes to tell the truth and be fair. Put another way, the more you refuse to give in to the impulse to lie or to be unfair, the more you build up strength in your will to act more positively under different circumstances. If you are fearful of public speaking, for example, you will get over your fear, if you take steps to practice your speaking in public. Bit by bit, you will build up the inner strength to overcome your fear. Virtue in this instance is stepping up to the plate and dealing with a fear or limitation of skill by working to overcome it. Vice would simply bemoan its fate and languish in inaction.

Conversely, isn't this why job hunting can be so annoying? You know that you can do a particular job, if only someone will give you a chance to become good at it, but all the employers seem to want people who are already habitually excellent at their jobs. This is a Catch-22 proposition that can only be remedied by education or acquisition of skills that the employer needs. Improving your job skills may get you a better career but practicing virtue will give you a better life!

DIFFERENT KINDS OF VIRTUE CAN HELP YOU TO BE BETTER THAN YOU ARE

Aristotle divided good habits into two major categories: intellectual and moral. Intellectual habits govern the development of mind, and moral habits help develop the will and what we refer to today as character.

Aristotle also described five separate categories of intellectual virtue and eleven categories of moral virtue. These are the activities of a productive mind and will; together they are your compass to the longitude and latitude of a meaningful life.

The Intellectual Virtues:

1. **Science**—in the modern sense of the word, as in technology and the uncovering of cause and effect

2. **Wisdom**—the ability to discern and adequately reflect on inner qualities; to analyze theory or a set of facts in their relation to one another

3. **Understanding**—the intuitive process that allows the mind to directly grasp truth—sometimes without going through all the intellectual steps that might ordinarily be necessary

4. **Prudence**—The ability to govern and control oneself through reason

5. **Art**—understood in the sense of artistic craftsmanship, as in sculpture, painting, music or a life well-lived

---

We publicly cultivate some of the intellectual virtues in this country and look at the tremendous results! Our lives have been enormously enhanced by intellectual products such as the telephone, television, trains, automobiles, airplanes, computers, hot and cold running water, money and satellites to name a few. The Moral Virtues, on the other hand, are those habits that help us to control our bad impulses, and are seldom the subject of detailed public discussion—with the exception of Justice. Most people think of appetite as only the urge for food or sex, which is most unfortunate because it robs us of a useful index for evaluating our desires and behavior. Aristotle delineates eleven basic moral habits or virtues that can be used to help manage the appetites and provide navigation for the will. Think of them as an ancient science of energy management.

The Moral Virtues:

1. **Courage**—the power to face adversity and struggle against evils

2. **Continence**—self-restraint in reference to your appetites or desires

3. **Liberality**—generous giving which overcomes greed

4. **Magnificence**—the ability to spend money on large, possibly useful and usually beautiful projects

5. **Magnanimity**—the magnanimous person is able to overlook slights and insults, and rise above pettiness. He or she is generous and able to get work done without complaint.

6. **Honor**—a state of character which is a result of the practice of moral and intellectual excellence

7. **Gentleness**—to deal with others on the basis of kindness and compassion

8. **Friendship**—friendship outside of casual acquaintances, requires effort to cultivate

9. **Temperance**—self-restraint in regards to pleasure

10. **Truthfulness**—the ability to see and affirm what is, and deny what is not

11. **Justice**—seeking for others and yourself that to which all are entitled under both moral and social law

The virtuous ride the will and the passions in the same way that good riders control their horses. The enduring image of horse and rider comes to us down through the centuries from both Greece and Rome. It is no accident that the knight and the cowboy, for example, are used as heroic images throughout western literature. The valiant knight and the good cowboy are always in charge of both their steeds and their character!

The failure to ride the horse of impulse is both a moral and an intellectual failure. If you will think of the ancient horses of passion as the modern ASS of the appetites and will, then the analogy is clear. The failure to ride your ASS is a moral failure that begins with an intellectual breakdown that is rooted in an entropy of character. We all have read about people who are unable to control themselves very well—those who have bad tempers, those who commit crimes of passion such as assault, unpremeditated rape and murder. Note how the expression "losing your temper" has acquired a meaning divorced from the meaning of temperance and self-restraint in general. It requires a very strong exercise of will power to say "no" to powerful appetites that have the potential to be harmful. The more you say "no" to things that are bad for you, the stronger your ability becomes to say no in general to bad habits. You create a habit of refusing to engage in bad actions. This has a spillover effect into other areas of your life. By saying "no" to one bad urge, you may also be better able to say "no" to excessive drinking, bad temper, taking harmful drugs, promiscuity, or laziness and other bad habits. In other words, you build up muscles in your will.

A person who cultivates good habits is called virtuous. We might want to think of virtue as being anti-entropic as it helps you use energy in a constructive manner. Good habits help build you up and bad habits tear you down. Virtue is a form of energy and information management as it applies to your moral and intellectual life.

An individual who allows himself or herself to be controlled by every instinctive urge that passes through their consciousness might be called vicious, a word the original meaning of which is "vice-ridden." We have only to think of Hitler, Pol Pot or greedy American slave traders to understand how dangerous habitual vice can be to others. There is no such thing as a vice that does not affect others in some small or large way. Unmanaged vice and misused Chi contributes to the entropy and decay of society!

Virtue, on the other hand, creates goodwill in families, the workplace, and in the community. Dick Management might be thought of as a practical application of virtue that can serve as a fulcrum for moral and social change, and ultimately, happiness.

Watch your thoughts; they become words.
Watch your words; they become actions.
Watch your actions; they become habits.
Watch your habits; they become character.
Watch your character; it becomes your destiny.

—Frank Outlaw

"To entropy."

MANAGEMENT TIPS

• Chi is an energy manifestation of your life force. This is the gasoline of your body; without it your life won't run. When you die, your life force goes elsewhere. If you do not use it well, you will be dead long before you actually die.

• The urges of your Appetite Survival System use your dick like a radar system. When you feel your genitals swarming in your trousers, you can be sure that Chi is flowing to your nether regions.

• You must have a moral framework to deal with your urges. Think of your moral framework as a harness for your ASS.

• Discovering your Golden Mean is the first step on the path to moral development. You will be able to take many other steps once you get to this one. The Romans used to say, "est modus in rebus"—there is a proper measure in things, i.e., the golden mean should always be observed.

• Remember that entropy is tugging at the fabric of the universe. It wants to dissolve everything into the primordial elements from which it came. The anti-entropic qualities of virtue can help you stand tall in a universe that is falling down.

CHAPTER 8

HOW A REAL MAN BEHAVES

I am a man; nothing human is alien to me.
—Terence (190-159 B.C.)

HOW DOES A REAL MAN BEHAVE? WHAT IS IT ABOUT SOMEONE WE ADMIRE and seek to emulate, and what is it about someone whose behavior and very demeanor repels us? Think carefully now. What are the qualities that we admire in a man? (Many of these same virtues and qualities we will also admire in women but in a different way.) The following are some key components of a real man's character and are indicative of life force energy well-directed.

- Kindness
- Toughness
- Thoughtfulness
- Caring
- Romance
- Sense of humor
- Hard Work
- Courage
- Magnanimity
- Honesty
- Justice or Fairness
- Temperance
- Wisdom

All of these qualities in a man would make him appealing to men and desirable to women, and in general, be the stuff of good citizenship and friendship. How does a man acquire these virtues and qualities of character? Some men are of course born pre-disposed towards some of these qualities, but others really have to struggle to be good. All men have to work at being better than they are. Is this not true of all human beings? How many of these things are compatible with a man whose dick is out of control? Are our prisons full of men with these qualities or without them?

- Kindness: how can a man be kind if his first priority is the satisfaction of his dick? No one else matters to the dick-infested mind.

- Toughness (when necessary): do we admire men who can be tough when it is truly called for? Such men stand up to the unjust and the unkind.

- Thoughtfulness: is it possible to be thoughtful of others when the satisfaction of all desires comes first? The egotistical person couldn't care less about others. The thoughtful man is usually charitable and kind.

- Caring: the caring man is aware of the impact that he has on others and seeks to be helpful whenever possible. His ego serves his deeper sense of self. The caring man is a custodian of the environment. If he must disturb the earth he is careful to do it in the best way possible.

- Romance: a sexually selfish man cannot be consistently romantic. He may be able to feign romance until he gets what he wants but then, watch out! He can be a snake or a lizard and deserves your contempt. A real man knows how to be romantic.

- Sense of Humor: a real man laughs at himself and his foibles. He faces adversity with good cheer.

- Hard Work: a real man does not shrink from hard work, and knows full well that many good things—including family, friendships, and freedom—require great focus, commitment, and effort.

- Courage: the courageous man stands up for what is right and true. He is able to do battle against himself. The courageous man is a defender and protector of women and children. Sounds like Superman? You bet.

- Magnanimity: the magnanimous man is able to overlook slights and insults, and rise above pettiness. He is generous and able to get work done without complaint.

- Honesty: this is the *sine qua non* of consciousness and spiritual or personal growth. The self does not lie. Deceiving yourself is tantamount to psychological treason.

- Justice or Fairness: a just or fair man seeks to consistently employ fair standards in evaluating himself and others. He neither seeks more than he is entitled to or less. He is as concerned for the welfare of others as he is of his own.

- Temperance: the temperate man realizes that his appetites have to be governed and that the failure to do so results in a kind of death to his deepest sense of self. Intemperance can cause the doorway to inner riches to creak shut or become obstructed by the rubble of vice and inattention.

- Wisdom: the ability to discern inner states. Wisdom always involves an inner self-awareness. The wise man recognizes the need to monitor, restrain and regulate the appetites whenever and wherever necessary.

If we look closely at each one of these qualities we will discover that a man, generally speaking, must able to say no to some of his wayward impulses in order to have some of these good characteristics in greater abundance. Another way of looking at this is to say that in order to have good qualities, one must be doing something on a regular basis that produce these qualities. Much in the same way that we say that a good carpenter builds a good house, a man or woman of virtue builds the house of character with good qualities.

Virtue is like a verb. It is something you must do in order to have its benefits. The action of virtue produces qualities that we may admire. Likewise, many of the things we don't admire are the product of a different kind of verb—a dead verb that hangs out and does nothing except soak up the excremental impulses of the Appetite Survival System. This is our friend vice, who literally and crudely speaking is a piece of shit.

In short, a real man practices virtue or is attempting to be an improved human being despite any failings he might have. A real man struggles to be better.

I remembered a grain of martial arts wisdom, a teaching about soft and hard. Proponents of the "soft" martial arts sometimes refer to karate as a "hard" style of fighting. Yet this is mistaken, for a stiff, hard technique is brittle, and is therefore easily broken. Hardness, by itself, does not signify strength, it augurs weakness. A hard body is neither flexible or subtle nor quick. To become a truly strong human being, one should cultivate a soft, supple exterior laid over a core of tempered steel. A person with these qualities is open and yielding, sensitive to shifting intentions, yet impervious to harm. As Ohshima-Sensei often says, strength is not [found in] mean extremes of hardness or softness, but in the distance between the two.

—Pamela Logan, *Among Warriors: A Woman Martial Artist in Tibet*

MANAGEMENT TIPS

• Wear your baseball cap correctly, bill forward. Wearing your baseball cap backwards may confuse your dick—your dick does not face backwards.

• Don't be a dick, life is too short. Treat others as you would like to be treated.

• Whores don't like to be kissed. Genital sex is not necessarily the most intimate sex. Think about it.

• If you want to put something up your ass get a colonic.

• If you don't feel like kissing a woman or looking her in the eye, you should not make love to her. Put yourself into her shoes for a change.

CHAPTER 9

DISCOVERING YOUR INNER ANIMAL

He who makes a beast of himself gets rid of the pain of being a man.
—Hunter S. Thompson, *Fear and Loathing in Las Vegas*

ONE WAY TO UNDERSTAND THE LANDSCAPE OF VIRTUE AND VICE IS TO discover your inner animal. The inner animal is whatever creature most closely resembles your life force's appetites in their most unrestricted and excessive form. Your inner animal is like a high priest or priestess zealously guarding the temple precincts of your ASS. (Unless you are a member of a culture that associates the inner animal with something positive or spiritual, please think of the inner animal as a metaphor for negativity and excess.)

Let's look at the Dog Analogy, which says that unregulated life force energy consumption (think Chi) leads to animal behavior. Watch what dogs do! An untrained dog is a simple creature. Dogs like to bark, copulate, defecate, eat and urinate on their territory, and sometimes fight with other dogs. They enjoy human company but most of all, dogs enjoy being dogs. Look at the following list and see what looks familiar:

- Mounting any bitch (female dog) in heat is done without hesitation.
- Puppies? That is the bitch's problem.
- Barking loudly is always acceptable at any time.
- Mark your territory with urine or excrement but make sure that the other dogs know what is your territory. It doesn't matter if the territory has already been marked.
- Fighting other dogs is no big deal and is always an acceptable way to pass time. Fair play is never considered. After all, one has teeth, which are for biting—biting is biting.

• Fighting alone is good but fighting in a pack is even better. It is a lot more fun to have a frightened victim that everyone can sink their teeth into.

• Some untrained dogs will eat until they are ready to burst.

• Hanging out is really the only way to spend time. There is nothing else to do.

• Licking your balls and sniffing backsides is an excellent way to pass the time.

An acquaintance once described an experience he had while passing a very provocative woman he had seen on several occasions. As he passed her, the words *fuck fuck fuck fuck fuck fuck* passed through his mind, slowly at first and then with great speed. The words sped up so much, he remarked, they actually came to resemble barking. It is clear that he felt like barking out his desire at her. However, being a rational individual, he calmed his impulses and merely said, "Hi."

But suppose he had followed his impulse and mounted the lady right there on the sidewalk? We call that rape. What does a dog call it? Good fun.

> Laws that protected rape in marriage—the right of a husband to penetrate his wife against her will, by force—were changed so that forced intercourse in marriage could be prosecuted as what it was: the act of rape. "But if you can't rape your wife," protested a California state senator in 1979, "who can you rape?" The answer is: no one.
>
> ◆
>
> —Andrea Dworkin,
> *Life and Death*

Now let's look at another slightly different but familiar list:

• Love 'em and leave 'em

• Deadbeat dads

• Males talking loudly and rudely, posturing and cursing

• Graffiti

• Bullies and gang fights

• Pack behavior and peer pressure

• Pigging out

• Watching TV all day long

• Sticking your nose into someone else's business.

The lists are familiar because the behavior is similar. Biological behavior is immediately recognizable due to its immediacy. There is no rational intervention between impulse and action. Your inner beast rises to the occasion whenever some juicy morsel comes its way.

Are you feeling anger or have a desire to take what does not belong to you? This is simply not a problem for your inner animal. What you impulsively feel is frequently what it does— as a matter of fact, it would much rather do what you *feel* like doing than

> Why didn't the pervert cross the road? Because his dick was stuck in the chicken.

what you *think* you should be doing. Every appetite and desire is an opportunity for your inner animal to express itself. You might want to think of yourself as an animal trainer. You will want to keep the creatures of your inner zoo under close observation.

Instead of a dog, you might prefer to think of your ASS as a huge hog, or a crocodile with huge snapping jaws lurking in the backwaters of your mind. Your inner hog is a master at doing absolutely nothing, or wallowing in the flow of every desire that washes over you. Your inner crocodile might be thought of as specializing in striking suddenly and without warning. Should you be eager to lash out with criticism or biting sarcasm at your fellow man or woman, your inner crocodile is quick to help you achieve your goals with a bit of extra savagery. Go the whole hog, as they say—no need to hold anything back—your inner menagerie is there to implement all of your wishes with no regard for anyone or anything.

Men who specialize in deceiving women for sexual favors are called dogs in many different languages. Think for a moment about the phrase "sexual predator." This suggests an animal stalking its victim. When we encounter obvious criminal types, do we not sometimes feel repulsed by their reptilian appearance? Likewise, why do we refer to some individuals as "snakes in the grass," "lounge lizards" or "sharks?" The answer is fairly clear. Those who have allowed their inner animals or their appetites to take over rational function begin to look like beasts. There are also con artists who, like chameleons, blend in artfully with their physical and social landscapes in order to avoid detection.

Society must identify those human beings who have seceded from humanity and forged alliances with their inner beasts. The GANDHI-HITLER INDEX found in Chapter 30 is a diagnostic tool to help you identify creatures masquerading as human beings in your places of business,

families and schools. In order to correctly identify and catalog the many
species of inner animals that you will encounter in your life, you must
have a system or structure upon which you can correctly plot the coordinates of good and bad behavior. In short, you must have a moral philosophy and system of spiritual metaphysics to map your social universe.
Psychology, like an old dog, scratches feebly at the door of the problem;
what we really need to do is to examine some ancient technology to get
a clearer understanding of your genitals' prime directive.

Ow the loot!
   Bloomin loot!
That's the thing to make the boys git up an shoot!
   It's the same with dogs an' men,
   If you'd make 'em come again
Clap 'em forward with a Loo! Loo! Lulu! Loot!
   Whoopee! Tear 'im, puppy! Loo! Loo!
Lulu! Loot! Loot! Loot!

            —Rudyard Kipling

Ballard Street By Jerry Van Amerongen

Garrett puts an end to the welcoming antics of
the Andersons' dog.

MANAGEMENT TIPS

* The insult "fuck you" is closely associated with inflicting violence of all kinds. Watch who you say the word fuck to; it may be a red flag to their inner animal.

* The hydraulic pressure in your balls is not always something to get rid of. There is a fountain of Chi behind that urge. See if you can tap into it.

* What is it about women shitting on glass tables that attracts you? Are fetishes wrong? Take some time to think about what you really want.

* Dressing loudly and talking trash helps you to become a dickhead.

* Your dick likes friction. This may extend to your social life. Watch it!

CHAPTER 10

ANCIENT DICK TECHNOLOGIES MEET MODERN SCIENCE

The intuitive mind is a sacred gift and the rational mind is a faithful servant.
We have created a society that honors the servant and has forgotten the gift.
—Albert Einstein

ALL LIVING THINGS OPERATE ON THE BIPOLAR (NEGATIVE AND POSITIVE) energy of Yin and Yang. This energy produces the Chi that are part of the workings of the life force. The life force is channeled to the body on different levels. These levels are interdimensional exchanges known as *chakras*. The energy they channel is called by different names in different cultures—Chi, Kundalini, Life-Force, Prana, Mani—but for our purposes they are roughly the same and no matter what term you choose, the management of this energy is the basis for many ethical systems, and the key to a better life. In order for you to learn how your dick is connected to this energy source, you must have some sort of model or way of diagramming how your dick and your impulses in general use energy.

The Hindus on the Indian sub-continent developed one of these systems many centuries ago. These yogis and philosophers described a source of life energy curled up at the base of the spine, which they called *Kundalini*, or "coiled serpent energy." This energy is converted or transformed into various grades of Kundalini known as *prana* at seven non-physical body centers called *chakras*. Chakra means "wheel" in Sanskrit. Think of the chakras as multi-dimensional wheels that have points of intersection with your body.

The power of Kundalini is legendary. You may have heard of yogis who can melt snow or levitate. The energy required to perform these kinds of psychic tricks, according to experts on Yoga, comes from applied Kundalini. Many of these same Yogis teach that prana must be cultivated and stored.

We have several common expressions that relate directly to the consumption of energy that occurs during sexual activity. We say things such as, "we humped our brains out" or "we lost our minds"—all indicative of a power drain or power failure. The cessation of thought that occurs in all moments of pure pleasure or pain indicates either a complete absorption in the activity or the kind of flickering that occurs with lights when the energy grid is oversubscribed by consumers. When was the last time your brain told you it didn't have enough energy? What do you think causes the kinds of depression that are apparently unconnected to loss or tragedy? Hold those answers; we first need to look more closely at the chakras themselves.

The chart below shows you how chakras might be visualized:

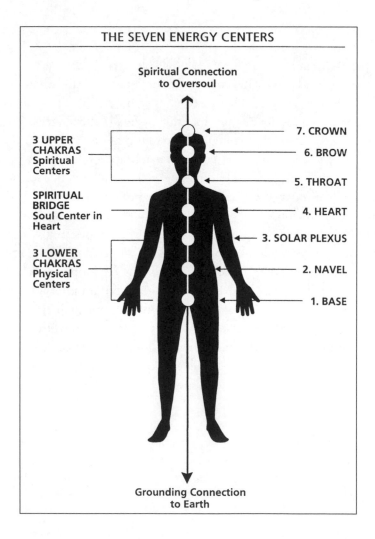

THE SEVEN ENERGY CENTERS

Spiritual Connection
to Oversoul

3 UPPER CHAKRAS
Spiritual Centers

7. CROWN
6. BROW
5. THROAT

SPIRITUAL BRIDGE
Soul Center in Heart

4. HEART
3. SOLAR PLEXUS

3 LOWER CHAKRAS
Physical Centers

2. NAVEL
1. BASE

Grounding Connection
to Earth

THE CHAKRAS EXPLAINED

Chakra 1   The Survival System—Basic Linkage Between Body and Life Force

Matter and life force are linked in the most elementary manner at this juncture. This chakra is the headquarters of your ASS. The first chakra governs the physical body, the base of the spine, legs and bones, rectum and the immune system. It is the center of basic emotions and instincts that relate to survival and security. Each chakra is associated with a color. The first chakra is associated with the color red. If too much of your energy is focused here, chances are you are selfish, and might be considered an "asshole."

Chakra 2   Sexual Instincts and Creativity

This chakra governs your sex drive and force of creativity. The sexual organs, the large intestine and pelvis come under the jurisdiction of this chakra. The second chakra is associated with the color orange. If too much Kundalini flows out this center, you will exhibit classic traits of a "dickhead."

Chakra 3   Will and Volitional Center

Power and mastery are the focus of the third chakra. It also governs the mid-spine, abdomen, spleen, liver and gall bladder. The third chakra is associated with the color yellow. (I should note that the first three chakras are focal points for most of the energy used by mankind. Your ego readily taps into these three centers.) If this is your major energy input and output center, you may be highly resistant to change or be what some would unkindly term "as thick as a brick."

Chakra 4   Emotional Center

This is the emotional center, often called the heart chakra or the center of compassion. Love and hate, grief, anger, forgiveness and hope are configured in this center. It governs heart, lungs and upper back and is associated with the color green. If your heart chakra is open, friends and family alike will consider you a loving person. Jesus is often associated with the heart chakra. This is why he is often graphically portrayed with his heart visible.

Chakra 5   Personal Expression and Time

This conversion center at the throat governs our sense of time, personal expression and our ability to communicate with others. It is our initial gateway to spirituality. The fifth chakra governs the throat, the mouth and thyroid gland and is associated with the color blue. Great orators, communicators, musicians and writers will have a very active throat chakra.

Chakra 6   Intuition and Truth Center

Sometimes called the wisdom chakra, the sixth chakra regulates intellect, and the ability to learn. Judgment, criticism, analysis, mathematical skills, and faith are all modulated by this center. The sixth chakra governs the brain and nervous system and is associated with the color indigo. This is Dick Management Central.

Chakra 7   Consciousness

This chakra is your uplink to divinity. Here your consciousness encounters multidimensional energy and entities outside our normal time and space. The seventh chakra, located over the top of the head, is associated with spirituality and the color violet. It is the doorway from humanity to divinity, the escape hatch from your inner crocodile.

THE SPIRITUAL PATH

The spiritual path in the yogic system might be described as a systematic use of moral, physical, and spiritual techniques to force the Kundalini energy to rise from the base of the spine through the chakras without stopping at the lower chakras, thereby allowing it to reach the overhead chakra and cause enlightenment and supreme happiness. The primary obstacle to spiritual growth, in this early moral schematic, centers on the notion that Kundalini (which for our purposes is a type of Chi or life energy) is constantly surging towards any open chakra. Enlightenment is slow because easy openings are always available for the Kundalini at all the "lower centers." This is a model for the management of sexual and psychic energy that antedates psychological explanations by many centuries. The biggest drainpipe for your energy, as it ascends through the chakras is your dick, so it is extremely important for you not only to manage the faucet, but first of all to know that there is one, and to learn to turn it the right way, at the right time. Dick Management will teach you how to do this but first you must understand how your desires work.

CATHECTION AND DESIRE

The conversion of energy that objects of desire induce in their subjects is not well described in Chakra theory. The ideas of this theory are most wonderfully perfected from a completely unexpected quarter. The founder of modern psychology, Sigmund Freud, utilized the word *cathexis* to describe how libidinal or psychic energy gets converted into appetite and desire. (Whenever you see the word "libido" just think of it as the source of psychic energy and appetite.) Freud inadvertently discovered a mechanism that perfectly describes how Kundalini works. Cathexis, even though it sounds like a clunky word, is a very useful way of describing how libido gets converted into other forms of energy. Likewise, by analogy, Kundalini might be described as lending itself to a similar energy conversion. One way of describing this conversion would be to say that your life energy attaches itself to and merges with the energy of various things as they become attractive to you. This attaching or *cathection* represents the first stage of your own energy conversion as it moves from potential to actual and is what actually starts the attraction to begin with. Your desires are the result of a cathection or fastening of potential that has already been made *before* it actually registers in your consciousness. Potential and actual are very strange concepts in this way. Which comes first, the chicken or the egg?

> Airports, the Dutch know, are all about flow control. Just visit the men's room. The tile under the urinals in the Arrivals Building…would pass inspection in an operating room. But nobody notices. What everybody does notice is that each urinal has a fly in it. Look harder, and the fly turns into the black outline of a fly, etched into the porcelain. "It improves the aim…if a man sees a fly, he aims at it."…Staff conducted fly-in-urinal trials and found that etchings reduce spillage by 80%…It gives a guy something to think about. That is a perfect example of process control [and cathection].
>
> ◆
>
> —Barry Newman, "Using Flies to Help Fliers," *The Wall Street Journal*

METACOGNITION, ENERGY AND YOUR IDENTITY

Metacognition is the pre-understanding and grasping of things that you don't yet fully know. You don't know what these things might be, only that they are out there and just beyond the grasp of your normal everyday consciousness. Potential events and things are within the realm of metacognition because your intellect can recognize not only what is actual in the here and now but also what is potential, i.e., what might be. How does the mind recognize the difference between actual and potential—between what is real and what is not yet real?

The argument of the ancients was that there had to be a form of actual energy that unfolded and wove potential energy into specifically existing things. This specific actualizing principle and coordinator of potential energy in non-living things was what Plato referred to as the *form* or *idea*. Aristotle referred to this same actual energy as *soul* when found in living things. Metacognition is an awareness that is rooted in the special abilities and actualizing power of your soul. Try exploring this power with the question: "Who is thinking?" You may note that you are in fact thinking these very words out loud but you will also notice that you were able to predicate this of yourself, as if you were outside yourself, looking at yourself. This metacognition would not be possible if you did not have the perspective of a larger actuality than you are consciously aware of. This greater actuality is able to seize potential—including *your own potential to be an object*. How can this be? Clearly there must be some part of you that is able to embrace the energy pattern of things, identify with them in the abstract—as being other than yourself—and then return that data to a memory device known as the brain. This is known as knowing "by becoming the thing itself on the plane of the act of knowledge."[12] This is more than just the process of calculation that we commonly refer to as thinking; it is a power that takes us out into the universe and enables us to be participants in the processes of reality, rather than automatons without either will or the power to change our reality.

Aristotle referred to this metacognitional power, specifically, as the *agent intellect*. Your agent intellect is able to "glom" onto both actual and potential things and become them in such a way that your *passive intellect* can faithfully mirror them. Your passive intellect is very much like hot wax—it takes the image that the agent intellect has absorbed and renders a faithful image to your senses. What makes this theory so very different from "the eye is a camera and the brain is an editor" view of modern thinking is that the brain is relegated to second place in the process. The brain might be better thought of as being like a radio that receives signals from a broadcasting station. The real power is coming from a force beyond the receiver. This is why scientists have so little information[13] as to how the brain really works—they are looking in the wrong place. Medical science is behaving like someone trying to take apart a TV set to find the people who are appearing on the screen!

Unlike many modern scientists, Aristotle and the Christian and Islamic philosophers who followed him centuries later were known as "realists." They believed that the agent intellect (as a power of the life force) could really know reality, and consequently, human beings lived in a real universe that ran on epistemological[14] laws that were not merely a subjective illusion projected by the structures of the human mind.

Relativists, on the other hand, do not believe that there is any objective reality to know. They believe that reality is a process that has no objective codification which the mind can latch onto. This argument had one of its clearest proponents in Immanuel Kant (1724-1804) who did not believe that you could ever know what he called, "the thing itself." If this were to be true, then we would have to conclude with the relativists that all moral laws and all cathections are ultimately subjective, and can neither be upheld or condemned under the magnifying glass of Ethics—except in terms relative to the given situation. Kant tried to avoid the consequences of his theory with what he called, *categorical imperatives.* These were universal rules that had to be obeyed whether or not you could ultimately know if they were true. Unfortunately, it is a hop, skip and a jump to relativism, if you cannot ascertain that an imperative or even a prohibition is rooted in something that you can really know.

Epistemology is the metaphysical science of how you can know things. The lack of a good epistemology can be the philosophical origin of much moral confusion: if you can't know reality, then the outline and the dynamics of what is true and false get blurred. This brings to mind Bill Clinton's famous line: "It depends on what you mean by is." Once reality is decoupled or deconstructed from cause and effect, knower and known—either by physicists or linguistic analysts—then meaning defaults to social contracts that are purely contingent on collective agreement or disagreement. In short, if cause and effect become completely subjective, Alice in Wonderland explanations fit just as well as any other.

Metacognition bridges the gap between the processes of reality that are external to you, and what appears to be evident to the senses. You don't need proof, for example, that you appear to exist, or that you are apparently in love. It is self evident to a certain extent for most us. Now of course you can question whether or not your reactions are not simply processes that you are attaching untoward significance to, but the majority of us would feel confident in ascribing objective reality to both our existence and our love affairs. The question arises, however, to what extent we can know the full significance of any process and its connection to the rest of all those things that are potentially true or false—meaning those things which are, or are not. Metacognition, as a form of intuitive understanding, helps us bridge this gap. This is what might be termed the faith in everyday reality. We make such acts of faith every day. The sun goes up and the sun goes down; it is raining or it is not. Most of us don't feel the need to question whether or not these things are true, or whether there is some hidden context we are missing that might suggest that what we are seeing is an illusion created by the warp and woof of our senses. We simply accept what we see. It is only when we question our metacognitional faith that we cast a pall of suspicion on objective reality, and ultimately, undermine common sense. When we do this, we hand over our thinking processes to linguists who are deconstructing language, and the legal profession, which at present is expert at decoupling the collective meanings that our culture ascribes to reality and replacing them with legal stratagems.

Whether we describe metacognition in terms of the mechanics of agent and passive intellect, or simply as metacognition, the reality is that your intellect and will are the eye of a force that cannot see itself, except in memory and time. Metacognition is ultimately that higher awareness of this force knowing itself and the world outside of memory, outside of time.

Who you may think you are is the past tense of who you actually are—much in the same way that what you know of the outside world is the past tense of what it presently is.

This does not mean that you do not know either yourself or the outside world. What it means is that you do not know its full significance from your present mental perspective.

This is why intuitions and hunches can be so powerful; they are rooted in a much more complex kind of temporal awareness than is found in just one body and one brain.

Metacognition is thinking outside the parameters of the brain and is an accessing of a greater consciousness than we are able to fully assimi-late. This larger consciousness is part of our future identity and is multi-dimensional. The energy required to access and bring this consciousness more fully into ourselves is intimately related to what we do with the energy of our life force.

The life force makes a supreme cathection with your life and your body at birth. You may have heard the expression, "lost the will to live." When anyone loses the will to live, it might be said that the soul relin-quishes its present cathection on this life and this body. This is an extremely dangerous condition that can lead to severe depression, suicide and risky behavior. It is critical, therefore, to recognize when the poten-tial of the sum total of cathections that your life force may have made during your life has been exhausted. Your life force simply needs some new challenges. This is why many conversion and "eureka" experiences come when you are at the very end of your cathection rope—all of a sudden your life force reaches out and cathects with something that gives you new hope, meaning and direction.

MODELING ENERGY CONSUMPTION

Metacognition and virtue, as forms of work, require energy and while this was implied by the ancient Greek philosophers, they never modeled the relationship between energy consumption, and the quality of the life force with quite the same visual power as did the ancient Chinese and Hindu sages. What they did, however, was provide a very useful schematic, using the concepts of virtue and vice, to show how the results of differ-ent kinds of behavior affect the metacognition of the soul. By using the classical map of virtue and vice, the energy system observed by the Chinese and the Hindus, and the concept of cathexis, as developed by Freud, we can get a more accurate picture of human energy systems. By having such a multi-cultural map, we can become adept at identifying those activities that produce actual energy or conserve potential energy, and those which tend to consume more than they produce. More im-portantly, such a map can steer us in the direction of activities that enhance metacognition, and help us to avoid those which distract us from this higher level of being.

Metacognition enables us to see our actions in such a way that we see their impact on both others and ourselves. Metacognition is at the heart of both compassion and Dick Management. The more clearly we can see the origin of our own and others' actions, the more we can sympathize with their difficulties and understand our own inclinations and desires. Metacognition enables us to see our cathections to the world more clearly. If you enjoy outdoor activities, for example, your Chi may be flowing back towards nature in a very healthy way. At other times, you may have a metacognition, or what most of us would call an intuition about our love life. If you find yourself thinking about someone that you may not have considered on a conscious level for a relationship, your life force may have already made a cathection with him or her that you are not fully aware of. Your intuition that something strange might be going on is a metacognition of the cathection that has already been made. You may experience this cathexis as a fleeting physical or emotional arousal, but rest assured that the other person has something that your life force wants or needs for balance. What is love at first sight but an instant cathection with the person of the other and a metacognition of your future together? Falling in love is of course a wonderful kind of cathection, but not all cathections are healthy.

STRANGE DESIRES AND CATHECTION

Some individuals may have desires that appear quite peculiar to the rest of us. How does one comprehend, for instance, the pleasure of sniffing someone else's shoes or underwear? Likewise, desires that manifest themselves in sado-masochism, necrophilia or in various kinds of self-mutilation (such as cutting oneself) reveal both the range and the curious structure of those things various individuals may find attractive. There is even an extraordinary and difficult to understand desire called *Apotemnophilia,* which is an attraction to the idea of amputating a limb. These individuals cannot feel "whole" unless one or more of their limbs have been surgically removed. (Apotemnophilia must of course be distinguished from *acromophilia*, which is the sexual attraction to amputees.) There are even web sites where such libidinally challenged individuals share information and the "porn" of hands without digits and legs chopped off at the knee. This has been journalistically and medically well reported,[15] and from the perspective of Dick Management shows the extraordinary degree to which the energy of the life force can be harnessed to self destruction when there are energy blockages or energy siphons.

The concept of cathexis helps us to understand strange desires by relating the movement of the life force to a river or stream. If a river is dammed in the wrong location, the water will flow into places where it doesn't belong. Likewise, your desires will flow into peculiar tributaries and backwaters if forces that you do not understand impede the basic flow of your life. Something in you seeks balance and will do almost anything to get that balance. Strange desires are almost always a result of psychological or spiritual imbalance. Cathexis, in this regard, is your life force's balancing tool.

The danger to you, of course, is that your energy, in seeking balance, will sometimes enter the habitat of your inner animal and be quite comfortable there. So what if you are shortening your life by overeating or taking drugs, by drinking, smoking or excessive sexual activity? So what if you're headed for death row because you've killed someone in anger? The inner crocodile does not care; it only wants primal satisfaction and metacognition is usually its first casualty.

CONNECTING TO EXCELLENCE

A more positive example of cathection may be related to your educational preferences. What you like in school is related to who you are and who you are to become. Reading and mathematics may open multiple chakras and help stimulate movement in the Kundalini, just as will exercise, sports, yoga, music, meditation, prayer, and various kinds of bodywork. The preferences of your life force will show you what direction you need to go in. They will also indicate to you your state of psychological and spiritual health. If you are truly obsessed with anything primal, such as eating or sex, you can be sure that your lower chakras are fully open and thereby reducing the flow of energy to higher evolutionary gateways. The lowest are the easiest chakras to engage, since they are larger and energy flows rapidly

I have suggested that if we are to be genuinely happy, inner restraint is indispensable. We cannot stop at restraint, however. Though it may prevent us from performing any grossly negative misdeeds, mere restraint is insufficient if we are to attain that happiness which characterized by inner peace. In order to transform ourselves—our habits and dispositions—so that our actions are compassionate, it is necessary to develop what we might call an *ethic of virtue*. As well as refraining from negative thoughts and emotions, we need to cultivate and reinforce our positive qualities.

◆

—The Dalai Lama

where it encounters the least resistance. Obsessions often indicate dangerous energy outflows that may be caused by blockages upstream.

The opening of lower chakras does not exclude the opening of higher chakras but you must remember that energy consumed at the lower chakras is simply not available in the same volume, so to speak, to the higher chakras. *This effectively functions as a visual model for Dick Management.* Energy consumed via the lower chakras tends to be depletive, whereas energy used in the upper chakras tends to be productive. The purpose of Dick Management is to maximize the effectiveness of your energy use. Likewise, in India, the energy of the Kundalini was harnessed by various yogic disciplines to bring body, mind and spirit in accordance with the idea of conserving energy and directing it to the higher chakras. These yogas use a specialized language that is remarkably similar in many respects to some of the concepts of virtue developed by the early Greeks.

Regardless of how you to choose to interpret these models, if you want to get the energy of the Kundalini (think Chi!) moving in the most constructive direction, you will need to understand and master the problem of entropy (see Chapter 7). Cathections of energy that require effort to overcome the "pulling down" factor of entropy can be referred to as the cultivated operations of virtue. Virtue directs the life force to higher rather than to the lower chakras. This movement of Kundalini from the lower levels of raw energy consumption to higher levels of energy abundant consciousness is the basis for a spiritual model that explains both enlightenment and the utility of Dick Management. The anti-entropic activity of the progressively enlightened being is the universal basis for excellence, and it is the platform for the observation of the social and individual destruction caused by the entropy of vice-driven behavior.

> If you think, you experience time.
> If you feel, you experience energy.
> If you intuit, you experience wavelength.
> If you sense, you experience space.
>
> —Fred Alan Wolf, *Star Wave*

MANAGEMENT TIPS

- Remember that your life force will make cathections for you, if you don't make some attempt to manage your internal processes.

- Watching talk shows on TV shows you how little people understand patience. Learn to wait your turn.

- Arguments will always test your virtue! Your Appetite Survival System prefers anger and impatience.

- The energy flows of conversation can excite your appetite. Manage the flow as it hits your consciousness and quiet your ASS.

- If you feel strongly about something, ask yourself if it is you or your ASS that really wants it.

PART II

Cyber-Kinetics
and the Soul

CHAPTER 11

HYPERSPACE AND QUANTUM SOUP

Electrons are negative charges and positrons are the anti-matter opposites of electrons. When they combine, they annihilate each other, releasing energy.

—*Science and Energy*

HOW CHAKRAS REALLY LOOK IS ANYONE'S GUESS, BUT IT IS PROBABLY SAFE to say that they are not visible to most of us. Perhaps they occupy a region of higher dimensionality called *hyperspace* by physicists. In order to get an idea of what hyperspace might be like, try visualizing a two dimensional world inhabited by flat creatures who know only the dimensions of length and width[16]. Now imagine one of the flat creatures imprisoned in a box drawn on that same paper. If someone from our three dimensional world were to pluck the creature out of his or her two dimensional jail, the other flat people would think a miracle had happened because up and down represent a third and unknown dimension[17]. In the same way, there are dimensions of a higher order contiguous with our own universe that may allow things like chakras to exist. Remember that these dimensions that are higher than three or four (four may be one of the dimensions of time) are collectively called hyperspace. Physicists are now claiming that there are at least twenty-six dimensions—if not more—some of which might appear to be infinitely small from our perspective, and would require enormous energy to access.[18]

QUANTUM WAVES

In order to understand how hyperspace works, we have to examine another concept from physics called the *quantum wave model*. There are two major theories physics uses to explain the universe: General Relativity theory and Quantum Mechanics. General Relativity theory, according to physicist Stephen Hawking and others, describes the force of gravity and the macro scale of the universe that solar systems, galaxies and quasars represent. Quantum mechanics, on the other hand, deals with events on an extremely small scale—the level of subatomic particles and associated processes. General relativity theory and quantum mechanics are unable, according to Hawking, to explain the origins of the universe on their own but when elements of both disciplines are combined, a larger picture of the universe emerges than can be predicted by either theory on its own. The so-called Theory of Everything or the Grand Unified Theory has not yet been found but many of the pieces are on the table. What physicists need now, in my opinion, is metaphysics. They need to make the leap from quantum mechanics to the multi-dimensional mechanics of the Divine Mind. Let us start with the meaning of quantum and move up the ladder.

The word *quantum* simply means: "one of the very small increments or parcels into which many forms of energy are subdivided."[19] Quantum Theory is based on the numerous processes involving *transference or transformation of energy on an atomic or molecular scale.*[20] Dig out the notion from the back of your mind that quarks have fractional charges and all of a sudden quarks and Chi are looking, from an analogous and metaphorical point of view, curiously alike. How would we measure quark flow when by and large, quarks are theoretical constructs inferred only through various smears that show up on photographic plates used in high energy physics experiments? I can't answer that question scientifically yet, but tuck it into the back of your mind for all future reflections on the nature of Chi. (There is a certain possible quantum felicity to the Chinese government's official spelling and pronunciation for Chi which is "*Qi.*")

Quantum waves, on the other hand, are a mathematical way of looking at events and things that enables them to be described in more than three or four dimensions. Physicists have theorized for quite some time that subatomic particles can exist as both particles and waves. In three and four dimensions (length, width, height and time) they might be described as particles but in dimensions five and above, they look like waves and are much more interconnected *through time* than they appear to be as particles. A quantum wave containing the particle components of a bicycle tire can as easily be on the other side of Jupiter in 1910, as it could be said to be passing through a sidewalk of New York City today. This is what is known as a *paradox*, i.e., something that seems to be contradictory or opposed to common sense but which also may simultaneously be true. It is something that cannot—at least on one rational level of seeing and understanding exist at all—but does.

Imagine that bicycle tire, as it touches the pavement, while you are riding down the street. At any given time, only a tiny fraction of that tire is ever touching the road. In the same way, what we see of the bicycle tire from a three-dimensional perspective is only the part that is touching the three dimensional road of space and time. We don't see the energy of that tire as it might look from the perspective of a five dimensional roadway. We only perceive things in terms of their three and four dimensional aspects (remember that time is the fourth dimension). This doesn't mean that the bicycle tire is not a bicycle tire—it certainly is—just in the same way that a brick thrown at your head is a brick. What these "events" might look like, however, from the perspective of higher dimensions is unknown. This is not the same as not knowing "the thing itself." We do know the thing itself—as it is consistently ordered within a given space-time framework—relative to our own position in that same framework. Knowing that an object may have a dimensionally higher reality may be metaphysically and morally useful, but is for all practical purposes, not determinative in such a way that we should disrespect or as they say today, "diss" reality or marginalize common sense. That being said, time and space are no barrier to the quantum waves that ultimately make up the energy of all things. What this means is that the energy of everything that has ever existed and will exist is floating together in some mysterious quantum soup that the equations of modern physics can point to but not completely define. Metacognition allows us to understand that this is so but it is up to us to make use of this knowledge in a practical way. Dick Management seeks to understand the quantum connections of your dick and your ASS.

EVERYTHING EXISTS IN TWO KINDS OF SPACE

The subatomic particles that make up the rubber of a bicycle tire don't just exist in three and four-dimensional space. They have an entire hidden existence, as you also do, in multi-dimensional space. This unified existence of subatomic particles and time, in the many dimensions of hyperspace, is what scientists refer to as *non-locality*. Looking at these same particles, things, or events from just a one-to-four dimensional perspective is known as *locality*. You live in a local universe, and your experience of yourself and reality at large is, for the most part, of the "local" universe.

This may be easier to understand if you consider locality in general as ac-tuality and non-locality as potential.

Within the context of non-locality, energy can be thought of as being more than one thing at a time and in more places than one. The Einstein, Podolsky, Rosen Paradox (EPR)[21] and Bell's Theorem, formulated in 1964, detail this craziness. According to these two theories, split particles seem to be linked in a way that indicates that some sort of *superluminal* or faster than light transmission of information occurs—*how*, nobody really knows. For example, if you were able to split a photon in Germany, at that very same instant, its partner—even though now theoretically in Alaska— would "know" exactly where the other particle was. This has been demonstrated in a number of labs throughout the world, but what does it really mean?

Both of these theories suggest that everything—from the farthest star to the small-est particle share some sort of underlying informational unity in the elemental potentiality of non-locality.

Another clue regarding the unity of all energy and information comes to us from holographic theory, which states that all events everywhere are immediately available as information, i.e., each portion of space contains information about all other spaces. This is of course now more than just a speculation, as holographic engineering can produce amazing images that demonstrate holographic theory as scientific truth. The holographic notion of a part, which contains all the information contained in the whole, points again to some underlying and unified linkage of all energy and information.

Non-locality is a little bit like a quantum soup in which all things and all times are completely connected and simultaneous. The only thing that keeps you from flying off and becoming a star, an ocean wave or a flower is your specific quantum nature, which tends to tie you to a specific time frame. Ultimately, though, your matter is not confined to four dimen-sions. There are higher orders of matter of which our four dimensional universe is but a dim shadow. Who you are is much larger than your day-to-day conception of yourself.

COLLAPSING THE CONTINUUM

So how do you move, conceptually speaking, from quantum waves to par-ticles, or from non-locality to locality? What does this mean in terms of everyday life? Quantum waves are said to *collapse* into four-dimensional space when we observe or engage them in some way. What this means is that every time you do anything, the movement from potentiality to actuality causes quantum waves to collapse. If you walk across the room, you are collapsing the multi-dimensional quantum waves of a particular future that will unfold for you due to the multi-dimensional interconnectedness of that action to the rest of the entire universe. In order to do this you must have some special ability to make the quantum jump from the actuality of locality to the potential of non-locality. Your life force consciousness not only has the ability to collapse quantum waves but it can also not collapse them!

Yes, your ASS can also collapse quantum waves and that it why you must not allow it to determine your reality! Have you ever snapped a wet towel at someone else's backside? The snap that you get out of the towel is based on a conversion of the potential energy of the moving towel, with the sudden jerk that you give it to retard its forward motion. That snap is in a way emblematic of quantum waves and action in general. You are converting momentum and potential momentum into the actual energy of the snap. This snap flicks across the buttocks of your victim like an electric tongue and you presumably enjoy the subsequent howls. In the same way, your desires can snap you out of your potential matrix and flick you like a bug kill across the windshield of your ASS. Learning to manage your dick will teach you how to hang on to that moving potential—the fabric of your being. Rather than flicking like a wet towel across the scrofulous ASSES of others, you will stay clean, dry and healthy.

Max Plank provided a clue to the curious activity of quantum waves in 1900. He discovered that energy only came in quanta (packets of energy) when *entering or leaving matter*. (Think about that wet snapping towel again; when you snap it hard, you will see water flying out of it.) What rules governed this strange in and out activity of quanta? Something appeared to be mediating the seamless non-locality of the quantum wave and simultaneously administrating its local manifestation. An entire category of wave-form functions was derived from this initial insight. It was later postulated that a certain type of energy wave known as a *carrier wave*[22] could locally snap the non-locality of quantum waves into a local manifestation—just like you and the wet towel. If this sounds suspiciously like Plato's Ideas or Aristotle's famous forms in a more modern guise, welcome to the club.

Physicists have long known that observation of high energy experiments can change their outcome. This has traditionally been attributed to the effects of general relativity theory but it is, perhaps, more understandable to say that observation of non-local events causes quantum waves to collapse into locality. Local energy, on the other hand, looks like subatomic particles interacting. These hundreds of tiny particles are governed by the rules of quantum dynamics under what physicists call The Standard Model. This model describes four conventional forces in physics and states that all the forces binding various particles operate by exchanging quanta or packets of energy. The four forces are:

1. Electromagnetic energy   (electricity, light, radio waves, etc.)

2. Gravity   (this particle remains elusive)

3. Weak Force   (exchanges between electrons and other particles)

4. Strong Force   (exchanges between quarks)

According to the Standard Model, many subatomic particles are not fundamental particles at all but also consist of even tinier particles known as leptons and quarks. Quarks come in "colors" and "flavors," and engage in a variety of activities that are generally incomprehensible to those not trained in higher mathematics. What is understandable is that physicists do not know why various symmetries or reoccurring patterns of energy interaction exist at all! The unifying principle of physics, the Theory of Everything or the Grand Unified Theory (GUT) remains elusive. However, non-locality as a metaphor, and not as a set of equations enables us to make the intuitive leap and to grasp without the benefit of mathematics, that the interconnectedness of the universe is based on some unifying and *non-standard* principle such as Chi that will continue to elude physicists as long as they continue to search for an explanation that doesn't point to a non-local source for both energy and consciousness. Alternatively, the strong force may in fact be evidence of Chi activity under another name.

MANAGEMENT TIPS

• Quantum soup is a metaphor for the mind, not something for your ASS to swallow.

• Your ASS prefers to stay local. Non locality is not its cup of soup.

• Chakras are non-local input output centers for many biochemical processes. Just because science hasn't yet identified these processes will not prevent you from observing them in your subtle inner consciousness.

• Your quantum address is like an unlisted phone number but that doesn't mean it doesn't exist.

• Going non-local frequently means that you have to let go of anger, fear and impatience.

CHAPTER 12

THE BIZARRE WORLD
OF THE ACTUAL

It's eternity in a person that turns the crank handle.

—Franz Kafka

YOU MAY BE SCRATCHING YOUR HEAD AT THIS POINT AND WONDERING out loud what *actuality* and physics might have to do with managing your dick or virtue. Understanding actuality (actual energy) holds the key to understanding your dick, virtue and physics, so pay close attention—slap yourself if you have to and make the decision not to be a metaphysical candy ASS. This chapter and the next two chapters will require some heavy duty thinking, but the rewards will more than make up for the effort. (If you are truly not comfortable with metaphysics, go straight to Chapter 14 and continue reading. It will still be worth your while!)

Actuality in the metaphysics of Aristotle was simply the unfolding of potential, but the closer you look at actuality and potential, the weirder they both seem. What is potential? The dictionary defines potential simply as: "something that can develop or become actual." We think we know what this means but when you work that backwards, at some point you come to something that has no beginning or is in itself causeless. Think of actuality in terms of fire. Fire represents the conversion of one form of energy (say wood) into another in the form of heat and light. Energy is simply changing form but what has given it the potential to do so in the first place? Actual energy is what allows potential energy to exist in the first place! This is another way of saying that energy is neither created nor destroyed—it just changes its form. *Potential is one of the disguises that actuality can assume when viewed through the Einstein lens of four-dimensional space-time.* Potential is actuality unfolding, slow motion style in time but what on earth is actuality or energy to begin with? Another way of asking the same question is: what is energy doing when it is not present in local three and four dimensional space as either actual or potential energy, i.e., what does non-local energy look like?

THE MASKS THAT ENERGY WEARS

Where, for instance, is the energy that makes your dick hard before it makes your dick hard? Your dick is only potentially hard at all times. What makes it actually hard, aside from the mechanics of filling with blood and the urgent testosterone signals of your balls? Where did the urgent potential of that itchy pool of semen, which is steaming your mind in x-rated thoughts come from? The "juice" that is making your Chi is coming from your life force, which in turn, is being generated by the multi-dimensional interaction of Yin and Yang. What is generating your Yin and Yang? According to Chinese philosophers, Yin and Yang emerge from a void that cannot be adequately described in words. The ancient Greeks, on the other hand, spent a lot of time speculating on the *regression of causation,* i.e., following the line of cause and effect backwards till they got to a source where they thought it might have originated. Since they were unfamiliar with ideas such as Yin and Yang, they developed an entirely different approach to causality that was based on a detailed chain of cause and effect.

These ancient philosophers had their own version of Yin and Yang in the notions of actual and potential and quite frankly, they are not terribly dissimilar in terms of what they are trying to elucidate. It would not be inaccurate, for example, to describe Yin and Yang in terms of actual and potential. If you drop the notion of Yin as female and Yang as male, you simply have positive and negative, which is another way of talking about actual and potential. The Greeks described the mixture of actuality and potential that we see in the present as being (lower case) and the larger actuality in question as *Being* (with a big "B"). The relationship between being and Being has bedeviled philosophers and theologians for centuries. A modern way of looking at the problem would be to say that being is local and *Being* is non-local.

A startling thought emerges from the perspective of modern physics: what we think of, as potential energy is really only a form of actual energy that is non-local. It just looks like and behaves like potential from our three and four-dimensional perspective. What this suggests is that the higher up the dimensional ladder you can climb, the closer you will get to the simultaneity and the "speaking togethering" of all the energy in the universe. The kind of information that the simultaneous actualization of all potential would represent is so staggeringly multi-dimensional and enormous in its complete actuality that we might think of our normal space and time as protection against its overwhelming power. This superluminal (faster than light) information and energy would indeed be present in all places, at all times and all at once.

How such energy and information would communicate itself in three and four dimensions is a great mystery, unless of course there is a negentropic energy and information interface that would enable the superluminal to function in what we consider normal space-time. That interface may be the evolutionary web of all living things. What is certain, however, is that the superluminal must exert an enormous force of attraction and evolutionary pressure on our four dimensional universe.

Your mind is a curious amalgam of surface potentiality combined with an actuality that pokes through many levels of awareness when you least expect it to. Conditions of stress and hopelessness seem to particularly favor personal encounters with one's own higher actuality. Mind in general, which seeks to regain the higher reality of non-local consciousness, simultaneously affects the potency of whatever matter it comes in contact with. Aristotle's definition of a soul as being "the first act of a body having life-potential" is useful here. What this definition means in modern parlance is that when matter becomes sufficiently complex in terms of material potential, *this potentiality itself must be thought of as the result of higher forms of actual energy attempting to manifest in a new way.* The whole notion of evolution being solely attributed to mutation and natural selection over large periods of time is entirely inadequate to describe the pressure dynamics of superluminal actuality. Natural selection or the survival of the fittest is only part of the evolutionary dynamic of superluminal and *negentropic energy transfers*[23] into the local universe. The startling complexity of your brain and your Appetite Survival System is the result of a local and non-local negentropic interface that has evolved between three-dimensional matter, time and the energy of higher dimensions.

Needless to say, the story is becoming more complicated. The pressure dynamics that affect evolution are the same pressure dynamics that are speaking to your balls and infecting your dick with some of those urges that occasionally overwhelm your conscious mind. Metacognition can be swept away by your ASS once it starts to push on your balls.

THE PRESSURE DYNAMICS OF EVOLUTION

A long time ago, when matter first started to evolve (we won't get into the nuts and bolts of how it started in this book), non-local force or energy became locally conscious. This is doubly confusing because non-local force is conscious in higher dimensions, but you do not have to understand this at the moment—just accept it as something to work with. You will get the hang of this as we move along. In order for non-local consciousness to manifest in our common space-time, a sufficient level of material complexity had to exist. For example, if your television were not sufficiently complex in terms of its technology, all the TV stations in the world would be useless. They could broadcast but you would not be able to receive. Non-local consciousness is a little bit like this. It exists and it seeks a material complexity in which to further express its potential, but before non-local consciousness enters locality, it manifests as Chi on various levels of physical and genetic evolution. As the wave-form of Chi collapses from higher dimensions on down, like an Origami bird, it enfolds its energy in ever more convoluted physical structures. Time and space are by-products, not conditions of its action.

The collapse of the wave-form function of non-local consciousness from hyperspace into particularity is a bit like an electron passing through energy levels or what are called shells (for those of you who know or remember college level chemistry) except that the collapse might be further thought of as creating dimensional interfaces within matter itself. One of these primitive and yet complex dimensional interfaces is the Appetite Survival System, which may be an early evolutionary feature of Howard Bloom's Global Brain. Other such in-terfaces include the human will and intellect, which may also be man-ifestations of the global brain, or universal consciousness as it tries to understand itself from an external perspective. Now this may sound like a great deal of intellectual gibberish, but take some time and think about this. These are not easy concepts even for biologists and physicists to explain but they are vital to your ability to understand and manage your dick.

Your consciousness, or what you loosely term mind, is a bridge between locality and non-locality. You are a non-local entity struggling with its own vast evolutionary, local and biological history and you are not happy about it. You and your Dick are part of the ancient pressure dynamics between the superluminal, as it exists outside of time and space and the superluminal, as it erupts into local space and takes on survival characteristics commensurate with its environment. Your ASS has been with you from the beginning, as has your spirit.

TACHYONS AND CHI

Norman Freidman, a physics enthusiast, outlines an extraordinary relationship between actuality and potential that is implicit in modern quantum wave theory. Freidman notes that when massless, faster than light particles called tachyons gain in energy, *their velocity decreases,* that is to say, as they increase in speed, they lose energy.[24] Tachyons are postulated to move at faster than light speed, which theoretically would require an infinite amount of energy to attain. What sort of cosmic activity could provide infinite energy? I leave this to your imagination but what this model shows us is that as some particles approach light speed, *what appears to be actual energy starts to disappear,* despite the fact that velocity is actually increasing. Where is it disappearing to? This is where our three and four-dimensional model of looking at reality breaks down. What is apparently happening is that energy takes on a higher dimensional actual form as it approaches the speed of light. The peculiar behavior of split photons "knowing" each where the other is that we see in Bell's Theorem is a testament to the dimensionally higher activities exhibited by light.

The most useful thing about tachyons is that they provide a model or a way of thinking about Chi. Any particle that can move faster than light, cannot move at this speed in three and four dimensional space (the fourth dimension being time). Actual energy (in this case tachyons or Chi) condenses out of hyperspace and acquires potential in three and four dimensions. What would appear to be happening with tachyons is that they are *acquiring potential energy as they slow down.* This acquisition of potential is precisely what pulls tachyons down into three and four-dimensional space. You might want to think of this in terms of rain clouds acquiring enough mass to release some of that mass as rain. In the same way, once tachyons acquire potential, they start to increase in mass and may no longer be thought of as tachyons but possibly some other unidentified and transitional particle. Now this is where speculation acquires enough potential to rain down thoughts.

Physicists still don't know what gravity is and no one has yet found the elusive *graviton,* the postulated particle that represent gravity. I respectfully suggest to the metaphysical community, the extraordinary and yet simple idea that gravity is the *energy signature* of the superluminal as it erupts out of its 26 (or even greater) dimensional matrix into three and four-dimensional space and starts to fall back to its point of origin. Gravity, as all scientists know, increases with mass and it is this increased mass that curves space-time and causes gravity. This is why gravity on the sun and on large planets such as Jupiter and Saturn is many times that of Earth's. What they don't understand are the superluminal particle dynamics that make this possible.

YOUR ASS IS LOOKING FOR SOMETHING TO GRAB

Thinking about such things as the machinery of the cosmos and tachyons also provides us with an interesting way of thinking about managing appetites and impulses. You give quantum potential to impulses by engaging them. They will pass through the atmosphere of your mind, if you ignore them. Your attention and indeed, your very actuality is *oxygen for your impulses* and helps precipitate them from the vast fields of quantum potential that surround us. When you mentally or physically engage anything, you give it some of your actual quantum energy, which is converted to further quantum potential. You cannot see this part of the cathection process but that doesn't mean it doesn't happen. The less you engage impulses and thoughts, the less they will be able to engage you. One of the ways that metacognition can help you with all urges is to help you step back and ignore them out of existence. This is virtue of a high order and one of the reasons that you will want to cultivate self-restraint in all matters of impulse. You retain more of your own actual energy the less you engage in the potential slowing down that the formation of impulsive activity creates. Metacognition allows you to live in a greater non-locality and avoid many of the sewage problems that your life force's ASS will get you into. Metacognition also enables you to reflect upon the meta-workings of the universe. In short, it enables you to be a philosopher, a theologian and a Dick Manager.

UP SHIFT TO THE SUPERLUMINAL

One of course might wonder in the abstract whether or not the Superluminal is conscious, or even whether or not it needs to be conscious, but the deeper awareness of our hearts tells us that yes, the superluminal is in some profound way, conscious and Divine. The haunting words of Genesis break the sky of our self-imposed limitations on what the Infinite might be like: "Let us make them in *our* image."

Whatever the Superluminal is—supraconscious and caring, or unconscious and indifferent (at least to our dimensionally limited thinking) it has been the source of many thousands of years of metaphysical speculation. Being, God, Non-Locality, Superluminal Energy, All That Is, The Unknown Force, The Divine, Supermind, The Ultimate Reality, Unmoved Mover, Tao—there are hundreds of names for it. Modern scientists are only the most recent group to attempt description of this apparently unchanging reality that seems to support the universe. It certainly is enough to make your head spin. Your soul, however, eats this stuff up—it can't get enough of it, even if all the big words and convoluted concepts give you a headache.

Your ASS, however, may be scrunching up its metaphorical butt cheeks—it senses that it is going to have problems, if all this thinking goes any further. So if you notice a deep resistance in yourself to some of these thoughts, ask yourself who or what is resisting? Is it you or is it your Appetite Survival System? Shift your identity to a higher level and observe the chattering objections of your ASS dispassionately.

THE HYPERSPACE METASYSTEM

Chinese philosophers refer to the interconnectedness of all reality (both actual and potential) as the Tao, the Way of Life, sometimes referred to as *Ta-Hua* or more simply as *The Way*:

> Ta-Hua makes every modality of being in the universe a dynamic
> change rather than a static structure. A piece of stone, a blade of
> grass, a horse, a human being, a spirit and Heaven all form a con-
> tinuum. They are all integrated by the pervasive Chi (vital force
> and material force which constitutes both matter and energy) that
> penetrates every dimension of existence and functions as the con-
> stitutive element for each modality of being. (Mircea Eliade, *The
> Encyclopedia of Religion*)

If you think of the Tao as a kind of hyperspace metasystem, which incorporates all of locality and non-locality into itself, it is perhaps easier to speculate that morality in general might be based on a superluminal (faster than light) negentropic energy and information transfer system[25] written into the very heart of everything that exists. This pre-existing and ancient system of energy accountability is the basis for what has been called the Law of Karma in Indian philosophy and in Western theology, Natural Law—a body of law or specific principle held to be derived from nature and deemed to be binding upon human society. They are both concepts that attempt to mine the universal insight that all life and all actions are connected on multiple dimensional levels of being and energy.

We are all aware that our actions have an effect, but the act that *affects* or causes the *effect* also has repercussions on the actor. This is key to the Indian concept of Karma. The idea that all actions have a karmic *affect* and an *effect* on the energy continuum of life can only be demonstrated in the context of a multi-dimensional metasystem of energy and information. Dick Management is the science that seeks to understand this metasystem and its relation to your life.

BEAM ME UP SCOTTY

If we assume that Kundalini and Chi are two ancient ways of trying to describe superluminal and negentropic energy transfers through a hyperspace metasystem, then an outline of the metaphysical domain of Dick Management begins to take on shape and clarity:

• Chi is non-local energy. (That is why most of us can't see it.)
• Your chakras are non-local energy processing centers.
• Your id is a primitive form of local consciousness
• Your ego is your contemporary, local identity.
• Your higher self is a metacognitional bridge between your local identity and your non-local identity, i.e., your soul.
• Negentropy is based on a superluminal energy exchange between local and non-local space.
• Morality is more than just a local problem!
• The Tao is an ancient model that integrates what physicists are now calling locality and non-locality.
• Dick Management is a way of counteracting the negative effects of entropy.

If hyperspace is a "real" place and not a figment of the scientific imagination, then we may have to rearrange all of our technical, moral, and spiritual thinking. Using the hyperspace model, it is easy to imagine that the technology behind the famous line, "Beam me up Scotty," from Star Trek may not be impossible. The conversion of three and four dimensional space back into the wave-form of non-locality means that you should theoretically be able to convert the wave-form back into local space wherever you put your coordinates. What this ultimately means is that objects in hyperspace should be able to move faster than light. But I digress. What it also means is that what you do with your schlong has cosmic implications. But do not be alarmed, or frozen into inaction; as you grow in wisdom, you will begin to see truth and consequences more clearly.

Since therefore God is the effective cause of things, the perfections of all things must pre-exist in God in a more eminent way...Inasmuch as He knows His own essence perfectly, He knows it according to every mode in which it can be known...Now it can be known not only as it is in itself, but as it can be participated in by creatures...God does not understand things according to an idea existing outside Himself. Thus Aristotle (Metaphysics IX) rejects the opinion of Plato, who held that ideas existed of themselves, and not in the intellect. God is the similitude of all things according to His essence; therefore an idea in God is identical with His essence.

—Thomas Aquinas, *Summa Theologica*, Q. 15, Art 3, Pt. 1

**"Let's work with what we've got--
Take some of the more promising apes,
and add some extra memory."**

MANAGEMENT TIPS

• Your ASS is an evolutionary, primitive thinking system that is perhaps an early offshoot of the Global Brain.

• Body and mind are not separate, but are manifestations of a higher dimensional, non-local entity called by many names such as: atman, core-self, dasein, ka, psyche, quantum entity, thetan and soul.

• The life energy has power that is derived from two sources: biochemical processes (local sources) and non-local energy sources outside of your body. This combined energy makes instinctive urges possible.

• Superluminal, non-local forces descending into four-dimensional space cause evolution.

• The pressure dynamics of non-local forces can affect your dong.

CHAPTER 13

WHO YOU REALLY ARE

Show me the Original Face you had before your
parents were born.

—Hui Neng (circa 650 AD)

YOUR TRUE SELF MIGHT BE THOUGHT OF AS A NON-LOCAL OR HYPER-space identity. This suggests that who you are is not limited to just four-dimensions of spacetime. This non-local identity, ultimately, might be thought of as your identity in the Superluminal and has traditionally been referred to as *atman*, *ka* or soul. The great German philosopher Martin Heidegger refers to it obliquely as *dasein*. It is a construct almost beyond our comprehension, but much like the concept of Chi, it is inextricably, the all linked to the All. I prefer to think of dasein as a convoluted German way of trying to get at the same fundamental reality that Thomas Aquinas postulates[26] and that Sri Aurobindo[27] refers to again and again. We are literally ideas in the "mind" of a Superluminal entity usually re-ferred to as God, who knows all things from all time. God is undivided, which means He has no moving parts or ideas that are separate from Him; He is His own thought and His own existence. How God's idea of you gets played out in time is how the local *you* happens to have come into existence. The consciousness-force that constitutes your life force is linked to God's own identity in a multi-dimensional continuum of con-sciousness and energy that is extremely difficult to explain in terms of four dimensional thinking patterns.

Your deepest self or dasein has partial dimensional access to this Divine Idea, which is your eternal and anti-entropic identity. We will talk more about soul theory in the next chapter, so hold the skepticism and the questions for the moment. Please use the idea of an identity in the Divine or an identity in the Superluminal as working concepts. You do not have to agree with the idea, or be religious to play around with it—and it has the potential of being more fun and rewarding than almost anything you can think of!

Who you really are cannot fully exist in time and space as we know it and this is why the matter of your body is under constant pressure from higher dimensions. This is also the basis for evolution. Think of your deepest or *core self* as a diamond, which is formed under the immense evolutionary pressure of the soul. Your consciousness, likewise, is formed through the pressures and dynamics of life. You cannot be born into your true self without the pressure of suffering and struggle. Like a diamond in the rough, your core self is a multi-dimensional construct that interprets the radiance of the soul, which in turn, is the sole interpreter of its blinding reality in the Superluminal.

> Our Birth is but a sleep and
>   a forgetting;
> the soul that rises with us,
>   our life's star,
> hath had elsewhere its setting
> and cometh from afar;
> Not in entire forgetfulness
> and not in utter nakedness
> but trailing clouds of glory
>   do we come
> from God, who is our home.
> Heaven lies about us in our
>   infancy!
>
> ◆
>
> —Walt Whitman, *Ode:
> Intimations of Immortality*

The non-locality of your core self is rooted in a twenty-six dimensional interchange that guarantees that it will always be one step ahead of your local consciousness. The core self is the master of entropy in much the same way that your ASS, in its negative aspect, is the love slave of that same entropy.

HYPERSPACE AND NON-LOCAL EXPERIENCES IN YOUR DAILY LIFE

What are called hunches, intuitions, and bright ideas are often nothing more than a glimpse or dip into the non-local perspective of metacognition. Those who are intrinsically gifted in these areas and those who work on developing them are called psychics, mystics, clairvoyants, channels, and lunatics. The more you notice and honor non-local experiences in your own life, the more you want to make sure that your non-local self does not hook up with any unsavory non-local characters such as demons, or engage in inappropriate local actions with the morally devolved.

The most significant issue as this relates to your dick is that the core self seeks creative expression. It is hungry to go about its business. If it is frustrated in its basic mission, it will release energy for cathection in whatever direction it is allowed to go. Mis-cathected appetites lead an individual to take pleasure in things that are hurtful to other people. The soul is aware of this difficulty, hence the notion of conscience.

Your conscience is simply the more developed aspect of the core-self trying to manage the lower aspects. Another way of saying this is that the non-local "you" which is multidimensional and quantum will always have to manage the local ego which is only three and four dimensional. The local you, for instance, may not believe in guilt or spirit but your non-local or quantum self knows otherwise. You may say you are a skeptic who doesn't believe in things he can't see, but no doubt you believe in both atoms and love. The fact is, you are the embodiment of and witness to titanic mysteries that any scientist or mystic worth his or her salt will tell you confront them every day. (A cultural aside—the common greeting in Nepal is to say *namaste* with folded hands and a slight bow. What does it mean? "I bow to the Divine in you.")

And so, unless you become the conductor of your own life or allow others to direct your Chi—teachers, parents, mentors, wise men and women, saints—your life may become disordered or side-tracked. Your life energy in the form of unregulated cathections can even become demonic. For example, if you allow the soul to taste the pleasure of torture, it may seek more and more of this pleasure in an inversion of its true values.

DON'T CHANNEL YOUR ASS

We all wonder how atrocities happen, how someone can kill their entire family or blow up government buildings full of innocent workers. Do you think that the people responsible for acts such as these did not "get off" on their actions? Think again; hedonism is not limited to excessive consumption of food, drink and sex. It is a taking of pleasure in energy release, whether it's from ecstasy or terror, semen erupting or blood gushing, life forming or life departing.

What your core self really wants is to fulfill its mission and refresh itself at its point of origin, which is the source of all life—the Superluminal reality. Have you ever wondered why it feels so good to be happy? When we are attuned to our inner being and behave accordingly, we become closer to who we really are, which is a reflection of our ultimate identity in the Superluminal. The converse of this is also true. The less we vibrate on the level of who we are, the less we will feel good about ourselves. Authenticity and truth are your connection to the Superluminal reality that transcends time. Obey these voices and you can never really be unhappy.

The spiritual adversary of the core self is the Appetite Survival System which has no interest in metaphysical thinking. This is pure gibberish to your ASS and if you don't watch it, your ASS will figure out a way to ignore anything that requires thought. This is why there is always a struggle between higher pleasures and lower pleasures.

"The spirit is willing but the flesh is weak," said Jesus; these words summarize the fundamental duality of your struggle with yourself as both a local and non-local entity. You are able to identify with both of these levels of your being—you can be an ASS or a saint or, an unholy combination of the

> "**B**efore I formed you in the womb, I knew you."
>
> ◆
>
> —Jeremiah 1:5,
> *The Old Testament*

two but what you choose most often is what you will tend to become. This is a tremendous power for good or ill, and it is also why virtue is so important; it enables you to "channel" your non-local self—the ultimate Dick Manager—instead of your ASS, and to surf quantum waves instead of pissing away your life.

THE POWER OF YOUR THOUGHTS AND ACTIONS

Your life force possesses superluminal power of an unimaginable magnitude, and its ability to do the work of your life is extraordinary. This energy however, is not fully available to your physical body—much in the same way as the higher energies of an atom are not readily available for our use, unless force-induced through fission or fusion. You can, however, better use the energy that is available to you by managing the local hemorrhaging of non-local energy that occurs with vice.

The wave-form of your consciousness collapses at the point of engaged desires or observation (as physicists note) and gives up some of its quantum energy. This is why it is so important to manage energy at the level of the wave-form, or non-locally, as opposed to its local manifestation. Once the energy has manifested locally, you may have a Management problem. Virtue at its highest level enables you to manage the wave-form functions of Chi. Your ego's job is to mediate between local and non-local influences. Only you can decide to listen to your ASS or to your core self who is the Dick Manager.

Whatever you think about and whatever you do has quantum consequences. You are an energy being, an entity that vibrates on a sliding scale between positive and negative actions. All positive actions bring you closer to the true nature of your own wave-form identity—your higher self. All negative actions bring you closer to your lower wave-form identity—your ASS!

The wave-form energy that is Chi may be managed through education, discipline or creativity but the management of energy does not explain the process, only that it can occur. Electrical energy is generated through friction, moving water, magnetic resistance, heat and photon containment, and so forth, but this does not explain the mechanism of energy conversion. Your psychic energy, as some psychologists call it, or Chi, needs to be converted in much the same way that the energy of falling water is converted to electrical energy by turbines. The virtues are like those turbines.

Chi may be converted to useful intellectual and moral cathections through sublimation or resistance to energy that is seeking to become other than moral or intellectual. Energy that is stopped at chakras that are "managed" will be forced to rise to the next available center. Chakras are quantum energy conversion centers or gateways, and you are the gatekeeper. By becoming a Dick Manager you will have the proper set of keys at your disposal.

Remember that this is just a useful tool in visualizing how life energy is converted. There are many different models for Chi usage. Some of these models work better than others but it is important to have a model. Without a model of life energy conversion, there can be no objective rationale for the kind of energy management that is required for moral actions and personal growth.

Virtue is an ancient technology that is rooted in a direct awareness of the higher self and its relation to either the chakras or some other moral schematic of quantum energy consumption. Virtue enables you to become a Dick Manager. This allows you to become aware of, and start to manage, the most powerful aspects of your energy consumption. Thus will you be able to more effectively achieve goals, turn dreams into reality, and be revered for your generosity of spirit and your ability to love others in a magnificent fashion, like the heroes and saints of old. Needless to say, the light of happiness will shine through you.

Personal identity is known to reside in memory, and the annulment of that faculty is known to result in idiocy. It is possible to think the same thing of the universe. Without an eternity, without a sensitive, secret mirror of what passes through every soul, universal history is lost time, and along with it our personal history—which rather uncomfortably makes ghosts of us. The Berliner Company's gramophone records or the transparent cinema are insufficient, mere images of images, idols of other idols. Eternity is a more copious invention. True, it is inconceivable, but then so is humble successive time. To deny eternity, to suppose the vast annihilation of the years freighted with cities, rivers and jubilations, is no less incredible than to imagine their total salvation.

—Jorge Luis Borges, *A History of Eternity*

MANAGEMENT TIPS

• Fear your own resistance to the power of the Superluminal.

• Clean your garage, or your closet if you don't have a garage. Break the habitual patterns of your ASS by challenging its complacency and laziness.

• Volunteer work can help open up your heart chakra and get your Chi moving in new areas.

• Raise a child. "Adopt" a child. This will help you connect to the universe in ways you never imagined.

• Be polite to telemarketers and solicitors. They are trying to make a living too. Your inner reptile likes to assault people.

CHAPTER 14

DIMENSIONALLY INTERACTIVE CYBER-KINETICS

Heaven doth with us as we with torches do,
not light them for themselves.

—Shakespeare, *Measure for Measure*

THE CONCEPT OF NON-LOCALITY ALLOWS US TO FOCUS MORE SHARPLY on the origin of the soul and to understand the *dynamic quantum interaction* between local and non-local space. The soul, if it exists, is in all likelihood non-local in nature, but the soul as it is presented by organized religion has all the local characteristics of a gas tank. If a soul is something that you *have* like money in a wallet or a car in the garage, then it can be ignored. If it is something that you are an expression of, then that is a different matter. You can't escape your soul.

Likewise, the Cartesian separation of soul from body—this "I think therefore I am," instead of "I am therefore I think" also plagues western thought. Once the body was separated from the soul, it was not long before the soul itself was discarded as a superfluous religious accretion. Without a soul to improve, the only things that can be improved are mind and body. Not content to be rid of the soul, some philosophers are working mightily to prove that we don't exist at all. If we are to believe some of these theories, we don't even exist except as disembodied processes that float like bubbles and foam on the mindless and random quantum seas of a universe that has no meaning other than what we make of it. In such a universe, whether you stick a knife in a child's eye, or labor heroically for social improvement matters not a whiff.

> It is scandalous that the philosophers entertain opinions that any common farm laborer would not hesitate to dismiss.
>
> ◆
>
> —Cicero (106–43 BC)

Likewise, whether you manage your dick or spend your life raping women is merely a matter of local convention. Gaze into the eyes of such philosophers and scientists and you will see a future that has died. Let us return to the philosophers of reality and resolutely turn our backs on anyone who maintains that the universe signifies nothing.

THE SCIENCE OF THE SOUL

Aristotle and other early philosophers in many parts of the world believed that energy for movement in living things came from the powers of the soul. Clearly the kind of energy that living things possess is different from the energy of non-living things. After all, rocks and other non-living things do not appear to have intellects, urges, the ability to move or to reproduce, so the early philosophers inferred that there must be some principle that distinguishes living from non-living. Hence the origin of the concept of soul or in some cultures, a life force or other principle of animation to be distinguished from the thing itself. Aristotle lists the following five powers of the soul:

1. Vegetative power—governs growth
2. Locomotive power—enables living things to move
3. Sensitive power—rules the senses
4. Appetitive power—runs the will and emotions
5. Intellectual power—enables the mind to abstract the forms of things

We tend to look at these powers in a fresh light when we think of them in terms of consciousness-force or even as quantum energy tools designed by the life force. These things are so obvious, that on one level, we tend to disregard them as distinguishing characteristics of life. We also often think that the concept of soul is a Jewish or Christian invention, but it was in use long before the rise of either philosophy or established religion. The soul has been known by many names: from the Ka and Ba of the ancient Egyptians to the Psyche of the Greeks. It was known as the Atman to the Hindus, the Po to the early Chinese and Buddha nature to the Buddhists. The soul has had as many names as there are cultures, but it is above all, a principle of animation and is the non-local mechanism that controls life.

The soul for Aristotle signified the "first act of a thing having life potential." Another way of saying this is that living things have an invisible energy and information template that makes them the way that they are—something that not only organizes their atoms and molecules once they reach a certain level of complexity but also paradoxically is the basis for that complexity in the first place. For Aristotle, plants and animals had souls because they had reached a sufficient level of complexity to sustain life-potential. Rocks do not have souls but they do have something that is like a soul. Non-organic matter has a "form" which is a kind of non-living soul. The important thing to remember is that forms and souls are a combined form of energy and information (consciousness-force) that makes a certain piece of matter look and feel the way it does—a kind of hyperspace or quantum energy map for the molecules and atoms. This map or template fuses with the atoms of matter to produce what Aristotle called *substance*. The Greeks knew about atoms long before the scientists of the nineteenth and twentieth centuries and physicists are only now beginning to discover the validity of the quantum patterns that the notion of substance represents. This quantum energy map which in-forms substance may exist in a higher dimension! As you now know, there may be many more dimensions than the four—height, length, width and time—with which we are familiar.

WHERE DOES THE SOUL COME FROM?

The energy of a soul is known in the Western philosophical tradition as the life energy or the life force. This energy, however, is not the soul anymore than the energy produced by a dam is the dam. The consciousness-force of a soul comes from its participation in the non-local and superluminal consciousness-force of Divine Existence. The life energy is part of a vast hierarchy of non-local consciousness and energy with multiple chakra input and output centers. Where it all begins and ends is lost in the utter non-local simplicity and yet complex local manifestations of the Divine Nature.

Aristotle's own words are instructive here:

But if there is something which is capable of moving things or producing them but is not actually doing so, there will not necessarily be movement; for that which has a potency need not exercise it. Nothing, then is gained even if we suppose eternal Entities, as the proponents of the Forms do, unless there is to be in them some principle which can cause change; nay even this is not enough, nor is another Entity besides the Forms enough; for if it is not to act, there will be no movement. Further, even if it acts, this will not be enough, if its Entity is potency; for there will not be eternal movement, since that which is potentially may possibly not be. **There must then, be such a principle, whose very Entity is act.**

Aristotle and other early philosophers speculated that this *Unmoved Mover,* whose very identity is pure Act, was in some way responsible for all actuality and all potency. The soul was also thought to represent some aspect of this same uncreated, and perhaps impersonal force with the concept of God being a handy way to describe the larger aspects of eternal actuality. This means that Uncreated Force or Act has always been in existence—it hasn't come from anywhere. Doesn't this sound a little bit like the Tao of the Chinese or the superluminal hyperspace metasystem we've been trying to sketch?

> Existence, by nothing bred,
> Breeds everything.
> Parent of the universe,
> It smoothes rough edges,
> Unties hard knots,
> Tempers the sharp sun,
> Lays blowing dust,
> Its image in the wellspring never fails.
> But how was it conceived? —this image
> Of no other sire.
>
>   —Lao Tzu, 604 B.C.

The soul possesses life force energy non-locally by participating in God's Existence. The local manifestation of your life force, on the other hand, is mediated through the quantum energy dynamics of Yin and Yang and other forces that we do not yet understand. Non locally speaking, you are distinct from the Act that has known you from eternity only by the *possession of that act*[28] as a gift. Your unique possession of the gift of life energy is a reflexive and self-limiting act of effortless Divine knowledge that makes you a human being instead of a butterfly or a tree. If you were to ask the philosophers or the theologians where God gets his uncreated energy, they would tell you that God is His own cause and His own Being. Scientists will tell you almost the same thing. They say that energy is uncreated and that it only changes form. Doesn't this also sound like an old time definition of God? You might want to think of the soul, in this context, as a mini-Unmoved Mover, a chip off the old divine block!

The Unmoved Mover that constitutes the core of our higher selves is existentially bathed in the very existence of the prime Unmoved Mover.

This Unmoved Mover, or the Superluminal if you will, while not other than its own "thoughts" is beyond the patterns that we customarily ascribe to thinking. We think in terms of time—past, present and future. The Unmoved Mover does not think in terms of time, as we know it. Everything is as the present to the Superluminal and lacking nothing, by being simultaneously the existence that powers everything into being, the Superluminal is able to share His/Her/Its infinite power with everything that is. The Superluminal is not diminished by giving everything, as there is no everything to give. There is simply no end to the giving.

Many religions believe that the Unmoved Mover has incarnated in human form, one of the most famous, to those of us in the West, being Jesus. But whether or not the Divine has incarnated once or many times is somewhat irrelevant. The Hindu religions, for example, have clearly understood that the Avatar, the God who descends to incarnate can do this as many times as He or She wishes. What the Divine wishes is what the Divine does and is certainly not bound by our behavioral and theological expectations.

OUR IDENTITY IN THE DIVINE

The mini Unmoved Mover that is your soul (you might want to think son or daughter of God) is also anti-entropic—it does not contribute to the downhill qualities of the physical world. Its actions are quite the contrary. It builds up rather than engaging in the tearing down of entropy. It is an offspring of what the Hindus call *Satchidananda*—a trinity of Existence, Consciousness and Bliss. Satchitananda is the hidden trinity that dwells at the heart of matter—a multidimensional existence, superluminal consciousness and transcendent ecstasy that supports the universe.

Satchitananda is labeled by the Chinese as the Tao and by Christians as the Holy Trinity. Chi is simply one manifestation, a local application as it were, of the vast multi-dimensional complexity of Satchitananda. By living your life at its highest level, *you* can bring superluminal energy into your work, your friendships, your family, and your society. And you don't have to be a monk or a eunuch to do it.

Scientists have searched through almost an endless variety of subatomic particles searching for some unified Theory of Everything. They are looking for an impersonal mechanism to account for the universe. They will not find it. What they have found and will continue to find is a mountain of compelling evidence for a unifying and conscious force that transcends their attempts to define or measure it. Whether you call this the Unmoved Mover, God, the Tao, Satchitananda, the Divine Consciousness or the Superluminal, the overpowering reality that these terms point to is the same.

The profound truth that Jesus points to in His sermons on the Father and the Spirit can be understood as a Triune relationship at the very heart of all being. We are children of a Divine Family and participate in the very nature of Satchitananda—Existence, Consciousness and Bliss. (You can find similar and parallel utterances in completely different traditions, such as Sri Aurobindo Ghose's *The Life Divine* or Satprem's wonderful primer, *The Adventure of Consciousness.*)

We have a timeless identity engraved in the nature of the Superluminal and it is our birthright to discover the dimensionally interactive mechanisms that link us in the present to a future that is without measure. The hyperspace metasystem that we inhabit runs on the multi-dimensional energy of Chi. However, as a working idea, Chi must be buttressed with a scientific link that will empower researchers in a creative direction. It is not an exaggeration to say that any information that would set scientists on the path to discovering a way to manipulate hyperspace would be nothing short of extraordinary. Let us bend to the task, no matter how rudimentary the sketch.

If we assume that the atoms of your genes act according to the energy map of the particular unmoved mover that is your soul, we must have a system to account for this negentropic energy transaction—even if we can't see the energy map! And if you have a life force or there is such a thing as a global brain it makes little sense to discuss it in merely abstract terms. It must affect and have theoretically measurable quantum effects on the body or it is of no compelling use as a concept.

THE MULTI-DIMENSIONAL KINETICS OF YOUR LIFE FORCE

Kinetics is the branch of science that deals with the effects of forces upon the motions of material bodies or with changes in a physical or chemical system. Kinetic energy is energy associated with motion. The unmoved mover or soul may be referred to as the helmsman of the soul's force and motion, hence the term Cyber-Kinetic. Cyber comes from the Greek word *kybernetes*, which means helmsman, pilot or governor.[29] This might be thought of as a branch of Cybernetics (which studies communication and control theory) as it applies to the operating systems of the soul. What we need to uncover is how exactly Cyber-Kinesis works.

How does the negentropic energy of the non-local mover that is your soul do its work? How does its non-local kinetic energy interact with matter in local space and time?

A clue provided by modern Physics comes from the study of vectors. A vector is defined as, "a quantity specified by magnitude and direction." How would you describe the quantity and magnitude of something that moves in more than four dimensions? A quanta, as a product of a quantum wave that is condensing out of non-local space would certainly qualify as a vector *in local space,* but what would be modulating unobserved quantum waves to precipitate the forming of quanta and subsequent vectors?

The outline of an answer to this question is found in something physicists are calling *Superstring Theory.* According to this theory, all matter is a manifestation of the activity of superstrings or vibrations of energy from the fifth to the twenty-sixth dimension. Superstrings that are theoretically *hundreds of billions of times smaller*[30] than subatomic particles are caused by nearly incomprehensible movements in these dimensions. Likewise, the quantum dynamics of your soul might be thought of as the product of incomprehensible movements in these higher dimensions. Superstring theory gives us valuable clues to understand how and why this might be the case.

METAPHYSICAL SUPERSTRINGS

Metaphysical superstrings might be thought of as being caused by some meta-dimensional Being in a metaphysical analog to the local and non-local dynamics of quantum waves. The eternal Act of a God who knew Himself in all the ways that He could be imitated would constitute a consciousness fragmented into an infinity of linear and multi-dimensional relationships in all possible directions, times, species, individuals and units of measure. Such strings of consciousness might be visualized and thought of as being infinitely thin, wide, long and timeless, and be present everywhere. This would constitute a web of consciousness that would interpenetrate and in fact be the root source of everything. In the context of metaphysical superstrings, your soul is simply one of an infinite number of ways in which the Superluminal knows Itself, outside Itself in a vast primordial Act of self-knowledge. These are of course metaphysical generalities, but doesn't this sound a lot like how we might imagine the Superluminal?

Superstrings might be thought of as a product of the Divine's own dimensionally interactive cyber-kinesis, which itself is a result of the multi-dimensional grasping of Itself, outside Itself, as Other. This grasping of itself as Other cannot occur in the trans-dimensional unity of its own consciousness, so it must take a form—and the form it takes is dimensionally interactive cyber-kinesis or movement in multi-dimensional space-time. Particle and wave, consciousness and force—the images comes back again and again. Dimensionally interactive cyber-kinesis is the wave form in higher dimensions and the particle analog is the superstring. The Divine's consciousness penetrates and is constitutive of every single and imaginable thing in the entire cosmos and yet simultaneously is not each and every thing. This is an enormous paradox and rather than being some sort of new and fortified pantheism, it is a testament to the independent yet contingent being of all things. God Is Existence and we are possessors of an existence that has been given freely to us. We possess the gift of God's own knowledge of Himself, as it is relative to each one of us—a Divine proportionality of cosmic knowledge. Each and every thing in the universe is part of the larger trans-dimensional and multi-dimensional movement of the vast wholeness that is the Divine. We are not God but rather jewels of consciousness in the vast and yet timeless movement of His Being.

Superstrings, tachyons, quantum waves, Chi and Cyber-Kinesis are simply different ways of thinking about the energy dynamics between local and non-local space. *Dimensionally Interactive Cyber-Kinetics* studies the metaphysical aspects of quantum dynamics as they apply to the negentropic energy exchange between local and non-local space. It attempts to reconcile an ecology of life force energy usage with human morality. As such it may provide a significant boost to the embryonic science known in some quarters as quantum psychodynamics.[31] *Both Dimensionally Interactive Cyber-Kinetics and superstring theory attempt to explain how energy moves in multi-dimensional space.* Superstrings are a theoretical outgrowth of scientific speculation. Dimensionally Interactive Cyber-Kinetics represents New Age and metaphysical thinking at its extreme. Both hypotheses are based on a need to account for the strange dynamics of being and energy. Physics and metaphysics have been on a convergence course for seventy five years but superstring theory—almost more than any other development—brings modern science not only to the door of metaphysics and religion but invites itself in for supper.

THE ZERO POINT

Scientific thinkers and New Age metaphysicians have identified the quantum exchange point between the lower dimensions and higher dimensions as the *zero point*. Unlike the singularities of physics, zero points are not generated by the gravitational and atomic collapse attributed to black holes. Zero points are simply theoretical interfaces between local and non-local space. The seven chakras, for example, might be thought of as *Zero Point Exchange Centers*. Each of the chakras converts negentropic energy locally into body part configurations and non-locally into a variety of intellectual and volitional (pertaining to your will) operations. The most powerful Zero Point Exchange Centers (ZPEX) are at the base of the spine and over your head. The one at the base of the spine is negatively charged and the one over your head is positively charged.

The Zero Point is an inferred construct much as atoms were in the 1930's before pictures could be taken of individual atoms. Inferred theoretical constructs enable both scientists and laymen alike to build a body of supporting data to support or deny various claims as to how the constructs operate. English biologist Rupert Sheldrake, for example, and other leading-edge scientific thinkers have argued for the existence of *invisible morphogenetic fields*, which guide the development of all biological organisms. This concept of invisible fields of energy is really just a more modern way of talking about souls and forms. However, souls, forms, and morphogenetic fields still do not account for the kind of multi-dimensional energy transfer that must exist in order for the invisible soul to

The energy flowing through the energetic continuum comes from one source. In India it is called the Divine Mother. Christianity calls it the Holy Ghost, and in many modern New Age spiritual teachings it is called Cosmic Energy. In modern physics it is called Zero Point Energy. It is important at this point to understand that Zero Point Energy should not be confused with a particular form of energy, such as etheric or astral energy. Zero Point Energy is the source of everything. All realms of subtle energies are just parts of the energetic continuum. Tachyon energy is the very first energetic structure that emerges out of this non-structured, virtually formless Zero Point Energy.

◆

—David Wagner,
Advanced Tachyon Technologies

affect the four dimensional universe of height, length, width and time that we are familiar with.

THE UNIFICATION OF PHYSICS AND METAPHYSICS

The Dimensionally Interactive Cyber-Kinetics of a dynamic energy system that would show the relationships between matter, form and the advanced forms that are souls is not fully developed in the metaphysical theories of the ancient philosophers, in morphogenetic field theory or in quantum physics but the principles of operation appear to be conceptually converging. *These hypotheses and theories are attempting to account for the negentropic energy transfer that appears to be occurring between hyperspace and local space.* This energy transfer can be understood from the perspective of string theory, using quantum mechanics as conceptual back up. Superstring theory does not tell us, however, where the vibrating energy of the strings comes from—only that it exists as energy from higher dimensions. Dimensionally Interactive Cyber-Kinetics, on the other hand, links the consciousness-force of God to the concepts of non-local energy and superstrings, and loosens the stranglehold that science has had on morals and common sense for over two hundred years.

Both science and metaphysics have been struggling to elucidate the qualities of local and non-local space in different ways for the past two hundred years. This is no accident, as the human mind approaches truth from these two very different kinds of space. What is most extraordinary, however, is that what was once called "sacred space" can now be thought of in terms of real and not imagined space. Non locality or hyperspace is really only a scientific elucidation of the much older and less conceptually developed "sacred space" of religion. How would prayers, for instance, be communicated to an invisible God? We might hypothesize that they are communicated through multi-dimensional space. What was unthinkable two hundred years ago regarding the convergence of science and religion is now quite thinkable.

The Chinese concept of *Wu Chi*, which is the formless source point of all Chi, for example, is sufficiently close in theoretical texture to the notion of zero points and the singularities of black holes that you have metaphysics anticipating scientific development by many centuries. We see this time and time again in the on-going dance between metaphysics and physics. Metaphysics throws a thinking party and sometimes makes a bit of a mess and dour old Physics comes in scowling and straightens everything up. They both need each other for clear and progressive thinking.

NON-LOCAL MATTER

Dimensionally Interactive Cyber-Kinetics is multi-dimensional in both wave and particle formats. This is a bland enough statement on the face of it but it also represents a shocking possibility. One way of thinking about this is to ask yourself what a multidimensional solid would look like. Does your higher self or even the soul, in some sense, have a subtle multidimensional material structure? Your core identity may have the characteristics of structure and energy and might be imaginatively thought of, as non-local matter that incorporates zero points into its structure. You may find this amusing but ask yourself this question: What kind of matter would make up the body of an angel or a god? Think about it for a moment, and you will understand what non-local matter must be like. Your cyber-kinetic core self is made up of non-local matter and has access to a hyperspace metasystem that spans the universe and makes the Internet look like child's play!

Who knows, perhaps the zero point is a tool from the twenty-sixth dimension and possibly beyond. This raises questions as to who the maker of this sort of tool might be but at the same time, there can be little doubt that this "Who" is the Master of all dimensions and all time.

Cyber-Kinetics are part of the divine highway that exists between Heaven and Earth.

Your Cyber-Kinetics, unlike those of the Master of time, are circumscribed or limited by the four and five dimensional evolutionary construct currently in use. Matter is under constant negentropic pressure from higher dimensions to evolve into a more complex kind of material that will better accept the full multi-dimensional power of the soul. 50,000 years from now we will probably be mentally and as physically different from ourselves as we are today from Neanderthals. Dimensionally Interactive Cyber-Kinetics are part of the evolving roadway between Heaven and Earth. Cyber-Kinetics is part of the multi-dimensional energy system behind you, me, and every human being who has ever lived and ultimately, every human being who will ever live.

Up to now, most scientists have been too occupied with the development of new theories that describe *what* the universe is to ask the question *why*. On the other hand, the people whose business it is to ask *why*, the philosophers, have not been able to keep up with the advance of scientific theories. In the eighteenth century, philosophers considered the whole of human knowledge, including science, to be their field and discussed questions such as: did the universe have a beginning? However, in the nineteenth and twentieth centuries, science became too technical and mathematical for the philosophers, or anyone else except a few specialists. Philosophers reduced the scope of their inquiries so much that Wittgenstein, the most famous philosopher of this century, said, "The sole remaining task for philosophy is the analysis of language." What a comedown from the great tradition of philosophy from Aristotle to Kant.

However, if we do discover a complete theory, it should in time be understandable in broad principle by everyone, not just a few scientists. Then we shall all, philosophers, scientists and just ordinary people, be able to take part in the discussion of the question of why it is that we and the universe exist. If we can find the answer to that, it would be the ultimate triumph of human reason— for then we would know the mind of God.

—Stephen Hawking, *A Brief History of Time*

MANAGEMENT TIPS

• Karma is not just something pre-ordained; it is metaphysical cause and effect. What you do affects the entire quantum continuum in the same way that a stone thrown into a pool causes ripples. All of your actions form a whole.

• You may find it helpful to think of quantum mechanics as the science of micro energy exchanges. We do not yet have the scientific instruments to measure these micro energy flows but their metaphysical significance can be inferred to be one of almost incalculable importance.

• At any given quantum moment, you can change your entire future. The fork in the road is always right in front of you. Pay attention to your choices; they can derail not only your life but the lives of others.

• The person in the heart is the person in front of you. Be ruthless in uncovering who you are—you are the only person you may be ruthless with.

• Discovering who you are is a life-long task but you will make no such discovery if you spend your time navel gazing. Who you are is a process and that process requires above all else, action.

CHAPTER 15

THE MISSING LINK AND GENITAL APPLIANCES

The gem cannot be polished without friction, nor man perfected without trials.
—Confucius (550–478 B.C.)

LET US STEP BACK FROM THE COSMIC MACHINERY AND RETURN TO YOUR dick. One of the biggest difficulties in discussing morality and "good" social behavior in general is that most people do not have an adequate model to interpret and evaluate bad behavior. You may watch endless TV shows discussing social problems but without a Dick Management model, the debate will generally degenerate into shouting matches between conservative and liberal points of view. Dick Management is the missing link that is almost always absent in discussions of crime and so-cial responsibility. Remember, sexuality, like almost all other activities, consumes energy. Genitals in particular use a lot of energy! Energy is defined as the capacity to act, or more generally, as the ability to do work. This energy has to come from somewhere and energy, as we all know, is never unlimited, otherwise we would never have to eat or sleep. We always have to acquire energy, by getting it from food and sleep or other sources, and we have to manage the energy that we have to make it last longer.

Morality, in this context, is a form of cyberkinesis whereby energy used thoughtfully is anti-entropic, or virtuous, and Chi misused, is vice, or a form of entropy. Cyber-Kinetic Knowledge and Dick Management can now be the basis for a new metaphysics and morality of personal en-ergy management. One might assume that the science of Ethics would address the linkage between energy management and morals, but to date, aside from the notion of sublimation as championed by a few psychologists and increasingly fewer theologians, there seem to have been few serious attempts in the West to link morality and the energy consumption of sexuality, other than those who have engaged the Eastern tradition. Western ethics attempts to address the nature of morality by focusing on the rightness or wrongness of certain actions. Unfortunately, without a science of energy management, these kinds of ethics remain largely an exercise in abstract thinking, with all the practical effect of pissing on a forest fire.

YOUR ASS LIKES DECONSTRUCTION

Morality and ethics have traditionally been thought of as branches of the science of metaphysics. Lao Tzu, Aristotle, Plato, Socrates and Confucius always included moral discourse as a common sense part of any serious philosophical discussion. Morality as a concept was always about the improvement or ruin of souls. Ethical thinking, however, as it is generally understood today, concerns itself with actions apart from any reference to the soul. Without some concept of the life force, appetites or the soul, morality and ethical discussions degenerate into deconstructions of language, word playing and the peculiar sniffing of academic backsides that passes for moral discourse on many college campuses and in many national newspapers.

How is it possible to arrive at a consensus on civil behavior when such behavior has no moral basis and the conventions of what we consider to be good behavior are constantly being challenged by an army of attorneys bent on deconstructing the meaning of language? How can we possibly arrive at any modern consensus on decent civility when wars become moral or immoral based on political propaganda and blowjobs are somehow considered outside the realm of having sex? One also wonders, with a growing and vague horror, if the abortion rights movement is not patterned after the same instinctive and low level of animal consciousness that motivates a polar bear to select a baby seal as its lunch or the male lion to kill the cubs of any lioness it mates with that are not its own. Mother Nature, or the Global Brain "red in tooth and claw" may act without compassion, but is that any reason for us to do the same? Human beings must act as the higher conscience of Nature; let us not listen to all the big ASSES she is speaking through.

Mother Nature is trying to get back into society. The present ASS infestation of modern times signifies that Mother Nature has found many willing ears. Rudeness, sexual harassment and violence are not the only ways that the Appetite Survival System of Nature reveals itself. Politicians, for example, are notorious reservoirs of ASS-dominated thinking. They have learned to play upon the collective ASSES of the public like a musician plays a xylophone. They know how to hit just the right note to induce other ASSES to release the foul wind of approval that is rooted only in mutual advantage.

> The emotions are not always subject to reason…but they are always subject to action. When thoughts do not neutralize an undesirable emotion, action will.
>
> ◆
>
> —William James

Let us not allow them to distort the syntax of morality and language with ASS-induced gibberish. My spirit revolts when I hear the word "choice" bandied about as if it were some sort of independent moral reality. The politicians who use such obfuscations should be taken out and whipped. Now my own ASS is rearing its ugly head, but that is what it is supposed to do when confronted with any evil proposed to it by intellect or instinct. Thus do wars and all conflicts begin. They begin with you and your ASS. So watch what your ASS is doing and watch what you are thinking!

CYBER-KINETIC POISONS

Morality is not just about referencing a legal code, playing mind-games with yourself, or asking God for permission to use your peepee. Morality is largely between you, your appetites, your soul, and the cosmic harmony of their existence when properly guided according to the principles of Karmic and Natural Law. Only you can discover what desires work for you and which ones don't. Chi consumption, for example, and its effects on your thinking and your life can only be monitored by you and no one else. Immorality, or making ignorant choices regarding your appetites and Chi usage (think life energy!) generally results in unhappiness and can poison your existence. Buddhism notes three pairs of poisons on the wheel of life: addiction and attachment (a cock), hatred and aversion (a snake) and delusion and indifference (a pig), which chase themselves to no avail. The cock chases the snake, which chases the pig, and around and around they go until the higher self or atman intervenes by decisively calling upon the will for moral action.

Your higher self knows the way to harmony and knowledge. Your instinctive appetites, mind and spirit are all part of a Dimensionally Interactive Cyber-Kinetic network of information which can tell you which activities bring you into the misery of the cock-snake-pig runaround, and which bring you out of it to happiness. It is therefore extremely important to understand the relationship between your ASS and your DICK, in order to avoid the cyber-kinetic poisons of addiction, hatred and indifference.

YOUR DICK IS AN APPLIANCE

Chi is the motor force behind the biological urges of your body, but your body cannot possibly handle the full power of all the Chi that Nature has to offer. Your Dimensionally Interactive Cyber-Kinetics are part of the invisible hyperspace metasystem of the Tao which integrates various relationships between the Unmoved Mover, traditionally referred to as God, the principles of matter and Nature observed by physicists, and the smaller unmoved mover commonly referred to as cyber, life force, or soul.

Your soul, as part of this hyperspace metasystem, has three major subsystems—the Appetite Survival System, the intellect and will. These three subsystems have a variety of operations that can be characterized as instincts, thought processes and intention. (All three subsystems are commingled in you, and in the murky and overlapping languages of different philosophies, so sometimes we have a hard time seeing where one begins and the other ends.)

Another way of understanding your life force's relation to this metasystem is to imagine your dick as a heavy-duty appliance. You plug a power tool, for example, into the wall and it gets juice. Your dick, just like a power saw or a hair dryer, gets its energy from somewhere other than itself. Similarly, the electrical outlet into which you plug an appliance gets its energy from the electrical panel installed inside your home. The panel gets its energy from the power company, which in turn gets its energy from a power generating station. The power from the power station does not come directly to you. It is "stepped down" by various transformers and voltage regulators. Your ASS is one such transformer and your DICK (never to be confused with your dick) is another.

Let's also say, for argument's sake, that there is a load controller (a solid state device which controls the total amount of wattage—volts times amps allotted to an appliance) on your ASS, which will only let you get so much energy a day. Your dick is like a 220-volt appliance; it uses a lot of energy, unlike your little finger, which may only use the amperage allotted by a 120 volt circuit. If you run a 220 volt appliance all day long, you are going to burn up far more of your allotted energy than you will if you are only running 110 volt appliances. Dick Management will show you how to run your dick on 110 volts when it is not being used, instead of flat out on 220 current. Think of this as a form of load control.

SUBLIMATION AND THE TWO HOGS

As we mentioned earlier, scientists tell us that the brain uses some twenty-five percent[32] of all the energy produced by the body. Thinking and running the central nervous system requires a lot of current. If most of this energy is being used by your dick or other power draining activities, your central nervous system may suffer an energy shortage. Chi energy shortages may lead to mental illness and depression, and can even lead to suicidal tendencies. This kind of energy is so important that Sigmund Freud and others had to reinvest the word "sublimation" with additional psychological significance. Resistance to the sexual instincts (of the Id) in psychological terms creates energy that makes other satisfactions possible[33]. Sublimation, in other words, enables your mind and your brain to use Chi that might otherwise be spewed out or squandered by your dick or other appetites.

The Romans used to refer to the male genitalia as "mentula," which means little mind. The human mind was referred to as "mens," so the average Roman male had to contend with the requirements of mens and mentula.

You might want to think of your mind and appetites as two hogs at the same dimensionally interactive cyber-kinetic trough. They are competing for the same energy source! Sooner or later, one of the two hogs is going to get the upper hand. Which hog are you going to let get the largest share of your energy? I call this the "two hogs theory" and it is a metaphor for the competition between intellect and appetites for life energy.

Your intellect and your appetites—particularly your sexual appetites—are like high voltage appliances that cannot run at the same time without blowing a fuse. Ever try solving an equation or fixing the toaster while you are ejaculating? Your dick is connected to your ASS and your ASS is connected to your Dimensionally Interactive Cyber-Kinetics. A handy way of remembering this is to recall that your ASS has two dicks; a little dick and a big DICK. You want the big DICK to manage the little dick.

Do you want to be more creative or do you want to be more of an animal? The choice is yours. It is either you or your ASS who is going to be in charge of your dick. Now that your intellect has been substantially fortified by metaphysics and cosmology, you have a much better understanding of the relationship between morals and personal energy consumption. Now you can begin to examine the social problems that arise in the absence of Dick Management. You know what to do. It is time to whip some ASS!

Sexual energy that gets preserved gets transformed into a subtle energy called ojas. This is similar to personal magnetism. It tones the entire personality, builds the nerves, improves brainpower and calms the mind. There is a similar word in English: ozone. In the early morning before sunrise we can go out and breathe the ozonic wind, which has a special vibration and energy to it. But once the sun's rays fall, this effect is lost. That is why the period between four and six a.m. is called brahmamuhurta, the Brahmic time or divine period, and is a very sacred time to meditate.

—Sri Swami Satchidananda, *Integral Yoga*

MANAGEMENT TIPS

◆ Your life experience is a building block for a moral system that works
  for you. Since you are a human being, many of the things that work
  for other human beings will work for you. This is the basis for any
  moral consensus.

◆ You are the Cyber (pilot) and you must identify the structure of your
  own cyber-kinetic links to the Appetite Survival System.

◆ Urges have kinetic energy. That means they are capable of motion.
  Curtail the motion when it first appears and you will limit the urge.

◆ Put some distance between yourself and your ASS at least a few times
  a day. You will come to enjoy being the Boss!

◆ Your meditations, prayers and thoughts may have more of an affect on
  the structure of all that is possible than you can imagine.

CHAPTER 16

VICE IS AN
ENVIRONMENTAL ISSUE

The social costs of drug abuse, including loss of work and disability have
been tabulated at $166 billion annually. On top of this, crime and related
violence costs Americans another $500 billion a year.

—Armstrong Williams

HAVE YOU EVER WATCHED TEENAGE BOYS TRYING TO GET THE ATTENTION
of a group of girls? Since many young men are not taught how to
approach young women or engage them in conversation, they fall back
on biology instead. Showing off, fighting, verbal posturing, grabbing at
breasts and backsides, insults directed at peers and adults, all are part of the
repertoire. This is an early stage of FIKI (fuck it–kill it), and is rooted in
evolutionary biology. In the animal kingdom, the strongest male generally
gets rewarded with the pick of the females. This isn't a question of right
or wrong for animals. It is rooted in natural selection, whereby the
strongest survive and reproduce. This is an ecology of the most elemental
nature, the interrelationship of organisms with their environment. By
showing their prowess, young men are re-enacting a dance between biology and ecology older than the Stone Age.

For human beings, controlling residual animal or biological instincts
that are on a continuum with the ASS and FIKI must be the basis of a
new moral and ecological paradigm. The behavior of teenage boys as they
try to impress females may be classic biology, but when this behavior spills
over into violence and various acts of juvenile delinquency (in order to
get attention or out of frustration) it becomes a moral issue. Remember,
the definition of morality we are using: *making good choices regarding
appetites.* Teenage boys will have these and many other appetites to contend with as they grow up. The most important issue, however, is what
they do with the appetites that they encounter. Do they move with the
energy of every appetite that happens to come along—like trees in the

127

wind—or do they try, akido-like, to move with the flow but make it constructive? The kind of mindfulness that is required for this kind of psychological akido requires an awareness of the energy flows of appetites and urges.

> As we rate boys, who being mature in knowledge, pawn their experience to their present pleasure, and so rebel to judgment.
>
> ◆
>
> —Shakespeare, *Anthony and Cleopatra*, Act I, Sec. IV

Prudence is the ability to govern oneself through reason, and is the hallmark of the energy conscious individual. It is a funky word to the modern mind—perhaps too redolent of "prude" and "prune"—but it is also one of the key activities of an awakened soul. Without the virtue of prudence it is not possible to be wise or to cultivate an ecological understanding of vice. The disciplining of the life energy required for virtue simply cannot proceed without a moral schematic that accounts for Chi misspent or well spent.

Vice for most of the early Greek philosophers was simply a habitual defect of behavior in regards to the regulation of the appetites. Mental illness or temporary insanity as an explanation for bad behavior would have been regarded as lunacy by the ancient Greeks. They knew that an undisciplined mind and will would jump from one vice to the other. No sooner was your average Greek dandy finished with one vice than he would find another. One minute an orgy, then large quantities of wine, followed by a visit to the stadium for a bit of betting on the chariots—then a great belch, a shit and finally sleep until late morning at which time it could all begin again! Aristotle lists the following vices. A modern day example is listed next to each.

- gluttony   eating three deserts
- greed   charging exorbitant rates or making excessive profits
- laziness   constantly postponing study or work
- intemperance   allowing yourself to "fly off the handle"
- incontinence   whacking-off every time the urge hits
- cowardice   habitually avoiding healthy challenges
- injustice   allowing what is wrong to stand without challenge
- lying   telling your girlfriend you love her when you don't
- stinginess   withholding resources and compliments from others

• rudeness   shouting at other drivers from your car

• ill-temper   allowing yourself to be mean-spirited

• impatience   not taking the time to listen or care

• violence   physically abusing others

• hatred   allowing anger to burn out of control and mutate

Go ahead, check a few boxes on the chart below!

	DAILY	WEEKLY	INFREQUENTLY	ALMOST NEVER
gluttony				
greed				
laziness				
intemperance				
incontinence				
cowardice				
injustice				
lying				
stinginess				
rudeness				
ill-temper				
impatience				
violence				
hatred				

These states of character are considered vices, inasmuch as they take away from the perfection of the individual (that is you pal) by allowing the appetites to rule instead of being ruled. A bad neighborhood in Los Angeles or the Balkans is where vice and brutishness—poor Chi management—is the rule. Have you ever wondered why we instinctively shy away from people with "shifty" eyes or "bad vibes?" Remember that the original meaning of the word vicious is vice-ridden! The motor force of vice is the ASS. We might even want to say that the vice-ridden are ASSES (Appetite Survival System Errors) devolving into something less than human.

While Aristotle's calculus of virtue and vice is pedagogically useful, its true value is as a steering mechanism that the soul or life force uses to allow itself to disengage from its absorption with the body and to consider its own greater reality. The insights of the Buddha in regards to non-attachment reflect this truth. The less the core self is attached to the outside world, the more it can focus on the multi-dimensional reality which generates the whole universe. Why focus on a part when you can have the whole? Selfishness and desire simply limit your exploration of who you really are. This is not to say that you should have no desires, but rather, that you see each desire in context and remain in the driver's seat.

We have this terrible idea that some psychologists have implanted, namely that desire should not be repressed, that all repression is bad. This idea has unfortunately "morphed" into the idea that repression and self-restraint are one and the same. They are not! Repression involves unconscious appetite suppression imposed on us by someone else, or unconsciously through circumstance. Self-restraint is the willful attempt to exercise some degree of choice over obvious appetites. For example, if my neighbor is playing loud music during the early morning hours, my immediate reaction might be annoyance, followed by anger. I might feel like wringing him or her by the neck—this is the biological or appetitive response that is rooted in FIKI and the death instinct. The civilized and prudent response, which involves exercising the virtue of patience and temperately suppressing anger (the first manifestation of FIKI) is to first go and politely ask the individual to turn the music down. This is moving with the energy of the basic appetite and prudently transforming it to a higher level. It also allows you to rationally gather additional information about your neighbor or learn something that may change your perception of the circumstances. Sometimes there are factors that make all the difference in the world.

> P atience is the best remedy for every thing.
>
> ◆
>
> —Plautus

Suppose your neighbor just got married or received a long-awaited job promotion? Perhaps you will end up dancing with him or her, or having a drink and becoming friends.

You will never know unless you think first and snarl later.

A friend of mine told me an interesting story in this regard. He was driving out of a parking lot when he noticed the attendant was shouting at him. Not thinking, he assumed the attendant was just being bossy, so he stuck his head out the window, cursed him, and continued out of the lot. Just as he was leaving, he heard his tires pop. The attendant had been trying to warn him that there were spikes set up to prevent exit at that particular location! A moment of self-restraint would have saved him several hundred dollars worth of damage and a badly deflated ego.

The ASS and FIKI are evolutionary survival tools, but for modern humans, they both need the moral adapter of prudence to be properly grounded. Our present reliance on psychology without prudent morality is like using ungrounded power tools in the rain. What good does it do, for example, to instruct young boys that they should not repress their sexual feelings, when, by and large, they live in their libidos to begin with? What they need is not just more information but *formation*. American institutions and schools are in dire straits because everyone has forgotten that FIKI and virtue actually exist. The first step in moving to solve problems such as teen pregnancy and juvenile crime is to understand that the solution to these problems involves managing the ASS and FIKI by cultivating the development of social ecologies of virtue. This means that without a moral code, we are bereft of the necessary structures to contain the ancient enemy of mankind. This enemy is not the devil or any other excuse for the evils that we all do; it is our reptilian-minded ASS who is the snake in the Garden of Evolution.

> If we have signs prohibiting smoking or guns, why not one for incivility? The universal symbol prohibiting assholes in public places should be a circle with a dark hole in the center. Stamping out FIKI could be represented by such a symbol with a line drawn diagonally through it. The Sign of the Sphincter would mean: "Assholes not welcome here."

For man, when perfected, is the best of animals, but, when separated from the law and justice, he is the worst of all; since armed injustice is the more dangerous, and he is equipped at birth with arms, meant to be used by intelligence and virtue, which he may use for the worst ends. Wherefore, if he have not virtue, he is the most unholy and most savage of animals, and the most full of lust and gluttony.

—Aristotle, *Politics*

MANAGEMENT TIPS

◆ Watching too much TV can become a really bad habit and waste an enormous amount of your time. Turn it off!

◆ Managing your dick requires that you cultivate moral and intellectual virtue.

◆ Your identity is more plastic than you think. Anger and lust are identities that you can assume faster than Clark Kent can change in a phone booth.

◆ Being generous may mean doing something your life force's ASS really doesn't want to do—like visiting Grandma or being patient with a screaming child.

◆ Who you are is largely a matter of what you do and the efforts you make to become that person you know you are. What you think about yourself is only the first step. The second step is to redeem your non-local identity from your local ASS.

CHAPTER 17

FLIRTING WITH FIKI

God sends lightning to strike the one he wants to be
his slave in heaven.

—African proverb

THE FOLLOWING TRUE REFLECTION BELOW SHOWS SOMEONE (IDENTITY withheld by request) on the shadow line or continuum between rationality and the power of FIKI. Note the close relationship between controlled violence and pleasure. The soul has an enormous attraction to energy outside itself and also to the discharging of energy. This is the sometimes the basis of temptation. Sexual management, on the other hand, consists of a dialog between the local you that wants everything now, and the non-local you that has different goals and is aware of the consequences of short-term pleasure. There is a delicious tension here that remains unresolved due to the character of the author, who in her own way, is exploring and seeking understanding. She clearly enjoys sadomasochistic activities with men and women and wants to know why this is so. There is of course no understanding of FIKI in the traditional sense of understanding. There can only be action and the action is potentially perilous, even life-threatening.

> I have to lock my hands behind my back. At times like this I cherish bondage, but I am not bound. I stand very still. I wonder if being held truly captive would make my desire to run away even stronger. As it is, I must control that urge. Does this distract me, or make me more vulnerable? He stands before me, hands outstretched, fingers grasping my nipples, pinching, twisting, making me rise up onto my toes. My eyes start to close, the pain, the fear...I try to block it out.

"Open your eyes" he snaps at me. My lids fly open, and his face is close to mine. I stare into his eyes, as he stares into mine. His eyes widen, his lip curls, and I can see his teeth bared, a snarl? A threat to my throat? I shiver, and my eyelids start to lower again, involuntary, this. "Open them!" and he pulls up harder, the pain stabbing, stinging, making me pant and gasp.

My head tips back as I stare, stare. I can see the beast. I've seen it before, it always looks the same to me. It doesn't seem to matter if the sadist before me is male or female. Age doesn't matter. The beast watches me hungrily. The beast looks cold, or is it hot? It's unbearably cruel. Why do I want to call it out? I am so very frightened by it. When he opens up, and lets the beast rise up, get close to me ... a whisper, or is it a hiss? "Kiss me" I lean forward, my lips trembling, and I kiss his mouth, a taste of iron, ashes, my mouth is dry with fear. A raw smell in the air, a sizzle like ozone. Is it from me, or him, or is it both of us, chemicals pumping out as the energy between us intensifies? My breath comes in gasps. My heart is pounding. Again my eyes start to close, again he growls. I know the beast takes the pain from my eyes, and I will yield this up to it. I don't like blindfolds, and this is why. I want to see my partner change. I want to know where he is, what he feels as he crushes and mauls my flesh, as the pain shoots through me.

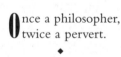

Once a philosopher, twice a pervert.

◆

—Voltaire, on sexual experimentation

Each time I've seen the beast it's left me shaken, knees weak, head light. Each time, too, I have tried to love the beast. This, I think, is why I want to call it up. I think about the chakras, the centers of light and energy. The energy flows up the body, along the spine, from the base to the top of the head. The lower energies, I know about those, I've spent a lot of time using them, my sex, my belly. I'm older now, and stronger, and smarter, and I want to move up further. I want to turn my heart onto the beast, I want to watch and see what happens…an exchange of pain and love. I want his teeth at my throat, I wonder if I can open up the chakra there, and pour that energy into the mouth of the beast, instead of the blood I think it longs for. What would happen then? I picture a golden flood filling his mouth. Would it hurt the beast? Would it kill it, or make it stronger? I daydream about this now. I think about Little Red Riding Hood, I know the fear she must have felt. I don't want a woodcutter to save me though, I want to see if I can save myself.

Am I strong enough? Will I end up in the belly of the beast? My mind tries to run, although my body holds its posture. Will I be burned, frozen, or lost? I want to do this, need to do this, to love the sadist beast.

I've seen the beast in several of my friends, people I like, people I care about. I've yet to see it in someone I love, and I wonder a lot about what that will be like. I think of the people I know who are able to bring out the beast. Most of them fear it, respect the power and the threat, the ones that don't I would never trust. The ones I do trust, I long for them. I want to look into their eyes, and see. Is it always the same? Is the beast the same? "Open your eyes" the beast says. Pain is easy to take from eyes, I know that. Let me stand before you, beast. Hurt me, and watch my eyes. Let me open my third eye, and you open yours as well. I want to build a channel, make a connection, weave a cable between us, I want to know what happens then.

The imagery I am using seems to me to imply that the beast is not human, but I don't believe that's true. It must be human. I want to understand. I am human, and that doesn't change when I stand before a sadist, baring my breasts, my throat, my eyes. I wonder though, does doing this make us less than human? More than human? I am so curious about it. I want to see it, I want to know. (Anonymous)

Did this story shiver your timber, or did it revolt you? The danger of playing with sadism is that it can allow the appetites of the ASS to completely overrule thinking patterns. The Marquis de Sade would have had no difficulty in understanding the little vignette above. (Interestingly, Camille

> When I was a prison instructor at Lorton Penitentiary, a man came up to me after class and said, "I've done some very bad things in my life. But what I want to know is, why?"

Paglia notes in *Sexual Personae* that the road from the shallow idealism of Rosseau leads inevitably to de Sade.) Likewise, serial killer William Bonin's moral elevator didn't go to the top floor: a prison doctor portrayed him as "a fairly open, honest, reasonably intelligent person who seemed legitimately puzzled by his predilection for sexual encounters which culminated in murder."

On a more fundamental level, virtue brings us closer to the quantum, light-filled side of our nature, and vice delivers us over to the Dark Side of the ASS. The quantum reality of our souls can be a strong counterbalance to some of the confusion that is generated by lower level collapses of the wave-form of consciousness into vice. Cyber-Kinetic virtue is really about deciding when to let some of the more powerful aspects of wave-form consciousness manifest at the local level. Do you let the wave-form collapse at a higher or lower level? You have a choice. Cyber-Kinetic knowledge helps you make good choices and manage your Chi according to the deepest desire of the multi-dimensional core self.

The first man who hit me
was my father.
A slap in the face
because I moved too slow.

The next man who hit me
was my high school boyfriend.
He said he was sorry,
but I made him do it.

The next man who hit me
was my pimp.
He said it was because the money
I made wasn't enough.

The next man who hit me
was a trick.
He said it was his pleasure
to make me submit.

The last man who hit me
broke my arm and kicked me in the face
because my period was late.

Now I have passed this legacy
to that child.
The first time she was hit
was because she had been born.

　　　　　　　　　—Zelma Brown, "School of Tough Love"

MANAGEMENT TIPS

• Get to know your inner Charles Manson before he gets to know you.

• Try watching dirty thoughts without engaging them. Imagine them as birds flying across your consciousness. Let them go before they shit on you.

• Your own inner filth is a tar baby. Touch it and you'll stick.

• Learn some yoga exercises for libido smoothing.

• Be kind to whores and avoid temptation.

CHAPTER 18

CONTINENCE AND INCONTINENCE

It is plain then that incontinent people must be said to be in a similar condition to men asleep, mad or drunk. The fact that men use the language that flows from knowledge proves nothing; for even men under the influence of these passions utter scientific proofs and verses of Empedocles, and those who have just begun to learn a science can string together its phrases, but do not yet know it; for it has to become part of themselves, and that takes time; so that we must suppose that the use of language by men in an incontinent state means no more than its utterance by actors on the stage.

—Aristotle

IF, AS OUR ANALYSIS OF VICE INDICATES, THE MORAL ENERGY LEVEL OF your life force can be changed or even drained by immoderate impulsive activity, then the ancient and useful concept of *continence* and *incontinence* needs to be re-examined. Continence has been relegated by modern usage to the ability not to wet your bed or your pants. If you don't pee in your bed or your pants, then you are continent, and if you do, you are incontinent. Contrary to this popular usage and as a general moral term, continence more fully refers to *the ability to restrain and redirect the energy of appetites*, particularly the sexual appetite. Moral incontinence is the inability to restrain or redirect appetites and sudden deranged impulses.

This is why we find in both the uneducated and the educated a common inability to restrain, let alone articulate, what used to be called vice (habitually cultivated bad appetites) by the ancient Greek moralists and "sin" by Christian apologists. What were the seven deadly sins of the medieval theologians if not the old vices with a religious twist? Unfortunately for most people these days, the idea of "sin" is old-fashioned because it has come to be associated with fire-and brimstone religion. Sin as an offense against God is dismissed from the minds of modern

138

individuals who do not believe in God to begin with. This leaves out the value of a more basic idea: sin is an offense against *yourself and who you might become*—even if life doesn't go beyond the grave. So we will want to keep it in the back of our minds, as a useful moral concept for human beings regardless of religious belief, or lack thereof.

THE SEVEN DEADLY SINS

The seven deadly sins were: Laziness (Sloth), Pride, Greed (Avarice), Envy, Lust (Incontinence) Anger, and Gluttony. Now what kinds of behavior do we commonly see in those whom we consider given over to immorality?

1. A lack of desire for work or the disinclination to study. This is laziness.

2. Inordinate sense of self-worth in relation to actual accomplishments. This is vanity (a form of pride) and should not be confused with a healthy sense of pride for accomplishments well done.

3. Taking other peoples' belongings or their work energy without reference to a moral or civil code. This is a manifestation of greed.

4. Painful or resentful awareness of an advantage enjoyed by another. This comes from the Latin *invidere* "to look askance at." This is envy.

5. Inability to say no to any sexual desire. Lust is incontinence in its most developed (one might say "devolved") form. A subspecies of incontinence involves loud abuse of others using as much foul language as possible, without regard to whom might be listening, including children. This is anger and incontinent behavior working in a common combination. How many homicidal brawls have begun in just this way?

6. Anger which can help you to overcome obstacles either real or imagined may lead to savage and thoughtless violence without the proper exercise of mindfulness to control it.

7. Allowing the appetite for food or drink to overwhelm our sensibilities to the point where resisting over indulgence becomes impossible. This is gluttony.

What is truly interesting about vice is what is least discussed. Some modern social scientists seem to have a great deal of difficulty in seeing a causal relationship between the excessive and imprudent use of sexual energy, and the consequent decline in intellectual and moral abilities.

Indeed, many will deny such a link exists, and refuse to investigate even the possibility of such a link. Of course they are fully supported in this refusal by many advertisers, marketing and polling experts, TV and film producers, who are aware consciously or otherwise that FIKI and vice sell, no matter how irresponsible the presentation.

ARISTOTLE'S INTELLECT VERSUS FREUD'S EGO

Aristotle claimed that the intellect had two functions: the moral and the intellectual. The moral function of the intellect is used to regulate the appetites by providing the will with alternative pathways to gross appetitive indulgence. Then modern thought in the guise of Sigmund Freud came along and said there is no moral intellectual function—only a calculus of benefits that an organism uses to best determine the quickest and easiest path to pleasure. Look at what Freud said, and judge for yourself:

> The power of the Id expresses the true purpose of the individual organism's life. This consists in the satisfaction of its innate needs. No such purpose as that of keeping itself alive or of protecting itself from dangers by means of anxiety can be attributed to the Id. That is the task of the ego, whose business it also is to discover the most favorable and least perilous method of obtaining satisfaction, taking the external world into account. The super-ego may bring fresh needs to the fore, but its main function remains the limitation of satisfactions. (Sigmund Freud, *An Outline of Psycho-Analysis*)

The ego for Freud was merely an evolutionary apparatus developed from the Id over time. This apparatus has no connection with anything like a self or soul (this is to be considered an illusion generated by the instinctive transposition of the energies of the Id) and ceases to exist when the organism dies. To talk about virtue or the self to anyone infected by such a point of view is futile; it reminds me of Nietzsche's "last men," who when asked what truth was would only blink.

Freud, unfortunately, reduced all human impulses to modifications of the intentionality and libidinal energy of the Id. He attempted to substitute the libido for the total power of the life force. Who would trade his soul for an ASS? This highly original and yet short-sighted attempt to reduce human beings to an expression of appetitive resolve ultimately results in the caricature of individuality that we see in the cartoon Beavis and Butthead. (This is odd, considering how much our culture claims to prize individuality.) This is also why we find it very difficult to define what is moral or what is immoral in our culture. From the perspective of all psychological schools that are even remotely Freudian or reductionist, human beings do not have good intentions or bad intentions; they simply have modifications of desire that are all ultimately equivalent and finally irrelevant. Ultimate relativism gives rise to the ultimate banality of petty evil and stupidity of which Beavis and Butthead is the perfect expression. General Butt Naked and Beavis and Butthead are both on the continuum of unexamined appetites. The tribal factions in Africa and the moral savages in Hollywood have much in common. They have never learned that their basic biology doesn't make the distinction between right and wrong. Only moral human beings who have whipped their ASSES into shape can make such a distinction. Biology speaks through your ASS, and what biology frequently wants is to indulge in its favorite pastime, FIKI.

THE DISASSOCIATION OF SENSIBILITY

There is another reason for the lack of linkage between vice and social dysfunction. The social scientists who are making evaluations in a moral vacuum, and the policymakers subsequently implementing their so-called findings are often themselves engaged in unmentionable activities. They are shielded from the consequences of their vices due to well-developed intellectual habits that cause them to automatically reject some of the grosser levels of vice and bad habit that you sometimes see among the downtrodden.

The academic wife-beater, for example, may have better manners than his counterpart on the "other side of the tracks" but their morals are both probably on a similar level. The wife-beater's inability to sympathize with his spouse is rooted in a completely ASS-dominated mind. The creepiness of such people will leak out but unless those around them have the discernment to see the workings of moral decay in front of them, they will only be able to focus on the gentleman's intellectual credentials. They will say things like: he is a good mayor, a good doctor or a good carpenter or plumber—as if such intellectual excellences could stand in the way of moral corruption. These same people might have noticed that there was something peculiar about the behavior of the wife-beater's spouse, yet were unable to link that feeling of unease to a concrete judgment rooted in a moral schematic. This is a disassociation of moral sensibility from the data of intellectual observation.

The politician who screams about the importance of public education and yet sends his or her own children to private school is also suffering from a disassociation of moral and intellectual values. Such an individual separates (consciously or unconsciously) what is good for himself from what is good for them, yet he thinks that he is for the masses. Instead of doing something about the quality of education, this kind of individual tends to engage the *posture of concern*, as opposed to really doing something about the problem. We see the posture of concern over and over again in politics and what it really amounts to is "make the right noises and maybe the problem will go away or take care of itself." The educator or politician who makes promises he or she has no intention or ability to fulfill is surfing on a wave of emotion and absolutely nothing else. It looks real and sounds real but is devoid of moral content. Such people are like air, you can never pin them down. This *disassociation of sensibility*, as TS. Eliot referred to it, is a product of the church-state like separation of moral and intellectual values. As long as we continue to pretend that moral issues are neutral and completely private, we will continue to have such ridiculous non-sequiturs as lawyers defending the innocence of clients they know are guilty. There should be a legally enforced difference between "explaining" a client's actions in the context of the law, which every American is entitled to, and otherwise simply lying on behalf of a client to reduce punishment. The failure of our society to honor this difference has resulted in such peculiarities as lawsuits directed at the tobacco industry for the vices of consumers, and murderers who get off the hook through the semantic deconstruction of evidence procedures and the psychological soiling of evidence.

> To educate a person in mind and not morals is to educate a menace to society.
>
> ◆
>
> —Theodore Roosevelt

MORAL ENERGY

Moral energy is a function of both moral and intellectual virtue. Vice is a function of entropy and decay. Another way of saying this is that virtue is anti-entropic and produces energy that *enables* morality, and that vice is entropic and wastes energy. This is a critical linkage that enables a society to determine that there are real reasons for suppressing vice and that it is not just a matter of bluenoses spoiling everyone's party. The endless hollow arguments about whether or not pornography increases crime is simply set aside in a moral ecology. If pornography causes arousal, then it may be activating FIKI (fuck it/kill it), and is at the very least using Chi that might be put to better uses.

How many times have you replicated in your own mind a particularly pleasing scene from a porno film or magazine? Note how you customize it to your specifications, using the software of your imagination. Did you feel less aroused after the imagery had its way with you, or did you feel an increased need to unload a load? How many times have you performed imaginary sex acts on attractive women who simply walk by you on the street? Has the thought of an unwilling participant who must be forced to your will ever crossed your mind? In other words, are you sometimes performing mental rape? Of course you are, but you are keeping it to yourself and thereby performing at least a primitive form of Dick Management. Yet clearly there are those who will feel the need to act out fantasies in the real world. The door to vice and violence is opened, and rather than gaze out as you or I might, the unformed steps through.

VIRTUE IS SOCIAL CAPITAL

Imagine what the world could be like if truthfulness were as prevalent as the telephone, or courage were as well developed as electrical devices. Visualize, if you will, a planet where continence is as important as money, or where thousands of Mother Teresas and Nelson Mandelas labor to develop kindness and charity, justice and magnanimity. While it may seem odd to compare the presence of a virtue like courage and the prevalence of electrical devices, the social consequences of what a culture values are every bit as important as the products it produces. Virtue or excellence is the power source or moral currency of any civilization and without it, a culture, no matter how intellectually developed, will fail.

In his book, *The Great Disruption*, Francis Fukuyama refers to shared values as *social capital*. The general restraining of impulses is perhaps the most common of all shared values in the western world, but an understanding of what this means in terms of a socially acceptable moral framework of virtue and vice is still sadly lacking. The Soviet Union, which placed a premium on the intellectual values of art and science, simply fell apart in the late 20th century due to the enormous moral vacuum in the hearts and souls of many of its leaders. Intellectual values without moral values tend towards an ever-greater dilution. Some African and Balkan countries, which in recent times have cultivated neither the moral virtues nor the intellectual virtues, are entering a phase of social meltdown, the likes of which may be seen as part of the rise and fall of civilizations, best exemplified by the fall of the Roman Empire. This spiraling deficit of social capital is characteristic of moral decline worldwide.

Why have we been drawn toward a culture of permissiveness? My former philosophy professor John Silber was correct when he spoke of an "invitation to mutual corruption." We are hesitant to impose upon ourselves a common moral code because we want our own exemptions.

This modern allergy to judgments and standards, of which attitudes toward the Clinton scandals are but a manifestation, is deeply problematic, for a defining mark of a good republic is precisely the willingness of its citizens to make judgments about things that matter. In America we do not defer to kings, cardinals, or aristocrats, instead we rely instead on the people's capacity to make reasonable judgments based on moral principles. Those who constantly invoke the sentiment of "who are we to judge?" should consider the anarchy that would ensue if we adhered to this sentiment in, say, our courtrooms. Should judges judge? What would happen if those sitting on a jury decided to be "nonjudgmental" about rapists and sexual harassers, embezzlers and tax cheats? Without being "judgmental," Americans would never have put an end to slavery, outlawed child labor, emancipated women, or ushered in the civil rights movement. Nor would we have prevailed against Nazism and Soviet communism, or known how to explain our opposition.

How do we judge a wrong—any wrong whatsoever—when we have gutted the principle of judgment itself? What arguments can be made after we have strip-mined all the arguments of their force, their power, their ability to inspire public outrage? We all know that there are times when we will have to judge others, when it is both right and *necessary* to judge others. If we do not confront the soft relativism that is now disguised as a virtue, we will find ourselves morally and intellectually disarmed.

—William Bennett, *The Death of Outrage*

MANAGEMENT TIPS

◆ I will not cut in traffic.

◆ I will not draw on other people's walls.

◆ If you feel like thumping the donkey, try skipping.

◆ Do not wave your bone in front of a woman unless she asks to see it.

◆ Your Johnson is not the President. You do not have to do what it says.

CHAPTER 19

PSYCHOBONDAGE

*Psychology is only the hope of a science and when someday the answers
are found, they will most likely be metaphysical in nature.*

—Attributed to William James

THERE IS POSSIBLY NO TERM THAT IS MORE CONFUSING THAN the word
"self." The teaching model that is used by many traditional psychologists
and psychiatrists is as follows:

Id—the unconscious source of psychic energy derived from instinctive needs in human beings

Ego—the organized conscious mediator between the person and
reality; a construct derived from the Id.

Superego—internalization of parental rules and social values.
Functions to reward and punish through a system of moral attitudes,
conscience and guilt.

This was later modified by more progressive psychologists to include
a fourth entity:

Self—the conscious mediator above and beyond the ego or more
simply, the sum total of all permutations of drives and consciousness
derived from a root energy source such as the Id.

In this model the self functions as the deeper level operative above and
below the traditional tripartite structure of Id, Ego and Superego. Note
the degrading of morality to something completely relative, an internalization of attitudes, which have no relationship to anything beyond that
internalization. This model, despite its shortcomings has its uses, but
where it really falls short is in historical continuity. For centuries, the soul
and the life force has been a subject of discussion for philosophers and

theologians. Has it only recently been rediscovered in the guise of the self by modern psychology? This is a bit like reinventing the wheel. What is the self but an attempt by psychology to return to some semblance of the soul without the soul? The basic rule to use when confronted with psychological terminology is the Duck Rule: If it looks, walks and quacks like a duck, then it probably is a duck.

Psychology is of course composed of dozens of competing disciplines, each with different theories and belief systems. Psychology has undergone the same fragmentation that appears

> The soul when in the body is the source of life, and this gives the power of breath and revival, and when this reviving power fails then the body perishes and dies, and this, if I am not mistaken, they called psyche.
>
> ◆
>
> —*Plato,* Cratylus

to happen with all religions. A master of some kind issues a teaching, it is taken as gospel for a while, and then one or two disciples will come along and add a teaching that the others will consider heresy, and suddenly, there is another religion or ideology competing for your wallet and heart. Psychology is a little bit like this, even though collectively, psychologists like to think of themselves as scientists. Given the fragmentation of the discipline, psychology cannot really be considered a science but rather a belief system that uses science to back up various ideas about human nature.

The main problem with modern psychology is far deeper than conceptual shallowness or historic forgetfulness. The greatest difficulty is that psychologists insist on using Newtonian tools to describe non-Newtonian events. Physicists long ago abandoned Newton as their model, but year after year, and one after another, learned treatises on Newtonian systems of psychology and sociology clutter valuable shelf space with university-sanctioned gibberish. Noted criminologist, Dr. Lonnie Athens observes that: "Violent crime is one of the most studied topics in sociology and psychology—just thousands of books. But almost everything I read, or we discussed in class, didn't make sense to me, didn't square with my own firsthand observations and experience of violence."[34] Some of my favorite cases involve inmates on work release, who have victims tied up at home while their psychologists are arguing for the outstanding character of their clients before parole boards.

The notion of a quantum entity like the soul is seldom employed by Newtonian psychology (with the exception of Jung and a few others) to explain how human beings can rise above the limitations created by abnormal subconscious structures. Indeed,classical psychology, as it is popularly understood, would seem to indicate that human salvation is accomplished by allowing the appetites to transcend conscious structures and thus become fully operative and free from the suppression created by the ego and superego. The assumption being of course that the appetites are naturally good and ordered, which is patent lunacy.

Modern psychology has created a gigantic, psychotic cultural delusion. Perhaps we could call it *psychodelusion*. Psychosis is defined generally as living and believing in a mental world that does not correspond to reality. If this is the case, then modern psychology might be said to be preoccupied with unreality. The source of an individual's psychological problems cannot only be attributed to deficient biology or environmental circumstance, rather they must be located in an inappropriate response or activity, as understood in relation to the life force's engagement or disengagement with reality. One of the best examples of this, "Being out of touch with reality," that I have ever seen is a description in *The Washington Post*, describing a visit to a youth detention center:

> I was at Oak Hill, the District's juvenile detention center in
> Laurel, to hear WRC-TV anchorman Jim Vance tell the boys how
> much he loved them and how they could make it if they tried. I
> also was asked to give an inspirational talk at a later date, but after
> sitting in a gymnasium full of these sullen, hunched-back, baggy-
> pants wearing teenage inmates, I began to wonder: Why? Channel
> 4's Vance gave a fine speech about going from a youth gang in
> Philadelphia to becoming a well-paid newscaster. But these kids
> had their own routes from gangland to glory. They made television
> news the old-fashioned way: They killed people. "Despite all of the
> pain and suffering you have caused, your neighbors voted against
> the death penalty," Terry Shelton, a detention center treatment
> specialist told the boys. It was the day after the election. The staff
> clapped. The boys, including a 15 year old charged with killing
> five people, looked at Shelton like he was from Mars…"How
> ironic though, that Oak Hill sits next door to the National
> Security Agency in Laurel, its high tech antennas and satellite
> dishes combing the skies for intelligence about international
> threats. And yet they can't even see the kids who cut through the
> razor wire-topped fence and escape through their yard.

The victims of these young men were as surely killed by the morally bankrupt social gospels of psychology and sociology as they were by guns or knives. Our society has abandoned young men and particularly young African Americans to the savagery of unexamined and uncontrolled appetites. How can we expect anyone to act in a rational manner when they have never been given the moral tools they need to understand either themselves or others?

Just saying "no" is not enough, we must have reasons to say "no" to something that may be bad. A moral calculus is required to determine the practicality and good sense of our actions, but beyond any moral calculus must be a communication with the bedrock of that morality. The core-self of the largely incommunicable soul is just such a bedrock.

Your reason for good behavior must be that it gets good results for you, and the reason that it gets good results can be construed as an objective standard that mirrors the internal reality that you are seeking to become. You are partially good and you wish to act in a manner that is consistent with the goodness developing at your core. Your biological nature isn't quite so concerned with what you think—it has its own agenda, so the struggle will always be between spirit and flesh, or what we might describe from a more modern point of view, as a struggle between non-locality and locality. What is really evil is to allow the healthy tension that exists between the core-self and biology to be erased by academic fiat. Once the tension is removed, out pops the ASS and its good friend FIKI, and social scientists are left scratching their heads at the results.

Philip Gold has a humorous description of his interpretation of the same phenomenon that I have been attempting to describe. He calls it Psychobondage:

> America as a civilization lives in psychobondage. By this I mean a civilization whose dominant value system is psychological

---

Statistics do not show the true severity of juvenile violence. According to recent figures from the Justice Department, nearly 58 percent of all violent and juvenile crimes do not get reported. These figures include **non-reporting** of 49 percent of sexual assaults, 60 percent of robberies and 58 percent of aggravated assaults. These shocking figures make a mockery of the assertion that violent crime has decreased in the United States. The *reported* figures have gone down but the actual figures have always been much higher than reported. One recalls the adage that there are three kinds of lies: lies, damned lies and statistics.

◆

—Statistics provided by the National Crime Victimization Survey

(How does this make me feel, especially about myself?) rather than overtly theological, ideological, scientific-rational, or even crudely materialistic. Feelings are of course universal. They are also powerful determinants of behavior. But in a civilization living in psychobondage, inner states act as more than motivation. They also provide the payoff, the goal; they become ends in themselves.… A civilization living in psychobondage cannot have a rational political life—the coming together of men and women to determine the structure and content of the common world. Electoral politics has long been degraded to the frantic pushing of various 'hot buttons' by therapeutic candidates and their handlers.… Nor can a civilization in psychobondage maintain its social relationships—the latticework of mediating and nurturing institutions standing between the individual and the state. When dealings between people are valued primarily because of their psychological payoffs, and discarded when those payoffs become inadequate or boring, horrendous behaviors and conditions result. What are spousal and child abuse save the adult inability to control emotions?

Superstition and warped beliefs are not confined to merely the gullible or fringe religious beliefs. Scientists are quite capable of entertaining ideas that are not much more than a combination of superstition and bullshit. The notion that life somehow just happens out of random combinations of matter with no coordination by a higher intelligence is really a fairy tale for adults. We owe ourselves a better story of our genesis than a mindless form of evolution based on random mutations unconnected to any larger purpose.

On a deeper level than many of us are aware, we know when something is true or false. (This is the essence of metacognition.) We may however be unable to consciously access our understanding due to a problem with our intellectual system software or perhaps too much clutter on the mental RAM. Your core-self is at the point of exchange between local space and your soul's non-local life energy, it is you. Your core-self knows truth; falsehood is alien to it. Your ego, however, may not always deal with this information gracefully.

There is sometimes a conflict or tension between ideas that get fixed in the ego and the ideas that the core-self believes in. The core-self is way ahead of the ego in this respect. Often you will have a hunch that something is not quite the way you think it is, but you just somehow can't quite bring yourself to look at it closely. Sooner or later, though, the core-self will insist that some issue or idea be focused on. If the ego suppresses the heartfelt desire of the core-self, depression or confusion will soon follow. Do not ignore any issue or warning that surfaces within your consciousness. If you do, you are courting unhappiness.

Imagine for a moment that you have found the almost perfect person to marry. He or she is very intelligent, wealthy, generous, funny, sensitive and industrious. You like each other a great deal and each finds the other to be a high grade physical and sexual specimen. Your ego says, "yes, yes, yes" but your heart says, "wait a minute." What does it mean when the heart hesitates? Doesn't it mean that the core-self does not believe or love what the ego believes or loves? In order to be truly in love, both ego and soul must be in love. The ego can be fooled, but the soul, never. In this example, if you allow the ego to determine your future, divorce and unhappiness is likely. The soul or self accepts no compromises.

What does the core-self believe in? When you examine the list, fundamental values surface. The core-self believes in goodness, truth, beauty, excellence, and joy. The core-self is innately noble, kind and courageous. The core-self also believes in evil as it knows fully what its dark twin FIKI is capable of.

PSYCHOMATURATION

The critical task for both philosophy and psychology is the cultivation of the awareness of the core-self. Psychologist V. Woolfe calls this *psychomaturation*. Woolfe's holistic psychology advocates the concept of a collective group mind that is universal. Individuals participate in this group mind without being aware that they are part of a larger whole. (Howard Bloom's Global Brain is scratching at the same mystery.) Psychomaturation is the process of becoming aware of this non-local connection and identity with universal mind. Universal mind is a source of both wisdom and power. By tapping into universal mind, human beings can become creative and larger than the confines of their own egotism.

> Urges are the waves constantly washing the island beach that is you. They are as regular and normal as the tides. How you harness their power and ride them is up to you.
>
> ◆
>
> —James O'Reilly

The most important conclusion that can be derived from a reflection on the significance of the soul is that this entity is, in fact, more powerful than either your dick or your ego. Whatever empowers the soul gives you a greater ability to deal with your dick. Stepping into the core-self of the soul creates an alteration of space and time and consequently of your perceptions and your desires. This is the essence of both psychomaturation and metacognition. One might disagree with the concept of a universal human mind, but the metacognition that each one of us can experience through multi-dimensional space is subjectively verifiable.

This critical linkage between the control of sexuality and the development of consciousness cannot be overstated. Sublimation is not merely a psychological oddity with occasional applications, it is the basis of good Dick Management, a starting point for all moral character development, and the means for up-linking to non-local consciousness.

Responsible behavior doesn't occur in some kind of magic vacuum, even though the core-self or soul can come forward in many ways and through many adverse circumstances. The place to start with any improvement is often the one that may not seem to be the most obvious. Look no further than managing your dick for the beginnings of self-improvement and expansion of consciousness.

It is difficult to get a man to understand something when his salary depends upon his not understanding it.

—Upton Sinclair

MANAGEMENT TIPS

- Your core-self is the most advanced consciousness of your own soul that you can claim as your own.

- Your values should not be arbitrary or completely relative to your situation; when anchored in truth, they are rock solid.

- You know who you are but you are afraid to claim this knowledge.

- By saying "no" to your dick, sometimes you say "yes" to yourself.

- A woman's spiritual consciousness is something to pay attention to. Her intuition is frequently much more developed than your own.

CHAPTER 20

THE PECER TEST

*Moral results can only be obtained through
moral restraints.*

—Mohandas K. Gandhi

YOUR PERSONAL ENERGY CONSCIOUSNESS EQUIVALENCY RATIO (PECER) measures the Chi available to your psyche, i.e., energy that has either not been cathected or used up by other activity. The higher the score, the harder is your virtue. Scoring is based on the hypothesis that there are four basic levels of Chi: (4) High, (3) Medium, (2) Low and (1) Running on Empty. Scoring is calculated using this four point system with four being the highest score and one being the lowest. Immoral activity in general consumes large quantities of Chi and will usually result in low scores. Higher scores reflect conservation of Chi and generally are indicative of virtuous activity. The PECER Test is a kind of rough measuring instrument that gives you an overall idea of how your Chi is being apportioned. (A sophisticated dong-o-meter to measure the Chi that is actually used by your dick would be most helpful but unfortunately such an instrument does not yet exist.)

This is not a psychological test. Do not confuse the results of this test with any sort of psychological profile. This test is profiling energy levels that professional psychologists are not able to evaluate. Such professionals may wish to test themselves, however, and come to their own conclusions.

Now, turn to the next page and begin The PECER Test!

BEGIN THE PECER TEST HERE

Circle the number to the right of the answer that most clearly applies to you. Positive questions (e.g. question 1) earn points from high (4) to low (1); negative questions (e.g. question 5) earn points from low (1) to high (4). Positive actions earn more points than negative actions. High scores indicate energy well used and low scores indicate energy misuse.

1. How often do you feel creative?
   Frequently (4)   Sometimes (3)   Rarely (2)   Never (1)

2. How often do you perform acts of kindness or courtesy?
   Frequently (4)   Sometimes (3)   Rarely (2)   Never (1)

3. How often do you masturbate?
   Frequently (1)   Sometimes (2)   Rarely (3)   Never (4)

4. How often are you happy?
   Frequently (4)   Sometimes (3)   Rarely (2)   Never (1)

5. How often do you overeat?
   Frequently (1)   Sometimes (2)   Rarely (3)   Never (4)

6. How often do you talk about people behind their backs?
   Frequently (1)   Sometimes (2)   Rarely (3)   Never (4)

7. How often do you feel hatred towards anyone? (To be distinguished from hating how someone behaves.)
   Frequently (1)   Sometimes (2)   Rarely (3)   Never (4)

8. How often do you get into fights just for the fun of it?
   Frequently (1)   Sometimes (2)   Rarely (3)   Never (4)

9. How often do you get into fights to help a stranger or to stop an act of vandalism or rude behavior?
   Frequently (4)   Sometimes (3)   Rarely (2)   Never (1)

10. How often do you curse?
    Frequently (1)   Sometimes (2)   Rarely (3)   Never (4)

11. How often do you lie?
    Frequently (1)   Sometimes (2)   Rarely (3)   Never (4)

12. How often do you take credit for other peoples' work?
    Frequently (1)   Sometimes (2)   Rarely (3)   Never (4)

13. How often do you steal?
    Frequently (1)   Sometimes (2)   Rarely (3)   Never (4)

14. If you have murdered, raped, or tortured an innocent person, and
    are not ashamed of your actions YOUR SCORE IS 26. Disregard
    your cumulative score. Write your score in the margin next to this
    question. This is your final score. You need to seek spiritual
    assistance.

15. How often do you smoke?
    Frequently (1)   Sometimes (2)   Rarely (3)   Never (4)

16. How often do you exercise?
    Frequently (4)   Sometimes (3)   Rarely (2)   Never (1)

17. How often do you have sex outside of marriage?
    Frequently (1)   Sometimes (2)   Rarely (3)   Never (4)

18. How often do you honor your appointments, commitments,
    promises and contractual obligations?
    Frequently (4)   Sometimes (3)   Rarely (2)   Never (1)

19. How often do you take care of relatives and friends including
    your parents?
    Frequently (4)   Sometimes (3)   Rarely (2)   Never (1)

20. How often are you courteous to those who are physically chal-
    lenged or old?
    Frequently (4)   Sometimes (3)   Rarely (2)   Never (1)

21. How often are you intolerant of other's beliefs or customs?
    Frequently (1)   Sometimes (2)   Rarely (3)   Never (4)

22. How often do you apologize when you make a mistake?
    Frequently (4)   Sometimes (3)   Rarely (2)   Never (1)

23. How often do you take illegal drugs?
    Frequently (1)   Sometimes (2)   Rarely (3)   Never (4)

24. How often do you give money to those in need?
    Frequently (4)   Sometimes (3)   Rarely (2)   Never (1)

25. How often do you get intoxicated with alcoholic beverages?
    Frequently (1)   Sometimes (2)   Rarely (3)   Never (4)

26. How often do you seriously think about having sex with someone besides your significant other? (Having a passing fantasy that you do not engage does not affect your score.)
    Frequently (1)   Sometimes (2)   Rarely (3)   Never (4)

The PECER Test is based on a series of twenty-six carefully formulated questions. Add your scores by totaling the numbers that you circled.

1. If your score is twenty-six to fifty-one, you have a serious Management problem. Your soul may be running on empty!

2. If your score is fifty-two to sixty-seven you are in need of Management.

3. A score of sixty-eight to seventy-eight qualifies you as a practitioner of Management.

4. A score of seventy-eight and above indicates a very high level of Management.

The following descriptive analysis may be more helpful in evaluating your score:

1. If your score was twenty-six to fifty-one your soul is running on empty and there is a good chance that you may be an ASSHOLE.

2. If your score was fifty-two to sixty seven your Management skills need serious work. You may be a LOSER.

3. If your score was sixty-eight to seventy-eight you are working within acceptable moral parameters and are probably a GENTLEMAN or a GENTLEWOMAN.

4. A score of seventy-eight and above indicates a high level of virtue. You may be a PRINCE OR A QUEEN.

Remember, on this test, a score below sixty-eight indicates energy deficits. You may be surprised by your total. The Psychic Energy Consciousness Equivalency Ratio or PECER shows how much of your allotted psychic energy (think Chi!) has been converted to consciousness, and how much to drive or appetite. Energy converted towards consciousness is useful and tends to produce a feeling of well being. Build up your PECER strength with virtue! Energy connected to drive is quickly consumed.

Additional test forms are available at www.dickmanagement.com

Agape means nothing sentimental or basically affectionate; it means understanding, redeeming good will for all men, an overflowing love which seeks nothing in return. It is the love of God working in the lives of men. When we love on the agape level we love men not because we like them, not because their attitudes and ways appeal to us, but because God loves them. Here we rise to the position of loving the person who does the evil deed while hating the deed he does.

—Martin Luther King, Jr.

MANAGEMENT TIPS

• There is a difference between being aware of sex at all times and engaging the impulse in your mind.

• Actively engaging in sexual fantasies starts to consume energy at the rate of a heavy-duty 220-volt appliance like a clothes dryer.

• Chi is the same energy that you need for sports, thinking and being creative.

• Nature also runs on life energy and its many different forms.

• Your ASS will generate many bad desires in the course of your lifetime. What you do with these desires is the measure of your management skills.

CHAPTER 21

NEGOTIATING WITH YOUR JOHNSON

There is no man so good, who, were he to submit all his thoughts and actions to the laws, would not deserve hanging ten times in his life.

—Montaigne

WHAT DO YOU DO WHEN YOUR DICK DOES NOT OBEY YOU? YOU HAVE told yourself several hundred times now that you want to exercise more self-control, but your dick ignores you. This is very much like having a disobedient child or dog that doesn't listen. The dog or child doesn't listen because it does not fear or want to obey the issuer of the commands. (Perhaps it does not even know how.) The first thing that you must have is something to restrain the Id (which is a lower manifestation of your life energy or if you prefer, your Global Brain) to control your dick at the very source. Your ego can in fact make deals with the Id and effectively restrain your dick. This is classic Freud but with a twist. Where Freud would have said there is no authority higher than either the ego, Id or superego, you have access to the higher authority of the upper echelons of your own core-self—not a subconscious but a supraconscious force. These higher promptings of the life force are your secret ally against its dark and less evolved twin—the Id that we also know as your ASS.

The key to understanding these higher promptings is to learn how to sidestep the embrace of your ASS and listen to your higher self. This is somewhat akin to dancing with a wild partner. You must first observe and learn how this partner operates by watching his or her dance steps and then you can anticipate their next moves. Observation and anticipation are essential for dealing with the patterns of behavior that your ASS will regularly engage in.

Imagine, for example, that you have a terrible craving for a cigarette.

Observe the desire as if you were a spectator and take several deep breaths. Now, try sidestepping and watch your partner continue its craving without you. Your "departnered" ASS won't notice your absence as quickly as you will notice the absence of your ASS. Once you are in this calm and detached position, your ASS, disturbed at being exposed, will try immediately to get back in synch with you.

You may have been able to achieve this disengagement from your appetite survival system only momentarily, but note that it worked for just a few seconds, if not longer! The essential principle is that you do not have to identify with your desires—unless you want to. It is difficult but not impossible. Ignoring pain is a similar drill; you simply detach your mind from the pain and pretend it is separate from you.

Remember that your ASS/Id, as the controlling entity of your dick, is looking for a maximizing of pleasure. At your deepest core, you long for happiness, which is one of the highest forms of pleasure. Your core-self can in fact make deals with your ASS who is currently the owner of your dick. Here is some hypothetical dialog to help you begin this process:

1. Okay, you met Miss Muffet at the local bar. You are both loaded to the gills and she invites you home. Yes, her tuffet is speaking to your dick but before you step over the threshold take a deep breath and consider some of the consequences. Are you in a relationship already? Is she? Imagine yourself waking up with her and she with you—the ghastly morning after syndrome.

   Visualize disease—nasty things like AIDS and other sexually transmitted diseases are not confined to the gay community. A little fun now may cost you your life or health later. Picture your dick falling off or your body covered with open sores. Wouldn't it be better to go with a woman to whom you are more deeply attracted?

2. Yes, the wallet left in the locker room is full of money and you could have a lot of fun with it. Put yourself in the owner's shoes, and remember how it felt the last time you had something stolen.

3. Let's say you have a weight problem and you just finished a superb meal. You are comfortably full. Dessert is introduced. Do you want to be wearing that food? As they say, "a moment on the lips, forever on the hips." You will be more handsome and the ladies will find you much more attractive, if you are lean and hard as opposed to looking like the Pillsbury Dough Boy. The best definition of discipline I've ever heard is: "Virtue is remembering what you want."

4. Your classmate or associate has just slighted you in a conversation that you overheard through a third party. You may want to ask yourself first of all: is this true? Secondly, you may want to ask yourself if it might be better to overlook the insult and treat the other person with compassion. How would you like to be treated under similar circumstances, if you perhaps uttered something in passing that was not for public consumption?

Notice how the element of time has been injected into the discussion with your dick's keeper. It is that moment of thoughtful questioning and reflection that allows the self to step forward, cathect with the future and rap your inner animal on the noggin before it starts to make trouble for you.

Yes, talk to your dick's master! This is the beginning of a long dialog and like all good propaganda, it must be repeated over and over again. This is similar to basic dog training. "Woof, woof," "down boy, heel—stay away from that backside! Yes, she smells good. No, you may not go in there today. I know you'd like a bite but let's show some class, etc." Do you let your dog do whatever he or she wants? Of course not. Then show your dick who is boss!

However, where deals fail to work, there must be punishment. Your Id, as a lower manifestation of the life energy can be made afraid—just like a dog. Your Id will always essentially work towards maximizing pleasure. That which is fearful or unpleasant can be used as a stick to cudgel your life force's ASS.

THE GIFT OF FEAR

Let's say that you are in a bank and you notice that there is a suspicious looking man hovering around the entrance of the building. You finish your transaction and are about to leave when the suspicious looking man whom you saw earlier bursts into the bank, brandishing a sawed-off shotgun and orders everyone to lie down. What do you do? Do you say, "I'm sorry sir, I just finished my business and will leave if you don't mind?" No, you lie down because you are probably scared shitless. Now the man tells the teller to hand over the money. She says, "I can't, I don't have the key." He

> There is more to be feared from the passions of men than from all the convulsions of nature.
>
> ◆
>
> —Edward Gibbon

says, "Open the fucking drawer or I'll shoot you in the face." Does she say "Sorry, I am not authorized?" I don't think so.

Fear is an extremely powerful motivator. Do we not fear losing our jobs, our health and our lives? You must become convinced that you will lose your inner life if you allow yourself to be completely ruled by your appetites. This means that if you only do whatever you feel like doing, you will be either mean or useless. Your ASS can be the cold-hearted man with the sawed-off shotgun, or an enormous hog that can only wallow in self pity. A sensible person wouldn't want to deal with either of them. What you need is a weapon or a stick to use against your ASS. Fear is one such weapon; it is a negentropic gift that your ASS hates.

The idea of Hell was at one time a religious whip for your ASS, and the very thought of it scared a lot of people into good behavior. Since most people now don't believe in the old time view of hell, we must develop an alternative punishment for the ASS, so that the beast obeys when we tell it to be quiet. Shame is another such punishment.

According to Thomas Aquinas, a heavyset and astonishingly brilliant Dominican monk who lived in the thirteenth century, there are six kinds or species of fear in addition to the simple fear of physical danger:

1. laziness

2. modesty

3. shame

4. amazement

5. stupor

6. anxiety

At first glance, you gaze in surprise at the items on this list. How can these things be different kinds of fear? But when you make an effort to think about it, they make perfect sense. Fear always involves avoidance or withdrawal from a perceived evil. Any time you encounter something that requires effort (a perceived evil from the id's point of view) or is an event you may not want to have happen, or is something that you must reflect upon or encounter with caution, then avoidance is called into play. According to Aquinas, it belongs to the appetite and will (the will is a part of the power

> A great many people think they are thinking when they are merely rearranging their prejudices.
>
> ◆
>
> —William James

of appetite) to pursue good and to avoid evil or lack of goodness. Let's look at the list from this perspective with a bit of explanation.

1. laziness: avoidance of work

2. modesty: avoidance of having the body seen by others, or of having one's achievements made much of

3. shame: withdrawal or recoiling from one's self; alternatively, the desire to avoid the deprivation of reputation, with the fear that it is already ruined

4. amazement: withdrawal from something that may be alternatively pleasing and frightening; (e.g. Houdini or an escape artist freeing himself from an impossibly difficult situation)

5. stupor: avoidance of effort or hard thinking, or attempts to rouse the intellect

6. anxiety: avoidance of unknown stresses

Understanding the six kinds of fear can be helpful in understanding how the Id/ASS operates. From the ASS's perspective, laziness may be more important than work, but the shame and fear of deprivation associated with not working is anathema to your ASS. Shame allows you to gaze upon yourself with loathing and exposes your Appetite Survival System for the whore that it is. Psychologists speak of shame as if it were something to be avoided. They are completely wrong, unless it is a shame that should not be a shame. For example, you should be ashamed of drug addiction, but not of having a disease or disability that you did not contract through any fault of your own.

Shame is not embarrassment either. One might be embarrassed, for example, by a cutting remark, but only ashamed if you are afraid to respond, or unable to shrug it off gracefully. Not wanting others to think badly of you isn't the same as shame either, it is more a concern for the truth of a situation that motivates us to seek correction of an perception that is misconceived or developed through mishap.

The careful use of shame and the avoidance of laziness can be used to break the hold of the ASS. Fear and shame are used effectively by the military in support of focused FIKI. Many young men are shamed by their drill instructors to exceed their pre-conceived notions of what they can and can't do physically or emotionally. If the military can successfully use fear and shame to motivate and shape young men, why is it such a leap for the bureaucrats who run our public high schools to philosophically understand and embrace discipline? The critical issue is probably not that these officials don't understand or want discipline but in order for that discipline to work, it must be located within the ethical and conceptual framework of morality, in short, virtue and vice. It is precisely the politically correct disavowal of this framework that renders even the most rudimentary discussion of values and responsibility to the realm of relativistic murkiness. This inability to grasp the value of carefully directed fear and shame leads to a general ridicule of public education. Who can respect any system of education where children might be afraid in their own classrooms of other students who are ruled by dangerous appetites that even their teachers cannot address for fear of censure?

How many of us, for example, would like to be publicly humiliated for our moral offenses? Why else are police publishing the names and addresses of johns caught picking up whores? Why do normal criminals routinely hide their heads under shirts or other articles of clothing when the television cameras are running? Could it be that they are ashamed or afraid of being seen by friends and family? Why is it so difficult for you to apologize sometimes? Making the leap from shame to doing something about it is the mark of the moral person! Remember, anything that increases your capacity or strength to act and to make decisions improves your ability to deal with your biology, and manage your dick. Your ASS is like a dishonest lawyer. See that you do not hire him to represent you. He'll take you for everything you've got.

Grandmother told Coyote to go out and hunt fawn. He went away and he saw new Indian potatoes. He stopped and asked his testicles if he should tell his grandmother there were plenty of potatoes, and take her back there with the digging stick so he could catch her and rape her. His testicles told him that he could do that, so he went back and told her there were many new potatoes. She took her digging stick and went with him and began digging. Coyote said, "Dig down deeper." So she dug deeper and deeper until her behind stuck up out of the ground. Coyote then grabbed her and stuck her head down in the sand so she could not see and he copulated with her. Then he ran so she could not see who did it, but she knew it was Coyote. She called out, "I know you now, you are Coyote." He said, "No, grandmother, I did not do that to you. I'm going to ask my testicles and penis if I did that to you and they will tell you." So he sat down and asked his testicles and they did not answer, so he asked his penis and it said, "Yes, that is what you asked me." Grandmother said, "I knew that, I know it now. It is a good thing that I'm an old woman or I would be having lots of little coyotes." She quit digging and went home. Coyote was so angry at his penis for telling on him that he was going to mash it on a rock. He sat down and started to hit it with a rock, but the penis drew back. Coyote pulled it out again and tried to hit it again, but it pulled back every time and Coyote never succeeded in mashing it.

—Malcolm Margolin, Bear River legend, *The Way We Lived:*
California Reminiscences & Songs

MANAGEMENT TIPS

- Find the best time for you to engage in sexual activity. If you are a day person, for example, regular sex during the day may use up too much energy.

- Try various kinds of discipline. Force yourself to exercise and periodically abstain from sexual activity.

- Observe how you feel about your dick and keep a journal of your reactions and your struggles with it. Observation helps you to differentiate the hidden structures of your psychic life.

- Pray or visit your priest, minister or Rabbi to help curb habitual masturbation or sex outside of marriage. This can be an unpleasant but highly effective activity to engage in because it tends to be embarrassing.

- Be courageous. Courage is required to fight with your appetites. Your ASS plays dirty—no ruse is too low to get you to comply with the prime directive of "getting off."

CHAPTER 22

A CYBER-KINETIC
EXERCISE PROGRAM

You are the invincible Atman, unaffected by the ups and downs of life.
The shadow you cast while trudging along the road falls on dirt and dust,
bush and briar, stone and sand, but you are not worried at all, for you walk
unscathed. So too, as the Atman substance, you have no reason to be worried
over the fate of its shadow, the body.

—Sai Baba, Indian mystic

IT IS ALL VERY WELL TO TALK ABOUT THE CORE-SELF AND THE SOUL IN theoretical terms, but how do you discover this multi-dimensional Manager, and how do you actually manage your dick? Is there any kind of program that will help you get results and keep your ASS from kicking sand in your face? The most important thing to remember is that the life energy of the soul occupies more than three or four dimensions. It is not possible to manage your dick from a three or four-dimensional perspective. This is why the "just say no" crowd has such a hard time saying no; a dick-powered Appetite Survival System will outmaneuver them every time. In order to grow in cyber-kinetic knowledge (soul knowledge) and restrain your life force's ASS you must do five things with vigor:

1. Distinguish truth from falsehood
2. Practice continence, which requires the full range of all the virtues
3. Behave with compassion and understanding towards others
4. Decide that you want options for your energy and work patiently on discovery
5. Cultivate an awareness of your higher self

These five categories of action are, ultimately, themselves the work of the higher self! In short, they are cyber-kinetic activities or processes, and are the hallmark of a soul emerging from the murk of everyday consciousness. Some individuals are engaged in more of these multi-dimensional processes than others, but unless all five are engaged the soul will limp and quite frankly, you may continue to be unhappy.

VIRTUE IS LIKE BODYBUILDING

The moral virtues, like the intellectual virtues, require work to be made part of your life. Practicing virtue is like bodybuilding. The more you do it, the better you will get at it and the better you will feel and look. The intellectual virtues of Science, Wisdom, Understanding, Prudence and Art are perhaps easier to grasp in terms of their practical application, and the need to work at them in order to improve, than the eleven moral virtues (see the Ninth Step of Chapter 23 for a further explanation of the moral virtues).

Let's take three moral virtues and examine the basic patterns that have to be engaged in order for a virtue to become a habit of will, i.e., something that you don't even have to think about very much because you will just do it. This is the Dick Manager's exercise program.

BUILDING COURAGE

Courage is something that we would all like to have more of. In order to practice courage, you must find something that you are afraid of, and then take some small steps towards become courageous by performing small acts of courage. For example, let's say that you are afraid of water and swimming in general. Ask yourself this question: are you afraid to take a bath? If the answer is no, then you are not afraid of water but you are afraid of something. So, the first question must always be: what am I specifically afraid of? Once you have identified what it is you are really afraid of, then you can get a handle on the situation. Something like a fear of swimming can mean different things for different people. Some of us may have a loved one who drowned, others may only be afraid of what might come out from under the water and bite them, and still others may be suffering from a childhood incident of suffocation. There could be many different reasons for having such a fear. There is no reason to be ashamed of anything you are afraid of. You are being honest. The only time you should feel shame about fear is if you are not doing anything to overcome it or to reduce its affect on you.

The next step is to take some small actions to acclimate you to your fear. A good example of this is how some individuals develop resistance to snake bites. They take small amounts of the venom over time, and ultimately become resistant to the snake's poison. If it is water you are afraid of, take some small steps to swim in water that is less threatening than a full sized swimming pool. Go to your local gym and find the biggest hot whirlpool you can find and swim in it. Find a series of larger pools, and build up your tolerance for larger bodies of water by slowly increasing the size of the pool and the time you spend at these facilities. Sit down with pen in hand and figure out a step by step process to engage your fear. Over time, you should become less afraid of the water than you were when you started your regimen. You will have created a habit of not being as disturbed as you used to be by being in the water on a regular basis. You still might not like swimming, but you could well cease being a such a "scaredy cat" by having made this structured attempt to overcome your fear.

CULTIVATING CONTINENCE AND TEMPERANCE

Continence is defined as self-restraint in regards to impulse or desire, so pick your pleasure and work at limiting your desire for it. Temperance is a form of continence as it specifically applies to pleasure. Cultivating continence calls on the tag team of continence and temperance to work together. Let's say that you have a propensity towards eating candy (I do) and would like to cultivate some self-restraint in regards to pigging out. First, try to understand why you are overeating. Are you lonely, unhappy or just have a craving for sweets? It could be many things. Next, start with something simple—like deciding before you eat the candy how much you are actually going to eat—and then not allow yourself a single bite more. Try this for a week. The following week, you might want to take one day of the week to deny yourself the pleasure of eating candy all day. You will notice that you really don't suffer that much if you eat a piece of fruit instead. Try this strategy for two weeks. You will notice that it gets a little easier the longer you do it. You may still want the candy but you've injected a little bit of a safety zone between the clamoring of your ASS for more, and what you *know* is enough.

Another form of self-restraint you may want to attempt is sexual self-restraint. This of course includes not playing with yourself. The program is very simple. Make yourself a one hundred dollar bet that you will give up sex, including masturbation, for one week. Write the bet down on paper. Under no circumstances can you welsh on this bet, even though it is with yourself. If you cave in, you must donate the money to charity—immediately. Okay, so you kept your money the first week. Now go to two weeks! Oh, some of you are sweating and some of you will lose your bets. Try again! You can only consider yourself having succeeded with this exercise if you get to the thirty-day mark. Yes, that is one month without thumping your johnson or using it in some other way. Whether you are gay or straight, it doesn't matter with this exercise. All are welcome to try it and everyone will notice some definite results. Some of you will be driven crazy by it, but it is well worth the effort to see if you have what it takes to be a serious Dick Manager.

DEVELOPING LIBERALITY

Liberality is defined as generous giving. If you are a tightwad or are not generous with your time, or do not give much of yourself to others, you may want to follow the steps of this exercise. First ask yourself for permission to investigate the difficulty. You may find it uncomfortable to be querying your motivations in regards to generosity. There may be many reasons for you to be tight-fisted with your time and energy. Perhaps you grew up poor, perhaps other kids stole money from you when you were young, or you could be just stingy with your time. Maybe you are just selfish. Be honest. Once you have determined roughly what the cause of your limitation might be, proceed to the solution. What is your regimen going to be? Here is a sample program. Once a week, you can pick a day when you will perform one act of selflessness, one act of generosity towards someone you might not like or care for. (You can do this with someone you like to begin with if that makes it more palatable.) Write the day down on your calendar and then make sure you perform a kindness on the appointed day. Under no circumstances leave it for another day. You must do it on the appointed day. If you practice this for three months, you may find that on the day in question, you will always be looking for someone to do a kindness to, or to be generous with. Liberality doesn't have to (although it may) involve the giving of money. Liberality is really about the giving of your time. (What is money but a kind of stored time?) You may find that you like how liberality makes you feel. Curiously enough, you may also find yourself performing kind and generous acts of self-giving on non-appointed days. Congratulations! You have just cultivated the virtue of liberality.

ASSUMING THE FINE GARMENTS OF PATIENCE

Patience is probably the single virtue that most of us are sorely lacking. Patience involves cultivating many aspects of virtue. It is often thought of by students of moral science as part of continence, but it is more than just continence. The patient person is almost always thoughtful and thoughtfulness almost always taps into the virtue of wisdom. It is difficult, however, for the selfish person to be patient or thoughtful of others due to the impulsive and self-centered nature of selfishness. We would seldom describe a selfish individual as wise. The patient person, on the other hand, is almost always able to cultivate continence and wisely wait for the benefits of patience to make themselves shown. Leonardo Da Vinci has a wonderful description of patience that more clearly than any rational explanation shows what a tremendous virtue it is.

Patience serves as a protection against wrongs as clothes do against cold. For if you put on more clothes as the cold increases, it will have no power to hurt you. So in like manner you must grow in patience when you meet with great wrongs, and they will then be powerless to vex your mind.

Patience will enable you to blanket the eruptions of your ASS before it dumps you into its emotional version of nuclear winter. If you are already suffering from intemperate eruptions, don't give up, put on the many colored blankets of patience and revive your spirit. Don't we all like working or associating with patient and thoughtful individuals? Be patient with others then and make the world a better place every day.

FIVE-STEPS TO BETTER DICK MANAGEMENT

You will note that the following five-step pattern for the cultivation of virtue is standard for all the virtues:

1. **Identify the problem** as closely as you can. Note that your ASS will usually be involved, so you may have to press yourself to come clean on the reasons for your difficulty.
2. **Plan on taking some small steps** to practice anything that you find difficult to achieve. Remember that virtue is something you must actually do—not something to be thought about just as a possibility.
3. **Write these steps down** that you will be taking—daily, weekly and monthly—on paper (a palm pilot or any other such device will also work—if you use it regularly). Writing the steps down,

like all scheduling is critical in order for you to actually do what you are planning. Do not under any circumstances allow yourself to miss an appointed virtue day. How you might feel about this has to be dismissed. Just do it.

4. **Just do it.** Continue to practice the good habits that you have cultivated during your training session and ignore any feelings of discouragement.

5. **Observe the changes** in your outlook and personality that these good habits engender and try to account for the changes in terms of your personal metaphysic and moral code.

EXPLORING YOUR HIGHER SELF

How do you go about exploring the larger sense of self that you may encounter during metacognitional acts of virtue? The most common way to observe your soul at work is similar to the manner in which astronomers discover planets revolving around distant stars—indirectly. For example, a planet's gravity distorts the gravitational field of its sun. Scientists can measure this distortion to predict the existence of planetary bodies. With this clue in hand, and by observing subtle shifts in consciousness during a variety of experiences, we too can observe the activities of our hidden selves.

You might want to think of your intellectual and moral powers as evolved processes or channels of your higher self, and your Appetite Survival System as an early evolutionary survivor of developing consciousness. Your Dimensionally Interactive Cyber-Kinetic self has the capability to reside on a higher or a lower level of consciousness but it must be managed or directed in order for it to go where you want it to go. In this sense, Cyber-Kinetics functions as the operating system of both your core-self and your Appetite Survival System. You must prudently manage your ASS and cultivate cyber-kinetic knowledge but if you don't know who you are, this will be a difficult proposition indeed. Virtue enables you to engage a system of ethics that gives you the intellectual structures to observe your ethic-less ASS and engage the transforming power and moral goodness of your higher self.

The virtues of courage, honesty, self-restraint, patience, and understanding are basic to the formation of any worthwhile culture. We simply cannot afford not to teach our young people how to cultivate these aspects of good character. They cannot achieve happiness without them, nor can a society flourish and endure without understanding these multi-dimensional processes.

As you investigate the dynamics of cyberkinesis, and explore the ecology of your sexuality and consciousness, you will begin to realize who the Dick Manager is. The discovery of this larger sense of self is one of the pivotal events in life. What we loosely call maturity is really a slow awakening of our deepest sense of self (the true Manager) and a growing awareness of non-local influences in life. The first call that we usually notice of this higher consciousness is for self-restraint, a kind of non-verbal "time-out." The higher self wants to put its local house in order by regulating the members of the 4F Club.

The Upanishads, the second earliest sacred texts of Hinduism after the Vedas, make it clear that charity and compassion are inextricably linked to self-restraint. The greater our self-mastery, the more we are able to develop our potential and help others. The opposite is also true: lose self-mastery, and charity and compassion will glow ever more feebly in your heart. No one says this more simply than the Chinese sage Lao Tzu, in his immortal little book, *The Way of Life:*

> The invincible shield
> of caring
> Is a weapon from the
> sky
> Against being dead.

The core self is your moral guide. It is your larger sense of self, the bigger multi-dimensional *you* that lies beyond the five senses of ordinary consciousness. Webster's dictionary defines consciousness as: a quality or state of being aware, especially of something within oneself. Consciousness consists of a disproportion between your non-local aware-

---

A ristotle points out that since virtue is related to action, it must also be related to emotion. Now pleasure and pain are a result of every action and every emotion. Thus, virtue must be related in some way to the two. It does not follow, however, that every virtuous action is a pleasant one. Other factors are involved.

For example, Aristotle believes that when a person goes after a certain pleasure at the wrong time or in the wrong way, they can become corrupt.

◆

—Barbara Jancar Ph.D.

ness and your local awareness. This is an ecology of consciousness and information inasmuch as it is a dynamic relationship between the environment of locality and the environment of non-locality. The disproportion exists because as you grow, you become aware of your self as a non-local entity, but you experience your self for the most part in a four dimensional universe. You have no way of measuring the non-local side of yourself, but you will intuit that it is much larger than your thoughts of it are. You will notice more and more in daily life all sorts of little events and "nudges" from somewhere else that you have always had, but usually were just below the threshold of consciousness.

The totality of your non-locality is your soul, but you are only aware of one aspect of this quantum entity. This is the Helmsman, the core-self, the mediator between you as a multi-dimensional quantum entity and you as a four dimensional observation of something that is largely incommunicable, except perhaps by analogy. Chi is the operating energy system of the soul, the way in which it propagates itself through time and space. How you use Chi has an ecological impact on your moral thinking. Dimensionally Interactive Cyber-Kinetics is the metaphysical system that describes the structure of this ecology. Dick Management is just one practical application of this new science of cyber-kinetic knowledge, which as you now know, is the language of the soul.

> If you are sitting in a hot bath and don't move, you don't feel the heat of the water. As soon as you move the heat is felt. In the same way, the human circuitry gives the vastness the possibility of experiencing its own vastness through what I call the undulation. The mind can't grasp this. But who you are is always grasping itself all the time. There is no one that has to start grasping for it to be grasping itself. It is occurring simultaneously with everything that is taken to be who you are.
>
> ◆
>
> —Suzanne Segal,
> *Collision with the Infinite*

AN ECOLOGY OF MORALS

The science of ecology states that an organism has an intimate and reciprocal relationship with its total environment. Energy fields are the quantum environment of your body and your core self, so you exist in an ecology of high energy physics. Imagine yourself as a quantum being, a glowing cloud of quarks with waves of fractional energy charges and bandwidths interacting continuously in many different dimensions. Obviously in this ecology what you do with your dick, your mind, or your heart is going to affect the rest of you, those around you, and indeed the rest of the world.

Many of us suffer from the mistaken idea that to have a bad idea float through our heads is an indication that there is something wrong with us. Nothing could be further from the truth. The healthy person has all manner of bizarre and peculiar thoughts pass through the mind. What makes for healthiness is having a lens through which one can examine the various kinds of shit that float in through the mental window. Thoughts of assault, murder, suicide, and perverse sexuality such as child molestation, incest, bestiality, necrophilia, and many others too numerous to mention are completely within the range of human sentiment. It is precisely for this reason that moral ecology includes, as part of its instruction, a teaching on Dick Management, which shows how to manage the corrosive, and debilitating urges that come from the ASS of evolutionary biology.

Dick Management takes the position that morality is far too important to be left to either religion or the sciences as we know them today. Both science and religion are fragmented into innumerable disciplines with competing and confusing ideologies, and methodologies that allow the unscrupulous to slip through the cracks and manipulate political and social agendas for their own gain. Dick Management is also opposed to any discipline that seeks to unlink the relationship between what the public does with its genitals, and symptoms of energy mismanagement deficiencies such as crime, divorce, vandalism and corruption of public officials. Psychologists and sociologists cannot continue to use a Newtonian or machine model for understanding the human mind and expect their disciplines to remain useful for long. The new tools given to us by modern physics, coupled with the wisdom of the ancients, can steer us in the right direction for taking corrective action. Nonetheless, standing morally upright is a difficult process. It is never enough to know the dynamics of good behavior or that you should behave properly; it is also critical that you actually practice good behavior and continuously make the effort to shoulder your ASS aside and act prudently.

The fundamental problem of consciousness is not to figure out how to predict the winners at the racetrack or to levitate—all of which would be fun—but how to manage the bad impulses that come from evolutionary biology, so that we can begin to become who we really are as humans, not two-legged dogs or smooth-skinned apes.

George Orwell said that a restatement of the obvious is sometimes the first duty of a responsible man. It is therefore worth restating what was once obvious: in extramarital affairs there are victims, beginning with the spouse and children. If marriage vows and commitments are still to be taken seriously, then adultery is a betrayal of a very high order. And when it is discovered, acute emotional damage almost always follows—often leading to divorce. In marriage, one person has been entrusted with the soul of another. That power, freely given, is unlike any other human relationship—and so, too, is the damage that can be done. This shouldn't be made light of, shrugged off, dismissed. In a current, trendy barbarism, some commentators claim adultery has a "humanizing" effect and that it makes public figures more "interesting." This, of course, corrupts the notion of what it means to be human. If betraying a wife makes you more "human," then does one's humanity grow too with the betrayal of one's parents? Or one's children? Or one's country? Just how many betrayals make you "fully human?"

—William J. Bennett, *The Wall Street Journal*

MANAGEMENT TIPS

- Your soul is an unmoved mover. How it is related to the Unmoved Mover is a question philosophers and theologians have pondered for centuries. You cannot exhaust this issue for its personal, political and social ramifications nor can you pretend that it is not related to your dick.

- Honesty is beyond being a critical requirement. If you are dishonest with yourself, you will never understand your place in the universe.

- Science will some day discover a way to view non-local energy. This more than anything else will be the basis for new sciences of energy management that will replace the presently limited psychologies that we use to analyze human behavior today.

- Energy must come from somewhere. Why do you think, for example, that you feel more refreshed if you sleep, instead of just lying down for the same length of time? Sleep is a way of going non-local, a refreshing visit to higher dimensions for your soul. Make sure that you get enough of it.

- You have rights. Do you think the Divine has any right to expect certain a standard of behavior from you? Act according to a higher standard than your own.

CHAPTER 23

TWELVE STEPS TOWARDS DICK MANAGEMENT

*A man who does not pay attention where he walks may get bitten
by a snake. Likewise sensual desires constitute serious dangers
for the present and the future.*

—Traditional Hindu wisdom

WHAT KIND OF MANAGEMENT TECHNOLOGY DO YOU NEED TO GO NON-local and develop higher consciousness? Upon close examination, you will find that you have much of the technology you need right at hand. Thoughts have a quantum weight that scientists have not been able to discover but they will. What you think and do *affects* the karmic and quantum structure of the universe. This doesn't mean that the world you see around you is created solely by your mind and actions but what it does mean is that your mind *participates* in the quantum processes of all reality. The Twelve Steps of Dick Management are a ladder to a higher consciousness that will enable you to more fully participate in life. Instead of being kicked around by the continuum, you can do some kicking back!

THE TWELVE STEPS

1. Mind–Less Observation
2. Interrogation
3. Mindfulness of Becoming
4. Decision
5. Kun Long
6. Energy Permission
7. Imagination
8. Intellectual Virtue
9. Moral Virtue

THE FIRST STEP

Mind-Less Observation (MLO) is the first step towards higher consciousness. It is the ability to watch thoughts without engaging them. This is the most basic operation of Dick Management. The thought is the parent to the deed, as Shakespeare said, so it is critically important to let thoughts of inappropriate activity just pass through your mind. You absorb the energy of the thoughts by not engaging them. On the other hand, if you start accepting and then morphing sexual thoughts, adding the redhead's thighs and lips to the brunette's breasts, as you mentally watch your organ sink into her backside—well, you are fully engaged. Chi will flow to those thoughts until you do something about it. An energy flow that is all out-going does nothing but turn out your lights. Mind-less observation is one of the first steps on the road to metacognition.

THE SECOND STEP

Interrogation is the second step and critically important. You must observe your reaction to everything that goes on inside, and outside your mind. You must catch your ASS in the act of going about its business without your permission. Effective interrogation is not possible without honesty. Interrogation can also take the form of thoughtful reflection. When you reflect on anything, you allow it to mirror itself in your consciousness, and in turn, you must try to faithfully accept the data as it is— not how you would like it to be. If, for instance, you begin to realize that you have a problem with laziness, it does you absolutely no good to point to the ways and times you are not lazy. You must accept the data of the observation and do something about it. You cannot manage your Dick without an adequate interrogation of your ASS. In short, your soul cannot awaken without truth.

THE THIRD STEP

Mindfulness of Becoming (MOB) is the third step. You must understand that the only reason that you know anything at all is that you become that thing—intentionally. Likewise, you can become your desires. The intellect is plastic and becomes everything that you allow it to become. If you entertain negative thoughts, for example, you will become negative. Conversely, if you dwell only on constructive and positive thoughts, you will become constructive and positive. You know reality by being that reality on the plane of intentionality. You become the quantum wave-form of a thing—that which it is before it manifests. Your everyday consciousness is not confined to the limits of your skull! The science of this knowledge is called epistemology. All this means is there is a structure to the way that you know things that is based on real processes that are ecologically linked to the entire continuum. You must be mindful of what you become. Learn to feel the inner shifts of identity—particularly when your inner animal decides that it would like to come forward. If you find yourself behaving incoherently, ask yourself what you have allowed yourself to become. Mindfulness of becoming is linked to mindless observation for a very simple reason—you need to assume an identity that does not react to every breath of energy that moves through your being.

Learn to listen to the small voice that speaks constantly to you. The Vedas describe the atman as "smaller than a thumb." There is a good reason that this is so. Your higher multi-dimensional identity has only a very small point of contact with your conscious mind. The matter of our bodies has not yet evolved to allow our higher consciousness to speak as clearly and loudly as we might sometimes like. By listening to this small voice our contact with the higher self is strengthened. Wisdom grows by being allowed to grow out from under the twin shadows of your local ego and ASS.

THE FOURTH STEP

Decision is the fourth step. It is an act of intellect and will, a partnership that prevents the emotions and your ASS from sabotaging your plans. For example, if you decide not to lie to a client during an important business meeting, you must follow through on your decision—no matter how difficult. This is known as the virtue of fortitude. Making a decision can involve many different virtues. The justice of your actions may have to be considered along with a prudent analysis of the consequences—particularly if you know that you might get fired for your honesty. Decision is the axis of all the virtues. There can be little virtue without decision. Do any of us admire those who are given to indecision?

THE FIFTH STEP

Kun Long is both the fifth step and a result of mind-less observation and appetite interrogation. It is the house of all virtue. You begin to grasp that there are levels to your consciousness and that you can shift levels with attention. Kun Long is a Tibetan word that might best be described as spiritual recall: a prudent moral awareness linked to the soul's multi-dimensional identity. Kun Long, as a form of metacognition, is the soul standing up and recalling its own identity, its own knowledge. This is mindfulness of a high order. We often confuse this sort of remembering with intuition. Intuition is frequently a result of unconsciously going non-local but memory is the vestibule of multi-dimensional space. Plato, for example, once likened all learning to remembering. Kun Long helps you to recall your superluminal identity. It is a metacognition that runs continuously in the background of your conscious mind. If you do not know who you are, you cannot manage your dick.

THE SIXTH STEP

Energy Permission (EP) is the sixth step. Once you are able to practice mind-less observation and begin to develop multi-dimensional metacognition, you will be able to learn EP. Energy Permission consists of refusing to allow energy to become attached or cathected to things that you don't want. Irrational fears such as phobias, for instance, can have no power over you if do not allow them to have the energy they need to survive in your being. Ignoring fear is one way of withholding energy from fear and letting it starve. This being said, there are many times when you want to pay strict attention to your more normal fears, as they are warning signals that have to be dealt with.

EP allows you to shut off the flow of Chi to unwanted mind parasites. Likewise, you either give your dick permission to do its thing or you don't. Managing energy will help you control the flow of energy that your dick indiscriminately craves. Ultimately, the attention you give to anything that passes through your mind is the oxygen that it needs to exist in your brain.

THE SEVENTH STEP

Imagination and the creation of new mental tools is the seventh step. Do not be afraid to use your imagination to visualize any aspect of consciousness that is unclear to you. Imagination is the surfboard of your soul! Become a homegrown philosopher and create road maps for your inner world. Even though it is difficult, you can develop an imaginative sense of chakras, or even the soul, as it lurks behind the consciousness of your everyday ego. Do not be afraid to experiment with images that help you to understand. Make up words if you need to and compare these terms to those of other thinkers. The great philosopher Martin Heidegger, for example, created many new philosophical terms to get at the realities he was attempting to describe in his landmark book, *Being and Time*. One of these terms was, as mentioned earlier, *dasein*. Dasein is being (little "b") understanding itself in terms of what we now understand as its superluminal existence and Being (big "B") understanding itself in terms of limitation. Dasein is the eruption of eternity into the present and a signification of the duality of human consciousness.

Dasein is of course the atman, core-self, quantum entity or soul. Heidegger was, in his own way, trying to reintroduce the concept of the soul back into western metaphysics in a way that would be appealing to post-Kantian and post-Hegelian philosophers. Heidegger understood that the greatest failing of modern philosophy was its refusal to acknowledge existence as something that could be discussed as other than a "useless and empty" concept.

At the same time, Heidegger realized that there was also something very wrong with traditional metaphysics and religion that tended to put existence under house arrest by tethering its full magnificence to dogma, church and ritual. Dasein represents nothing less than the recovery of existence for everyday living and as such represents a remarkable development in human thinking. As a concept, it is an excellent way of thinking about the soul and the higher self in terms of its superluminal origin.

Stretching Heidegger a bit, we might say that the concept of Dick Management is a requirement of dasein. The moral and intellectual virtues might also be thought of as the processing tools of dasein. Metacognition is dasein!

THE EIGHTH STEP

Intellectual virtue is the eighth step. Virtue is an energy transformer. Electric current is "stepped up" or "stepped down" by transformers. Virtue habitually channels energy in certain useful directions or changes the energy into something that you can use. Moral virtue "steps down" the wild energy that your appetites are hungry to embrace, and converts it to free and available libido (think Chi!) that your will and intellect can use for cathections other than short-term pleasure. The intellectual virtues "step" energy up, and the moral virtues "step" energy down.

Another way of looking at this is to say that the soul injects time or more correctly, its own space-time into every situation that it fully engages. This means that the full dimensionality of the self can be brought to bear on situations requiring the exercise of virtue. This changes the space-time of the experience. Remember that your soul occupies a much larger space-time than does your four dimensional ego. By engaging the core-self or dasein, you warp space-time and the situation, whatever it is, can never be the same. Understood in this way, virtue is a way of accessing the true power of the soul. Think of virtue as both accessing and channeling various aspects of the soul. Ultimately, when you access dasein, or go non-local, you change because you become the *actuality* that is you, and that *you* is much larger than what you think it is. This is the essence of metacognition.

I will never forget my first experience of this kind of metacognition. I was eleven or twelve years old and I had just thrown a wet toilet brush at a friend while he was on the john in a public park. He was furious and chased me out of the bathroom and up towards a hill—threatening all the while to beat the living daylights out of me. As I was running up the hill, an enormous clarity of *understanding* descended upon me. At that moment I knew I had nothing to fear—how I knew this did not matter—*I knew*. I turned around and calmly waited for my attacker. I watched his face. He had slowed his running and a look of confusion and hesitation showed itself on his normally confident face. He hesitated as if confronted with something that was very different from what he was expecting. It was very different indeed when I threw him to the ground and slugged him a few times until he yielded. I did not beat him with any rancor, I simply stopped him with little more concern than I would have had closing a window. The taste of that moment of youthful dasein or metacognitional clarity is still with me thirty-eight years later.

The most extraordinary thing about this little vignette is that while I was the wrongdoer, my wrongdoing was secondary to how the event played out. My bad intentions were not the issue in this case and it frequently is not the issue with Being—it is what you do about being wrong that is important. I later apologized to my friend but the larger reality of what had happened transcended its point of origin, which happened to be my bad behavior. An old friend once told me that "good things often come in on their negatives." Pay attention to gifts that are presented to you under poor auspices!

Virtue can help insulate you from the ASS-driven power surges of your dick and also protect you from low voltage and depressive situations that can damage your psyche, but only you can make the choices that virtue requires. Remember, your mind requires energy to run but your appetites couldn't care less about the needs of your mind. The two hogs, your mind and your dick, always want what you need to access your core-self. Looked at in this way, vice blocks access to the transforming power of metacognition by sucking your energy down the tubes of impulse.

Think of the Aristotelian virtues listed below (you've seen these before) as both modalities of access and real manifestations of the presence and activity of the core-self. The virtues are processing tools used by the soul for personal transformation.

The Intellectual Processes

1. Science—in the modern sense of the word, as in technology and the uncovering of cause and effect
2. Wisdom—the ability to observe and adequately reflect on inner mental and spiritual states; the ability to understand cause and effect as it relates to locality and non-locality
3. Understanding—allowing the soul to directly grasp the truth as it may be presented
4. Prudence—the ability to govern oneself through the use of reason
5. Art—understood in the sense of artistic craftsmanship, such as in sculpture or painting

THE NINTH STEP

Moral Virtue is the ninth step. Think of moral virtue as a way of accessing and uplifting the power of your life force. This will frequently involve tapping into the power of your balls.

1. Courage—the power to face adversity and struggle against evils
2. Continence—self-restraint in respect to pleasure

3. Liberality—generous giving

4. Magnificence—the ability to spend money on large, possibly useful and usually beautiful projects.

5. Magnanimity—The magnanimous man is able to overlook slights and insults, and rise above pettiness. He is generous and able to get work done without complaint.

6. Honor—a state of character that is a result of the practice of moral virtue.

7. Gentleness—this is really what we would call compassion and is a practical result of self-restraint.

8. Friendship—friendship, outside of immediate ties, requires effort to cultivate.

9. Temperance—self-restraint in regards to pleasure

10. Truthfulness—the ability to see what is and what is not.

11. Justice—seeking for others and yourself that to which you are entitled under both moral and social law.

You will note that virtue in each instance harnesses either the intellect or will, or both, to manage Chi. Virtue habitually channels energy, and allows the soul to absorb and manifest it in a higher form, rather than becoming a pass-through entity, that simply acts as an interface between higher dimensions and the energy sinkholes of a three dimensional world. Virtue increases your capacity to act by providing energy for the consciousness of the core-self. The quantum entity that is your higher consciousness requires nourishment to be present in any truly conscious manner. You must engage in actions that feed your soul.

Energy that is not dispersed or squandered attracts energy much in the same way that "money attracts money." This is always the opposite of a Catch 22 situation. You get the energy for action by keeping the energy of the Id under control. If energy is being absorbed by creative structures, it will cease to go with energy flows that are on the express train to oblivion. Gambling, for instance, has often been thought of as a vice because the energy of money—which is often hard earned capital—is wasted on possibilities that have little chance of preserving or increasing that capital. The excitement of gambling is like the pretty swirl that the energy of falling water makes as it gurgles down the drain. Virtue is a way of going non-local, and this requires the extra energy that vice consumes. Vice is a way of staying very much local and this consumes the energy that you need to go non-local. Your dick is a major faucet of this energy. Turn the damn thing off once in a while!

THE TENTH STEP

Quantum Channeling (QC) is the tenth step. The greater actuality of your own soul is drawing you towards itself. Your recognition of this "drawing" or "unmoved movement" constitutes a potential pathway that is lit up like an airport runway by the actuality lamps of your soul. The path of your life is an attempt not only to arrive at the source of this actuality but also to fulfill its purpose. Quantum channeling is the setting of goals and the actualizing of potential as required by who you actually are, and the need you may have to get to God. There is very little room for wishful thinking here; you have to follow through on achieving goals or there will be no energy payout and no runway to your future. There is always a proportion between your actuality and your potential—your Yang and your Yin. I call this the YY ratio. If your ratio consists of too much actuality, you will flit all over the place and have few coherent plans; if too much potential, then you will have too many plans and not enough action. Your potential is like a sun and your actuality the hydrogen that makes it burn. Go from sun to sun like Apollo on a road of fire.

When I find myself becoming irritable and short-tempered, or even confused, it is usually because I have exhausted the fire of one goal and not yet properly set another. In order to set a new future for yourself you must look for a new pathway, a new destiny. Set fires in your own sky— keep moving on the pathways of being. You do this by throwing out your agent intellect into the sky of all potential pathways and feeling around like a blind man until your passive intellect identifies the Braille of a new quantum roadway. Suddenly, the way is lightning charged with the particles of actuality. This thing is now real, the quantum channel is open and a new karmic future awaits you.

Understanding QC is important when evaluating major life-changing possibilities such as a new job, partner in marriage or religious conversion. Your future may appear to you in a vision of glory or it may be as simple as a sudden understanding of what must be done. However quantum channeling comes to you, self-initiated or even out of left field, it comes with the force of revelation. You *know*. Make sure that your future has a goal and that you have chosen one way or the other to go there. If not, chances are that you are drifting. Drifting is only useful as a form of rest; it can never be substituted for goal building.

Quantum channeling is particularly useful for Dick Management. Too much energy consumed leads to Yang (male energy) imbalance. The overall balance of Yin and Yang requires the requisite amount of Chi, which in turn, requires that neither Yin nor Yang be out of balance to begin with. Sexual energy is referred to as *Ching Chi* in Chinese medicine, and like all forms of Chi, is composed of negative and positive, or Yin and Yang energy. One might cheekily say that if you drain your Yang, then your Yin will be out of whack, and you will lose the masculine energy that you need to be a man. Quantum channeling will help you to set the kind of goals that you need to manage your energy and act like a human being instead of an animal.

THE ELEVENTH STEP

Prayer and Meditation is the eleventh step. All of the techniques and knowledge that you may acquire from metaphysics and physics, or any other discipline are just that—techniques. To know how to build a car, for example, is technical knowledge, but unless you actually build or repair cars, it may not be of much practical use to you. Similarly, you must use the eleven steps to actually bring your higher self to the forefront of your consciousness. This is very difficult to do without prayer and meditation. Prayer and meditation are two guaranteed ways of going instantly non-local. You give yourself permission to go non-local when you pray or meditate. This is a tremendous benefit because most of us can pray or meditate to some degree. Prayer and meditation is your passport to non-locality. Since God is a non-local entity, when we pray, we engage the greater non-locality of His Being. This creates a powerful non-local channel to Divinity and can be a source of tremendous refreshment. Your actuality merges to a small degree with that of the Divine in prayer and this creates an enormous additional potential in yourself. The ultimate source of actuality gives you some of its own actuality in grace and power.

Your ASS's ticket to non-locality is usually via drugs and alcohol—this is the easy way to go non-local, and your ASS can then operate freely from the confines of your moralizing higher self. It is no accident, for example, that pimps will try to get their streetwalkers addicted; it takes their rational minds off the irrational things that they may end up doing. Drugs may at some time be an aid to going non-local, but the dangers of drug taking are well documented, and even experimental use can potentially lead to various unhealthy cathections and ultimately to addiction. Generally speaking, the healthy person's consciousness does not require mind-altering drugs, and indeed the wise person will seldom enjoy such processes, as they tend to disrupt the orderly development of higher knowledge

THE TWELFTH STEP

Understanding Your Dharma. This is your non-local channel to divinity, and is the twelfth and last step towards Dick Management; it is the end that is also a beginning. I can't describe the Buddhist concept of Dharma more eloquently than Howard Rheingold does in his useful book, *They Have a Word for It: A Lighthearted Lexicon of Untranslatable Words and Phrases.* He says:

> "Dharma is there to be discovered, however, and it is the answer for the individual up against something too gigantic to comprehend. Dharma means to be yourself as fully as you can, acknowledging that each human consciousness is a unique precious experiment in finding the way to the essential truth. It can also mean, as it does in the Buddhist tradition, the teachings and practices that can lead to self-realization....The dharma does not mean blind acceptance of this god or that doctrine; it is, rather, an acknowledgement that the right way to live one's life will lead to the enlightenment of all sentient beings and a declaration that each human being has a unique opportunity to discover that essential truth."[35]

Once you have discovered and come to understand dharma, which is your life's purpose, you will be firmly on the Road to Dick Management.

My life has been devoted to poking around in the outer reaches of myself. In the same way that the universe unfolds as it is explored, so does my own. No sooner do I arrive at some new, inner galaxy than I can see heretofore-unimagined worlds that invite further exploring. But the acceptance of external authority as my overriding authority blocks all discovery of the self. Such acceptance inhibits all growth and mimics death, for no act is more suicidal than casting aside one's personhood and replacing it with the alien authority of another.

—Gerry Spence, *How to Argue and Win Every Time*

PART III

CIVILIZATION:
PUBLIC VERSUS PUBIC POLICY

CHAPTER 24

WHAT PRIVACY TELLS YOU ABOUT YOUR DICK

Your privates are no longer private.

—The Shepherd

IMAGINE YOURSELF AS A PEACEFUL ALIEN FROM A DISTANT GALAXY. YOU land on earth and set up an observation post unknown to the earthlings. You watch what goes on, and since your technology enables you to see through buildings and clothing, the things that you see are most interesting.

First, you go to the capital of the most prosperous and most powerful country on the planet. You observe that every day, in many of these offices, the men who seem to be in charge are walking around with hard penises for part of the day. You see many of them putting their erect organs into the mouths or backsides of female employees who work in their offices. The men seem to enjoy this a great deal, the women less so. This is evidenced in that most of the females spit out or clean up the contents that the organ has deposited so quickly in whichever orifice has been used.

The alien observer also notes that females with symmetrical faces, large breasts and round backsides seem to make up a large percentage of the work force of the most powerful offices of the Capitol.

The observer notices some other peculiar things also. There are some men who seem to enjoy having organs stuck into their mouths and backsides also. There are also men and women in the Capitol buildings who engage in self-service. If a female is not available or vice-versa, a hand motion appears to produce the desired result.

The alien observer notices that in almost all instances these acts occur in private—they are not for public consumption, and indeed many of these men and women will go to great lengths to avoid being discovered engaged in genital activity. The alien observer can only conclude that these people are engaged in some kind of illegality, but he is a bit confused, as this seems to be the center of government.

So what do we tell our alien? Why is all this sexual activity so hidden, so furtive? "Shame," you say casually, as if that is a full explanation, dependent on nothing else. What exactly is it that we are ashamed of? "We humans are just embarrassed by certain things in general," you might say. True, but that is an obfuscation. Why don't we say, after eating five large cheeseburgers—if asked what we were doing— "I just finished eating five big cheeseburgers?" We might prefer to say, "I just finished eating." What is the relationship between shame and privacy?

We are ashamed of what is immoral because activities covered by the cloak of privacy are revealed to be moral or immoral by the degree of self-restraint or lack of self-restraint that can now be plainly seen once that cloak is lifted.

Being seen defecating in public might be embarrassing but being ashamed and embarrassed are two different things. You might not be ashamed of taking a dump in public—if there was simply no other way of attending to the task. You would, however, probably be terribly embarrassed but not as ashamed as you might be if you were caught jerking off in a company toilet by your boss.

Sexual activity is private by degree. That is to say, as a species, we generally don't like to disclose the detailed contents of private activity with anyone other than our associates, friends or family. (Of course if we have slipped into brutishness, we may want to inform everyone as to our prowess, but most people will find this loutish.)

If sexuality as a bodily function tends towards privacy, then why would we engage in sexual activities that might become public? Bear with me on this. If sexuality at its best is private, then sexual acts that tend towards becoming public may be much less desirable. Now if someone finds out that you are having sex with your spouse, no one cares, but the moment you have sex with someone who is other than your spouse, everyone is interested. (By the way, when was the last time you heard a married man boast of getting laid, i.e., having sex with his wife?)

Having good sex with someone who is not your spouse is good (so you think) only as long as it remains private. It ceases to be quite so good once your wife discovers the activity. Privacy allows us to both hide what is shameful, and secure from the gaze of others, events and actions that might not be fully understood outside the subjective context of the people involved. The subjective context of experience, however, is not always good, and likewise, the objective analysis of subjective experience may be incomplete or even undesirable. On this side of the coin, privacy shields us from unnecessary embarrassment. Picking our noses, prying food out of our teeth, or passing wind are sometimes requirements that we do not wish to share with others, as we ourselves would not like to view others engaging in similar actions. What could be more grotesque, for instance, than watching someone on a public bus picking their ears and then smelling their own ear wax? We just don't want to see it—just as we don't want to watch anyone hurl the contents of their stomachs anywhere near our shoes.

Therefore, privacy can be a shield for the best of what we do and the worst of what we do. Privacy is morally ambivalent. Unfortunately, the ambivalence of privacy is popularly used as a blanket to somehow sanction actions that have historically been considered immoral. Copulating with a dead body is certainly a private act, but is it a good act? This is what advocates of "privacy as morality" overlook. There is the implicit assumption that because an act is private it is not subject to the moral scrutiny of universal rules of good behavior. The difficulty of drawing a moral line in the sand cannot be equivalent to the assumption that there should be no line at all.

Sexuality creates its own form of privacy whereby there is a process of inclusion involving the persons involved and an exclusion involving those who are not allowed to participate. Privacy, like the dual-headed god Janus, has two faces. There is good privacy and there is bad privacy. Good privacy builds on a moral life but bad privacy destroys morality. Privacy is made good or bad by what goes on inside the world of privacy. If you are mounting dogs or dead bodies in your private sexual world, let's just say that you have bad privacy. Who would want to be part of your world, except maybe other dog "lovers" or necrophiliacs? Certainly not your mother.

We might judge the goodness of our actions and indeed our lives, by the number of people whose lives are improved as a consequence of our activities or good example.

What is good tends towards the greatest improvement of self and others. This is goodness by inclusion. What is bad tends towards exclusion. If private sexual actions consistently exclude everyone but yourself and improve no one's life, including your own, you can be pretty sure they are unhealthy.

Somebody figured it out—we have 35 million laws trying to enforce the Ten Commandments.

—Anonymous

MANAGEMENT TIPS

• Are you ashamed to be seen in public with the person you are having sex with? This is not the sign of a healthy relationship.

• If you do not feel like talking to her after sex, what kind of relationship do you think you have?

• Do not lie about your feelings to a woman. If you do, this will come back to bite you in the ass.

• Do you think that just because no one sees what you are doing that it is good?

• If you feel ashamed after sex, your feelings are probably right. Shame can be the function of a soul that knows itself better than the ego does.

CHAPTER 25

ARISTOTLE, FATHER OF DICK MANAGEMENT

Since happiness is an activity of soul in accordance with perfect virtue, we must consider the nature of virtue; for perhaps we shall thus see better the nature of happiness. The true student of politics, too is thought to have studied virtue above all things; for he wishes to make his fellow citizens good and obedient to the laws.

—Aristotle, *Nichomachean Ethics*, Bk. 1: Ch. 12

CONSIDER THE QUOTATION YOU JUST READ. CAN THE READER IMAGINE an American politician discussing the soul and happiness in conjunction with the notion of politics? You probably find it difficult to imagine because the majority of American politicians do not know what virtue is, let alone the proper definition of the soul or politics. There is a connection between the idea of the "good," the soul, and excellence (virtue) that is lost on most politicians.

Aristotle defines politics as the "Science of the good for the many." If this is so, how is it that politics has become a science of the good for the special interest group? How is it that the soul or the "good" as concepts are seldom utilized in either modern politics or education? Do we say that these are old ideas that only applied to the Greeks or do we assert that these are timeless ideas?

There are those who will say that because Aristotle had slaves and didn't believe in women's rights, his thinking shouldn't be used in discussions about modern morality. This is a legitimate criticism of Aristotle but it is important to defer, within reason, to the spirit of the times he lived in. We do not condemn Moses for taking more than one wife, Jesus for not saying anything at all about slavery or homosexuality, or Mohammed for starting Holy Wars. It is quite evident, however, in the larger context of these great leaders' teachings, that many things that were not said, might be inferred. We also have to remember that all of the books that we have on Aristotle were essentially his class notes. There is much that we do not know about his "real" beliefs. However, Aristotle provides a structure which both non-religious and religious may consult with profit, and as he was neither Buddhist, Christian, Hindu, Jew or Moslem, he is the least ideologically and religiously "tainted" of all the great moral philosophers. There is much that we might use in Aristotle to provide a sound basis for the science and art of Dick Management.

POLITICS AND MORALITY

If politics is not linked to an understanding of the "good," excellence, and the soul or life force, this deviation will result in an impoverishment of politics and civic life. In his *Nichomachean Ethics* and *Politics*, Aristotle gives us perhaps the most comprehensive and penetrating inquiry into the meaning of politics and its relation to the "good," excellence and the soul. Aristotle's discussion of the science of politics is as relevant now as it was two thousand years ago.

> Every art and every inquiry and similarly every action and pursuit is thought to aim at some good; and for this reason the good has rightly been declared to be that at which all things aim.... Now there are many actions, arts and sciences, their ends also are many; the end of the medical art is health, that of shipbuilding a vessel, that of strategy, victory, that of economics, wealth.... If, then, there is some end of the things we do, which we desire for its own sake...clearly this must be the good and the chief good. Will not the knowledge of it, then have a great influence on life? Shall we not, like archers who have a mark to aim at, be more likely to hit upon what is right? If so, we must try, in outline at least to determine what it is and of which of the sciences or capacities it is the object. It would seem to belong to the most authoritative art and that which is most truly the master art. And politics appears to be of this nature; for it is this that ordains which of the sciences should be studied in a state....it legislates what we are to do and what we are to abstain from, the end of this science must include those of the others, so that this end must be the good for man. (Aristotle, *Nichomachean Ethics*, Bk. 1, Ch. 1)

Amazing! Politics is a science that legislates what we are to do and what we are to abstain from. (This is cultural and political Dick Management.) Obviously, those people who insist upon their right to be free of government interference in all moral matters must be unaware of this. How many times have you heard, "What you do in your bedroom has nothing to do with your job, and the government has no right to legislate morality." And yet I think we can all agree that a politician or educator who likes to dress like a poodle and be whipped in the privacy of his bedroom is hardly a candidate for public office or stewardship of young people. Aren't murder and theft illegal? This is legislating morality.

The difficulty in evaluating immoral behavior in individuals who are otherwise functionally productive stems from confusing the intellectual and moral virtues. They are not absolutely related, i.e., a deficiency in the moral virtues does not prevent the acquisition of intellectual excellence. (Noteworthy examples of this are Bill Clinton and Richard Nixon, both from different ends of the political spectrum.) A man could theoretically be a good dentist and engage in bestiality. Immorality is a problem because the moral virtue of self-restraint or continence is required as a practical matter for superior intellectual and moral development. Perhaps it seems too obvious, but incontinence and its more developed cousin, vice, cause moral habits to devolve. Try to be a good student, employee, spouse, friend or parent on a daily diet of sex, beer, marijuana and violence and you may understand the difficulty.

Unfortunately, there are those whose intelligence is so great that no matter how they abuse themselves, they are able to excel intellectually. This only confuses those who are less intelligent or capable. They point to the bright ones who are corrupt and think that they too ought to be able to get away with the same excess and do well at their studies or personal development. What is overlooked is that the corrupt geniuses would be able to do far greater things if they exercised moral discipline.

For the majority of mankind, the energy required for advanced intellectual or emotional development is directly tied to overall life energy (think Chi!) usage. Sublimation is the missing link between moral and intellectual development, and excellence. The discipline required to manage sexual appetites is useful in all walks of life for achieving ends that require great effort. However, if you do not believe that there are any appetites to regulate, then what you do, or don't do, won't necessarily appear to make any difference to you—other than contribute to your personal confusion and disorder. However, don't tell me that you would visit or trust a doctor who in his spare time puts rodents up his rectum for sexual satisfaction, or elect to public office a pederast whose preference is for boys under the age of twelve.

Clearly, the government does legislate morality. Many immoral acts are prohibited, such as the taking of harmful narcotics and spousal abuse. If you don't think that you have an appetite for murder, think about your last encounter with someone who was extremely rude to you, or a bad experience with a lover or spouse. Obviously, we do have an appetite for murder, most of us just don't indulge

> All good philosophy is but the handmaid to religion.
>
> ◆
>
> —Francis Bacon

it. Unfortunately, some of our citizens are now in the unhappy position of being so uninhibited that murder is no longer an unthinkable option. "What, he insulted you? Let me blow him away." Does this kind of activity produce happiness? I think it rather produces a stupefying satisfaction, which allows the appetites to increase both their range and hold over an individual. The wild irrationality of Idi Amin, Stalin, Caligula or Saddam Hussein comes to mind here. The appetites are a harsh ruler; every whim must be gratified. "I feel like cutting his head off—no problem—and while you are at it, execute the foreign minister, I don't like his shoes." Think about it, how many of us are that close to the craziness of unregulated appetites? Consider the following words of Aristotle:

> Perhaps, however, it seems a truth which is generally admitted,
> that happiness is the supreme good; what is wanted is to define its
> nature a little more clearly. The best way of arriving at such a
> definition will probably be to ascertain the function of Man. For
> as with a flute-player, a statuary, or any artisan, or in fact anybody
> who has a definite function and action, his goodness, or excel-
> lence seems to lie in his function, so it would seem to be with
> Man, if indeed he has a definite function. Can it be said that,
> while a carpenter and a cobbler have definite functions and
> actions, Man, unlike them is naturally functionless?
>
> —Aristotle, *Nichomachean Ethics*

The primary function of man, according to Aristotle, is the rational ordering of the appetites in conjunction with intellectual development. Happiness comes to the man or woman who is able to fulfill his or her primary function. If we were to put a more global label on this rational ordering of the appetites, we would say that the development of personal potential—both intellectual and moral—is the foundation upon which a life of virtue, and consequently, happiness, is built. Happiness, like sun-shine, is a product of fusion. Likewise, the fusion of intellect and appetite in the production of virtuous or worthwhile activity produces, or can produce, happiness. No such fusion can take place where either intellect or appetite is unbalanced. Conversely, the lack of worthwhile activity, such as can be found in excellent school programs and good jobs, pro-duces unhappiness, as the intellect may be unable to carry out its func-tion of ordering the appetites and developing the intellect.

> If there is nothing good there to pervade that society, it will destroy itself, or be brutalized by the triumph of evil instincts, no matter whither the pointer of the great economic laws may turn.
>
> ♦
>
> —Alexander Solzenitsyn

Aristotle, as we noted earlier, links the notions of soul and virtue. Virtue is defined as: "an activity of soul in ac-cordance with reason." It is precisely for this reason that much of the deeper meaning of Aristotle is lost on college students. Mention the words "soul" or "virtue" and many students will draw a blank. There can be little under-standing of Aristotelian politics and the notion of the "good" or even hap-piness without an understanding of the structure of the soul, its life energy and the development of virtue. Likewise, the foundations of Dick Management must be built on a life of virtue or at least a life tending towards virtue (the zigzag theory of moral growth).

American politics does not consider the notion of the "good" but rather, the notion of "self-interest." Self-interest is a way of allowing everyone to choose what he or she thinks is good without a third party taking an objective position as to whether or not it actually is good. The substitution of meaning here, of the "good" by self-interest, constitutes an incredible failure not just of linguistic discrimination but a failure to deal with over 2,000 years of moral discourse. Whether you are religious or not, your children should not be denied exposure to the inner life of man as it has been developed over many centuries, and represents a huge reser-voir of cultural wisdom.

The rational ordering of the appetites which constitutes the basis of prudent Dick Management is particularly vulnerable to the notion of self-interest. Self-interest conceptually severs the link between goodness and transcendence, by rooting the notion of goodness in appetite, and ul-timately in subjectivity rather than reason or objectivity. When goodness is defined solely by your appetites instead of reason, you enter the world of the butthead.

Moral consciousness is the guardian at the frontier of our biological past and the angel waiting at the gates of our transcendent future. Those with demonic appetites shall not pass through those gates, nor shall those who claim they don't give a shit. The development of higher consciousness needs to be on everyone's agenda.

The cultivation of the language of consciousness, as it was referred to by one of the early cartographers of consciousness, George Simon, involves mapping the relationships between the core-self (which represents the higher, multi-dimensional future of the life force), the personality, and the animal genetics that manifest as FIKI. This is everybody's business and will, for all practical purposes, be the essential political and social task of the next few centuries. Moral consciousness is an ecological project that involves both the development of a psychic language, and the cultivation of time-honored intellectual and moral practices.

Could not the crisis of responsibility and accountability for the world as a whole and for its future be but the logical consequence of...a conception which does not question the meaning of existence and renounces any kind of metaphysics or any kind (of understanding) of its own metaphysical roots?
—Vaclav Havel, former Czech President

MANAGEMENT TIPS

- No matter how you might feel about it, you must follow through on decisions when you know that they are right. Your feelings are frequently based on the subjectivity of your body. The core-self remains undisturbed by the antics of the emotions—the desperate begging, the ultimatums.

- By looking at filth obliquely or by practicing non-local observation rather than directly or locally engaging it, you actually have greater enjoyment on a subtle basis—more than by indulging the thought itself. Practice this daily and discover the secret pleasure that virtuous people have slyly enjoyed for centuries.

- Caution: If you are even vaguely masochistic don't strike your dick with heavy objects. This may turn into a fresh source of pleasure.

- There are varying degrees of sexual appetite, so we have to be careful in our assumptions, but generally speaking, there is a sexual mean, or balance, for all of us. The key is to find out what that mean is and act accordingly on a regular basis. A simple thing like the time you engage in sexual activity can make an enormous difference in how you feel.

- Every woman has the potential to be naked. This Naked Factor was first elucidated by the Shepherd. Your dick takes this idea very seriously, as should you. In every situation of temptation, the Naked Factor rises in direct proportion to the hardness of your dick. Conversely, if your dong is kept leashed, the Naked Factor stays in the background which is where it belongs. The Naked Factor has been implicated in numerous studies as a contributing agent to marital discord.

CHAPTER 26

THE NON DICK MANAGER

The things that will destroy us are: politics without principle; pleasure without conscience; wealth without work; knowledge without character; business without morality; science without humanity; and worship without sacrifice.

—Mahatma Gandhi (1869-1948)

THE SHADOW LINE

ISN'T IT AMAZING HOW MANNERS HAVE CHANGED OVER THE PAST THIRTY years? If you look at someone with passing interest on the street, a common response might be: "Hey motherfucker, what you looking at?" Perhaps you were only interested in their colorful clothes or interesting shoes. What happens when you swerve in traffic? Fists are shaken at you, curses and sometimes bottles fly in your direction or worse, guns and knives are produced. Welcome to the world of the Non Dick Manager—NDM for short.

There are other instances when you may be completely minding your own business and suddenly you are in an ugly situation because an NDM is moved by a stray appetite for violence or mockery that happens to cross their decayed mental threshold. These NDMs come in all races and all shapes and sizes. NDMs are now getting younger and younger due to the general lack of moral formation in our educational institutions. There are also female NDMs whose lack of self control and general moral decay gives them this status by way of analogy. NDMs love guns and death—in short NDMs love FIKI.

Several years ago, there was a chilling article in a national newspaper about young men in Liberia (curiously referred to as "technicals") running around in wigs and Donald Duck masks, shooting people for the sheer pleasure of killing. "Give me five feet" was how death was announced. The perpetrator did not want to be sprayed by the blood of the victim, as blood will spray or spurt up to three or four feet out of a body that is shot with an AK–47. Is this not FIKI in full flower? Do you think that any of these men or their Caucasian counterparts in Serbia were practicing any kind of impulse management?

There is a line on the continuum of human behavior that, once crossed, allows very little turning back. It is the threshold of evil that we have called the shadow line. How does it happen? Over a period of time an individual is almost imperceptibly taken over by the ASS of biology, but only if there is little or no self-restraint practiced. Perhaps it started with drinking or taking recreational drugs every now and then. Masturbation and casual sex might have become commonplace. Small and large acts of theft and falsehood may have been perpetrated...before he or she knows it, they find themselves doing things they might once have found unimaginable. Little by little, the Id, as it expresses itself through the appetites or ASS (Appetite Survival System) can start to take over rational function as the moral brakes are released. This is a form of biological possession or full-blown FIKI. What is a demon but a Non Dick Manager given over completely to the fulfillment of appetite?

ANGER

Anger is a common topic among psychologists and social commentators when describing rioters: "These people are angry, they are frustrated by lack of jobs and decent housing." This is the kind of mantra repeated over and over by the media, but a distinction needs to be made between righteous anger and the vice of anger. It is one thing to revolt and riot against an oppressive government or racist business practices, but quite another to riot because it is fun. Part of FIKI is venting displeasure at anything that does not please you. What this means is that we have an appetite for anger in any situation that doesn't move in the direction we think it should. If you have a small child who has difficulty keeping food on his or her plate, it is very easy to get angry with them. The question is how much anger is justified and how much is unjustified? If you reprimand a child in a stern voice that is one thing, but suppose you beat the youngster black and blue?

> It is easy to have principles when you are rich. The important thing is to have principles when you are poor.
>
> ◆
>
> —Ray Kroc

Appetite is always on, always on that scary continuum with FIKI that goes all the way into abandoning reason and common sense altogether.

The only person who can say no to a bad appetite is you, and you better have some good reasons or your appetites will get the better of you every time. If, for example, you allow yourself to engage in sexual activity each and every time you feel the slightest urge, then how on earth are you going to restrain yourself against a little thing like anger? Suppose your wife doesn't feel quite up to sex after both working all day and taking care of your children? "Beat the bitch"—that is the immediate reaction of appetites denied in some individuals. Others may treat their spouses like dirt, if their every whim is not met. There is no end to the petty bickering and family violence that can arise in appetite-dominated, NDM households. The most terrible thing of all though is that ASS-dominated males pass on the same survival characteristics that they learned, to their children.[28] Young boys in particular learn at an early age that violence is how you get your way. There is absolutely nothing worse for other adults to have to deal with than the delinquent children of NDMs. You can't correct the children because the parents themselves are frequently the problem and either will not or cannot correct their own offspring. I would imagine that you could fill a book with stories about the "neighbors from hell." NDM activity on the part of families could be greatly reduced in a society that practiced Dick Management.

Resistance to or sublimation of the sexual impulse is the absolute benchmark of appetitive and moral self-restraint. If you can control your dick, you can control anything. As Augustine said, "The man who is busy waging war against himself has little time to wage war on others." Likewise, the torments of the heart—anger, pride, ignorance, fear and frustration, which the Buddhists consider contrary to both right mind and good intention, can only be contained and directed by those who are able to manage their most powerful appetites and impulses. The kind of anger that leads to assaults and gang beatings is what happens when dicks are allowed to do their thing without reference to a moral code. Sexual self-control is usually the critical missing factor. The management of difficult appetites helps create habits or muscles in the will that can empower individuals to be their own masters, rather than instinctual slaves.

The consumption of Chi by all sexual activity needs to be monitored in the same way that you periodically check your gas tank. General depression, for example, can be a very good indicator that the psychic gas tank is low. Pythagoras taught that semen was "a drop of brain containing hot vapor within it." Conserve your brain's Chi, cultivate continence and lay off the baloney pony for a while. Recuperate and channel energy into a worthwhile project. You will feel much better, and so will those around you.

CURSING

Why has cursing been commonly viewed as uncivilized and rude behavior? There is in some quarters a growing point of view that says that cursing is harmless. Think again. What is cursing? What happens when you curse? Cursing is an expression of anger that has traditionally been considered a vice. Cursing is just another way of letting appetite control your rational functions and allowing valuable energy to be dissipated. Cursing is a kind of incantation or conjuring up of the latent demons in your appetites. You curse because it feels good to curse—good to let out some of those frustrated appetites. According to some surveys, as many as ninety percent of all high school teachers have heard abusive language from their students. Cursing may be thoroughly enjoyable but can become seriously disturbing, when it leads to smashing windows or heads. This is precisely what can happen to those who give in to anger. They do whatever flows with the moment of anger, and all of a sudden, all hell has broken loose. Cursing creates a double defilement. You debase yourself and defile others with your tongue. Ease up on the cursing, and anger will be restrained.

Moral values have a primacy among all other personal values; it is a greater good for the person to be endowed with them than with any other. Thus Socrates could say, "It is better for man to suffer injustice than to commit it."

◆

—Sean O'Reilly, MD,
Bioethics and the Limits of Science

What is graffiti, if not cursing in paint, or marking your territory like a dog peeing and crapping on neighborhood lawns? The message of graffiti is very clear, "Untrained dicks at work!" Restrain your dick and you will have a good strong leash to restrain those other appetites—particularly the ones that lead to FIKI and the collateral property damage and destruction characteristic of the Non Dick Manager.

DEPRESSION

Everyone has some experience of depression, but why is it that some individuals seem to have more crushing depressions than others? The easiest way to think of depression, barring serious medical conditions, is to think in terms of energy gluts and energy deficiencies. When you feel good, you usually have a glut of energy or, after a workout, for example, you bask in the after-glow of energy well spent. Energy deficiencies, on the other hand, involve not having enough energy to make the cathections or instinctive urge connections to things that bring pleasure or satisfaction. Psychologically speaking, an energy deficiency is related to a lack of motivation, or a loss of hope in the future. Hope is what motivates the soul but motivation requires energy. This is a little like the question: which comes first, the chicken or the egg? You need Chi to be motivated, but how do you get the Chi to be motivated? Hope accesses the future by causing the collapse of a set of quantum waves that constitute that very future. Energy pours in from whatever future it is you have accessed, but you must access it. Energy comes from the collapse of the quanta.

Depression is a dimensional condition that blocks access to the quantum collapse of futures your soul requires to survive. Depression comes in two basic flavors. Unipolar disorders consist of depressive episodes that occur several times during an individual's life span. Bipolar disorders involve an alternating cycle of depression and mania. This is more commonly known as manic depression. The most common form of unipolar disorder is known as dysthymia which like a low-grade fever permeates the consciousness and will with an eroding lack of aspiration. Double depression is a deeper form of depression than dysthymia but not as serious as manic depression. Rounding out the field, we have seasonal affective disorders (SAD) that seem to be related to the decline of light during the fall and winter months. Depressive disorders, according to recent studies published on the Internet strike approximately twelve million Americans annually and have been described by international experts as the "cancer of the 21st century."

Depression is sometimes caused by chemical or genetic imbalances, but a large number of dysthymic and double depressive episodes are caused by energy deficiencies or NDM energy imbalances. For depression to be considered the cancer of the 21st century, there must be something very wrong with modern life or modern thinking. The enormous gap between common sense and reality that some schools of psychology have generated with absurd and morally disconnected explanations of behavior is partly responsible for this new "cancer."

Vice is an energy siphon. If you want to pretend that what you do with your moral life has no effect on your mind, you are entitled to do so, but you may pay a price with either depression or a serious lack of motivation. Cathections are energy conduits. You may buffer your sexual activities for instance with other, perhaps more productive cathections, but sexual cathections are frequently a major drain of Chi. Utilitarian or toilet sexual cathections (beating off or using your wife or girlfriend as a receptacle) on the positive side have no more value than taking a crap. Negatively speaking, however, they can puncture your energy gas tank.

THE IMPORTANCE OF GOING NON-LOCAL

The soul cannot be fooled. You cannot give it false goals or false hopes. The soul desires a future commensurate with itself—nothing less, nothing more. What distinguishes the hopeful person from the individual who has lost hope is a soul that is awake to itself. Depression is a particularly modern psychological dis-ease because modern man has socially banished the soul. Socially speaking, the soul is considered the province of religion or New Age philosophy, but if you are neither religious nor New Age, then the soul may not be given much space in your life, or in that of your society. The awakening to self always begins with hope for the future. Your soul or your deeper self is intimately tied to that future. The futurity of the soul allows for endless delight because there is no end to it. You will never run out of futures.

> Sacrifice your littleness, your limited, finite self
> The minute you sacrifice this, you realize the supreme self in you. That's why sacrifice is the law of life. Stop this I, me, mine.
>
> ◆
>
> —Swami Satchidananda, from *Tying Rocks to Clouds* by William Elliott

Confining yourself to locality is a prescription for depression and failure. There is only one cure for depression and that is to get more non-local consciousness into your life. This may involve meditation, religion or the practice of some kind of intellectual, moral or spiritual virtue, or all of the above, but if you are depressed, do not ignore the non-local solution. The key to initiating a non-local solution in many instances is to admit both failure and helplessness. Accept your limitations, accept your failures; face yourself honestly and then ask the Divine for help. Paradoxically, the moment you *let go* of your own locality, you open yourself to the infinity of non-locality. This is paradoxical because it requires that you *let go* in order to go anywhere. Suicides, for example, are those who have gotten themselves so locked into local thinking that there is no exit, except the ultimate non-local solution—death. If you think about it in these terms, suicide becomes symbolic of the desperate need some people have to cure their non-local deficits. Depression is likewise an experiential metaphor and symbol for just such a deficit. Pay attention to depression; it is a warning from the future.

GUNS, CARS, MOVIES AND WHORES

What do guns, cars, movies and whores have in common? While this may seem to be a ridiculous question, a bit of reflection on the nature of movement and pleasure will quickly lead to the conclusion that there is a powerful link. Movement is fundamentally about the conversion of potency to act. Moving energy is more attractive to the soul than stagnant energy. The soul's business revolves around the conversion of potential and sometimes non-local realities to local applications. An inventor, for example, gets an emotional kick or high from translating potential ideas into actual working concepts. On a more mundane level, there can be an enormous amount of pleasure derived from going out for a walk or a drive which is really only another way of converting some potential energy into actual energy.

The dark side of this for the lazy or undisciplined Non Dick Manager is that immorality can provide a quick and convenient energy fix. "Getting off," for example, might be as sloppy as visiting the local massage parlor or as deadly as pumping bullets into pedestrians at the shopping mall.

Your life force is attracted to energy, and anything that causes energy to move through the soul is appealing to it. If the soul feels that murder will bring it closer to non-locality, then murder is its game. This is where the ego must guide the life force to safer ground.

Violence causes energy to flow! Terminating another life force, for

> Culture is not culture unless it induces, and sustains when induced, the one type of mind in the world which will never assist, never even indirectly assist, at any kind of mental or moral tyranny. Culture aims at producing a free spirit, in the deepest sense: free, that is to say, from the fanaticisms of religion, from the fanaticisms of science, and from the fanaticisms of the mob.
>
> ◆
>
> —John Cowper Powys

example, involves a transfer of energy from the victim to the killer. All killers might be thought of as psychic vampires. Watching it on film is on the same spectrum. Do some individuals get a thrill from watching such things? Of course, and where do you think the energy from that thrill comes from? Energy flows nearly as well from watching it on film, seeing it at the theater or even as they did in Rome, watching it at the Coliseum, as it does from watching the real thing, so how does it work?

TELEPORTATION IS A PROBLEM

Your dimensionally interactive cyber-kinetic self is able to transport itself with ease to real events that may have occurred in the past, present or even the future, and suck up energy from the minds of the participants. Over the past twenty years, for example, there have been a number of serious government sponsored programs on what is called *remote viewing*. There are numerous documented instances[29] of ordinary individuals being given numerical and other coordinates representing longitude and latitude by a controller (another person who knows what the coordinates represent) and subsequently reporting on things they could not possibly have known without receiving information from an unknown source.

Your multi-dimensional, core self can literally teleport itself to all sorts of illicit places but first it needs an address. Every act and event has a causal or quantum address. (Energy maps itself and everything is remembered at the quantum level.) Immoral movies and books can be dangerous because the soul reads quantum addresses that you may have no conscious idea exist. Do not allow your core self access to addresses you would not normally frequent. What is insanity but a bad psychic address that your mind has cathected, and cannot or will not let go of? Remember, your life force is pure energy and it is attracted to anything that has power—good or evil. It will go wherever you let it go. This does not mean that your soul is immoral, it is just hungry for energy—anything to get it back on track towards non-locality.

A riot, for example, is a bunch of NDMS whose life forces are like dicks at an orgy. There is so much energy being unleashed that some untrained souls practically levitate with excitement. Next time you watch a riot on film, note the enthusiasm of the participants. No one is suffering except the victim.

Snuff films, which feature real murders on film, are simply the next logical step for those who are not willing to qualify their soul's thirst for illicit sources of energy. They are also, frighteningly, becoming more common.

Fast cars might be thought of as sexual aids, or penis-extenders, which help stimulate the appetites of those spindly and impoverished souls who expend sexual energy frivolously. What red-blooded male is not thrilled to hear mighty engines roar? What battle is ever fought without lots of noise? What are bullets, if not similar to tiny penises capable of ejaculating hundreds of times a minute for the pleasure of the shooter? What is a powerful car, if not a swollen penile advertisement, a flag for fast and easy women? Not the paid kind mind you, but those vacuous young ladies who, low on energy and virtue themselves, are looking for an energy fix with almost any moron carrying drugs or money.

And my friends, what do whores and fast women in general do? Do they soak up those unseemly urges that might cause us to loot and pillage our neighbors? No, they remind the Non Dick Manager how important it is to get what he wants, whenever he wants it. Whores and fast honeys teach his dick that a woman is an object, a bitch for his satisfaction, and that the rest of the world is just something for him to spear.

GETTING OFF AT THE MOVIES

"Getting off" and attempting to increase the psychic juice available to already drained loins and minds seems to be the common denominator between guns, cars, movies and whores. On a deeper level, these are illicit trips to non-locality and represent a desperate search by the soul to replenish depleted reserves of Chi.

The more closely guns, cars, movies and whores are examined, the more one is inexorably led to the conclusion that they are a major component for the fulfillment of FIKI. Guns, cars, movies and whores give you what you want and when you want it, which is usually now—no preamble, little foreplay. Is it any wonder, given our cultural approval for the satisfaction of almost any impulse, that cars, guns, movies and whores are becoming increasingly important as both necessities and status symbols? The rapper Ice T was perhaps being honest when he said that "Crime is the most exciting thing you can do. You get off on crime more than anything else." From this perspective, why should a little thing like violence stand in the way of our enjoyment of life?

Many of the most well attended movies are about—you guessed correctly—guns, cars and whores. Several years ago, several friends and I watched a movie starring Antonio Banderas called "Desperado." There were five of us watching this movie with several of the viewers watching for the second or third time. Among us were a psychiatrist and his wife (a nurse and mother), a psychologist and others who were authors and editors. As heads were being blown off and gunfire exchanged in all directions by individuals with huge, rapid firing weapons, howls of laughter and encouragement were being directed at the screen by this well-educated audience of five quasi-NDMS. Had there been any violation of half-naked women, the pleasure would have been more muted (in deference to the female in our midst) but the enormous satisfaction generated by the violence would have only been augmented by sexual violence.

What on earth were we doing? Indeed what on earth are most of the movie viewers doing when they are watching multiple acts of violence on the screen? Are they shielding their eyes, averting their gaze at either nakedness or violence? No, they can't get enough of it, and neither could we.

FIKI IS EVERYONE'S PROBLEM

FIKI or the indulging of your ASS is the *sine qua non* of many successful movies today, not just because producers are immoral and greedy but also because the audience loves it. The satisfaction and indeed pleasure of FIKI seems to manifest overtly in criminals who are more directly engaged by it and covertly and subconsciously by the vast majority of those for whom the real thing is not an option. There appears to be nothing wrong with anyone enjoying murder and mayhem on film, but once it steps off the screen into real life, then and only then do we get morally enraged about the content of our movies. For this reason, many violent criminals might be better prosecuted as hedonists guilty of moral transgression, rather than as simple law-breakers.

We really need to grow up as a culture and realize that many of our so-called criminals are simply individuals who are unable to control their impulses. Many of these unfortunate people were unceremoniously booted out of childhood and forced into adult life-styles by movies loaded with salacious comments and multiple role-model-type examples of adults who are cinematically exalted for not practicing any form of Dick Management. Even something as seemingly innocuous (by today's standards) as a James Bond movie is loaded with dick-goading examples. Doesn't James mount all the beautiful women in between blowing all sorts of people off the map? Isn't it portrayed as just too cool? Why should we be surprised when children seek to be as cool as Mr. Bond—never mind the ghetto gangster next door who drives a limo and always has a hot babe on each arm, powder up his nose, and a TEC-9 in the trunk.

What is needed is an ethically acceptable science of self-control and art of Dick Management—not the kind of pseudo science we have today which encourages the public to get in touch with impulses, as if they were automatically enlightened by doing so. Let me ask you—would you prefer that high schools distribute condoms or copies *of How To Manage Your Destructive Impulses With Cyber-Kinetics?*

The ASS and FIKI are evolutionary components of daily life that have to be monitored and regulated, socially and politically. A public morality that recognizes this is critically important if we are ever to get beyond the vacuous dialog that is taking place about crime and values today. Without an education in morals and personal energy management, not enough prisons can be built to stem the tide of devolved Non Dick Managers coming to your neighborhood soon.

A few years ago, while living in northern Europe, I came across a phenomenon that represented everything conservatism should mobilize to refute. A group of sadists and masochists formed an organization to lobby for tighter regulations for their brothels. They wanted a special fire-fighting apparatus, as it would take people who are handcuffed or tied up longer to leave a burning building...

—David Brooks, *The New Conservative*

Ballard Street By Jerry Van Amerongen

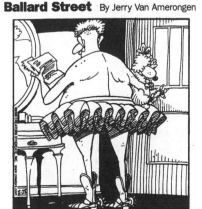

Chet peruses his dismissal notice from
the rodeo cowboy's association.

MANAGEMENT TIPS

• What drives you shapes your thoughts, so take care as to what you allow yourself to be driven by. The Dick Manager is always watching his ASS. The Non Dick Manager (NDM) is an ASS.

• The NDM generally ignores both his own intuitions and the feelings of others. If you find yourself slipping into intemperance, pause and ask yourself if this is what you really want.

• Leave your bone alone today. Give it some privacy. You might be surprised at the subtle changes in your energy level and self esteem.

• When making love, do not be mean with your peepee. A gentleman allows ladies the proper amount of time and wants to know what she likes. As a medieval troubadour once sang, "In my lady's bower, none is more courteous and debonair…"

• Remind yourself daily that pain in the form of depression or low energy can be the result of too much mindless sexual activity or a poor God connection.

CHAPTER 27

CHARACTER DEVELOPMENT

One who recognizes all men as members of his own body
is a sound man to guard them.

—Lao Tzu, *The Way of Life*

If, as Aristotle and the founders of many great religions have argued, virtue is a state of character, how might we go about developing the concept of virtue into a philosophy of character for modern man? What is it about good character that we like? Don't we admire courage and fair play? Aren't we impressed with people who are able to exercise self-restraint and who seem to be happier for doing so? Does anyone admire a coward or a glutton, or someone who exposes himself to young children? Why not? These are things that most of us feel are undesirable traits and yet we are often unable to express the "why" in terms of a philosophy.

We are almost afraid to call something a vice for fear of offending someone who is unfortunately vice-ridden. The public equality of self-interest prohibits our saying that anyone else's values are less than our own, when in fact they might well be. A moral philosophy that borrows from the world's greatest teachers allows us to determine why some actions are good and why some, relatively and objectively speaking, are bad. This is not the same thing as standing in moral judgment of anyone. If an objective moral code or natural law exists, the vice-ridden are guilty before the code. They stand self-convicted by reason. Cicero, in his treatise *On the State*, describes how a person's actions relate to non-local law, which gives us a local or objective standard to evaluate our actions:

> True law is Reason, right and natural, commanding people to fulfill their obligations and prohibiting and deterring them from doing wrong. Its validity is universal; it is immutable and eternal. Its

commands and prohibitions apply effectively to good men, and those uninfluenced by them are bad. Any attempt to supersede this law, to repeal any part of it is sinful; to cancel it entirely is impossible. Neither the Senate nor the Assembly can exempt us from its demands; we need no interpreter or expounder of it but ourselves. There will not be one law at Rome, one at Athens, or one now and one later, but all nations will be subject all the time to this one changeless and everlasting law. (Cicero, 40 B.C.)

Virtue or moral and intellectual excellence is humanity's way of relating itself to the law of Reason or Natural Law. This is just another way of saying that virtue connects us to the non-local structure of the universe in all the right ways. Natural Law is quite simply God's idea of how we should behave. It is your duty and pleasure to seek it out and understand it.

> Natural law strikes many as something extrinsic, an almost arbitrary, certainly onerous imposition by the lawgiver, especially if the latter is Divine. Misdeeds are not wrong because God says so; rather they are wrong—self-deceiving and self-gypping to the perpetrator. The problem is that our human nature is undeveloped, unorganized and ambiguous, until we start building it by living in accord with it, i.e., finding what assuages in part our gnawing appetite for bliss and transcendence.
>
> ◆
>
> —Milton Meier, Ph.D., *The Examined Life*

Following Aristotle and Plato, theologians of the Middle Ages, divided moral excellence into the Four Cardinal Virtues: Prudence, Justice, Fortitude and Temperance (self-restraint or continence). These virtues had parts that consisted of other lesser but nonetheless important virtues. For example, patience might have been considered part of temperance and courage a part of fortitude. Although some medieval theologians made courage a part of fortitude, it makes more sense the other way around. Fortitude is defined as a strength of mind to encounter adversity without wavering—in short: guts. It requires courage to exercise fortitude. Likewise it makes more sense to make prudence a part of wisdom. Is it not wise to be prudent?

The present Dalai Lama, like many of the great philosophers, has a remarkable insight into the relationship that the virtues have with one another:

I believe that developing the compassion on which happiness depends demands a two-pronged approach. One the one hand, we need to restrain those factors which inhibit compassion. On the other, we need to cultivate those which are conducive to

it. As we have seen, what is conducive to compassion is love, patience, tolerance, for-
giveness, humility and so on. What inhibits compassion is that lack of inner
restraint which we have identified as the source of all unethical conduct. We find
that by transforming our habits and dispositions, we can begin to perfect our overall
state of heart and mind (kun long)—that from which all our actions spring.

THE FIVE VALUES AND IMPROVING THE SOUL

A formulation of the these virtues that might make more sense for modern man would be the five values of the soul:

1. Wisdom (with an emphasis on prudence)
2. Justice (with an emphasis on fair play)
3. Courage (with an emphasis on fortitude)
4. Self-Restraint (with an emphasis on moderation and continence)
5. Compassion (with the emphasis that compassion is not possible
   without the other virtues)

All other values might be thought of as being derived from these five
anti-entropic values. The two results of having and practicing these values
are the additional personal attributes of honor and happiness. Neither individuals nor a society can survive without happiness and honor.

If, as Aristotle argues, virtue is an activity of soul in accordance with
right reason, we must attempt to understand what this means for your
soul and your personal development. Your inner self or the higher consciousness of the life force is buried under the carapace of the ego. The
extent to which we allow the soul to emerge is proportional to the effort
that we make to cultivate excellence. The metacognition exemplified by
kun long is contingent upon the cultivation of virtue.

Your soul's movements may be a complete mystery to you, but it is
always attempting to engage in a greater manifestation of itself in the present. Only you can allow this to happen by paying mindful and honest
attention to what is actually happening in the vestibule of your own consciousness. This is the beginning of the kind of wisdom that is called
mindfulness. Your genitals are of course not interested in this kind of sub-
tlety, so part of being mindful is a kind of spiritual or yogic observation of
what your dick is up to. Generally it is always up to something.

Metacognition (the Buddhists refer to this as mindfulness) consists of
being aware of energy shifts; proportions and disproportions of feeling
that come across the threshold of consciousness. All of us experience these

subtle inner states of self-awareness, but few of us have the language to interpret what is going on. There is a vast danger in not heeding inner promptings and subtle shifts in time and spatial orientation. How many times have you ignored a gut instinct about something and paid a heavy price for not paying attention to it? Far too often this inner or non-local consciousness is confused by mistaken religious or social beliefs that constrict the relationship between you and your core-self. For example, the person who doesn't believe in God will deliberately ignore some subtle promptings out of a fear of becoming religious, and some religious individuals will ignore their inner consciousness for fear that it will take them to a place traditionally forbidden by religion.

Homosexuality is of course one of those socially forbidden places that may be attractive to your ASS. Honesty is critical. Your dick simply wants to get off, so whatever is handy is just fine as far as the Appetite Survival System is concerned. However, you are not your ASS, so you need to interrogate choices that may be suspect, rooted in laziness or psychological trauma. "There is only one sin and that is being stuck"(George Simon). Whatever your sexual preference, make sure that is where you really want to be. You have a choice and a will; exercise both of them. The moment you discover that you are unhappy with your sexual choices, that is the moment to be hard on yourself. Unhappiness is always a cyber-kinetic message from your soul that something is wrong. Heed your soul and walk the path that has been set down for you—no matter how difficult.

DEPRESSION IS A MESSAGE FROM YOUR SOUL

There are many individuals in our society who suffer from depression because they lack the vibrant energy conferred by honor and wisdom. Honor and wisdom are required in order for the soul to fully express itself but depression is a message of energy deficiency. These energy deficiencies can be closely related to depression when they are not adverted to. Nothing feels more dishonorable, for example, than sexual or business relationships that are not honest or con-

> Livy, the Roman historian [59 B.C.] in the preface to his work, asks how Rome had come to such a point of disorder "that we can tolerate neither our vices nor their remedies—*nec vitia nec remedia pati possumus.*"
>
> ♦
>
> —Rev. Seumas O'Reilly

structive. Your sexual happiness and personal integrity cannot be fabricated out of anything that dishonors moral and spiritual excellence.

Happiness, like moral excellence, makes more sense when it is understood as a state of the soul or the product of a well-directed life force. The significance of happiness becomes clearer when it is seen as the result of moral and intellectual excellence or what might be loosely termed "good character." Good character is, in turn, the prerequisite for the cultivation of wisdom and consciousness as a whole. Good character enables you to silence the noise of the chattering ego and quiet the appetites that would otherwise occupy all of your time.

REGULATE YOUR DICK AND YOU CAN DO ANYTHING

Good character is produced by the prudent pursuit of honor and the desire for excellence. Honor is the hidden image of itself that the soul longs for. The quest for honor and excellence produces happiness by fulfilling the life force's desire to come forward and be manifested. This is the root meaning of concepts such as *kun long* and *dasein.*

Happiness is a manifestation of the soul's eternity in the present, a window on the infinite. This constitutes a moral paradigm of the highest order. I call this the *Venus Paradigm.* The Venus paradigm states that happiness, like honor, is a product of the love of moral and intellectual excellence, and that such a love leads ultimately to knowledge of the soul, and the Divinity. Your ASS plays an obstructing role in the achievement of any moral or spiritual standard. Be aware of your ASS's NDM agenda and half the battle is won.

Whatever else they may have believed, the Stoics of Cicero's time were certain that all men shared in the divine spark of God's existence and that virtue brought humanity closer to God. These same Stoics also believed in a progression towards virtue. They understood that there was much stumbling on the path of virtue but that all human beings should continue to

> The three hardest things in the world are neither physical feats nor intellectual achievements, but moral acts: to return love for hate, to include the excluded and to say, "I was wrong."
>
> ◆
>
> —Sydney J. Harris

make the effort. This was a cosmopolitan and pre-Christian view of morality that we would do well to consider for our present age. What this means is that we adopt a dynamic attitude to what is frequently called sin.

Sin is not a place to build a life, even though everyone may feel the need to make a pit stop every now and then.

Aristotle's moral and intellectual virtues should be taught in depth as part of a moral curriculum. How could anyone argue that moral excellence such as courage, self-restraint, wisdom, justice, generosity and kindness is not useful and necessary for the preservation of a society? Let the religious and social issues surface as they may but let us take a step in this direction. Aristotle provides a powerful counterweight to the herd consciousness of fundamentalists of all religions and in fact, may be the philosopher so needed, to maintain tolerance and impartiality in these matters.

Do not believe in anything simply because you have heard it.

Do not believe in traditions because they have been handed down for many generations.

Do not believe in anything because it is spoken and rumored by many.

Do not believe in anything simply because it is found in your religious books.

Do not believe in anything merely on the authority of your teachers and elders.

But after observation and analysis, when you find that anything that agrees with reason and is conducive to the good and benefit of one and all, then accept it and live up to it.

—The Buddha

MANAGEMENT TIPS

+ Prayer is dimensionally interactive communication with God. You can't have too much of this. The Superluminal consciousness can utterly transform your spirit, but you must first open yourself up to change and pay attention to the truths presented to your heart.

+ If you piss on the floor or toilet seat, clean it up.

+ Spend a day without cursing, even to yourself.

+ Try a sexual fast for two weeks. You will find it enormously clarifying.

+ Use your turn signals.

CHAPTER 28

DICK MANAGEMENT FOR CHILDREN

*Perhaps the greatest social service that can be rendered by anybody
to the country and to mankind is to bring up a family.*

—George Bernard Shaw

AS YOU HAVE NOTICED, YOUR CHILDREN HAVE GENITALS. WHEN THEY ARE young, they generally have no use for them other than as something to pee with or play with once in a while. Even though they come to know how babies are made and how sex works, aside from curiosity, their genitals do not seem particularly moved by this knowledge, until the onset of puberty, which occurs generally between eleven and fourteen in boys and a few years earlier (generally speaking) with girls. The period of time from birth to puberty is known in psychological terms as *latency,* meaning that their sexuality is inactive or hidden until puberty. In other words, a child's ASS does not fully awaken until puberty. So, take care not to awaken your child's sexuality before it is ready. Put those dirty magazines away and make sure they watch as little violence and sex on TV as possible.

Even without sexual awareness or sexual play, a child's life force may have a very active ASS and if not suitably monitored by adults, some children may easily develop into monsters. Violent television shows are a particularly dangerous thing for your children. FIKI slumbers in every breast and if television shows violence as something cool—and particularly as something that there should be no remorse for—then some children may be on a slippery slope without suitable moral guidance.

According to many studies, nearly three times the number of American children have behavioral disorders than they did twenty years ago. Now it is certainly clear that we are much better able to diagnose such problems than we were in the past, but how many of these so-called disorders are disorders at all? There is a great deal of nonsense today, for example, about attention deficit disorders. Clearly there are some hyper-active children who have problems based on their biology, but it would seem that many of them are arbitrarily put into this category due to the failure of modern psychology to identify problems of character. How many children assigned to this group have absolutely nothing wrong with them other than a lack of exercise due to too much TV and lack of disci-pline by overly indulgent parents? You will find psychologists who will argue on both sides of this issue without finding a common ground to understand the nature of the behavioral problems that are clearly visible to all. Chemical imbalances and neurological dysfunction can be assigned a sensible role in many an individual's personal difficulties, but it is impor-tant to distinguish behavioral problems that are rooted in biology from bad behavior that has a moral or even a spiritual origin. In any event, those who are chemically challenged need to make an even greater effort to gain control over their biological estates.

The unofficial teaching of the medical/psychological establishment is that physical punishment for children such as spanking is detrimental to their psychological health, and gives children the wrong message by showing them that violence is acceptable. On the face of it, this seems like a plausible argument, but when you observe the bad behavior and vio-lence that children who are seldom disciplined sometimes exhibit—something seems to be seriously awry with this line of reasoning.

Have you ever observed a teacher attempting to discipline or reprimand a group of teenage boys? Unless the teacher has the ability to either inspire the boys with fear or respect, the re-sponse he or she gets may range from sheer boredom to outright disre-

> It is easier to build strong children than to repair broken men.
>
> ◆
>
> —Frederick Douglas

spect—and in some instances is met with the threat of assault—unless of course the teacher backs off! The teachers who usually inspire the most re-spect from teenage boys are the ones whom the boys know will kick their butts or severely and quietly discipline them unless they behave and behave quickly. Fear is a most salutary thing when brought to bear on wild ASSES. Women often don't understand this—that males need to be cowed by physically or morally stronger males or females. The basic principle at work is that the smaller monkeys are only really afraid of the bigger monkeys.

What is wrong with the argument against corporeal punishment is a misunderstanding of who or what is being punished. It is the ASS which must be punished and to this end punishment must be dispassionate, fair, timely and firm. Your children can understand that it is certain behavior that is unacceptable, rather than thinking that there is something wrong with who they are. They may have to work to understand this but the life-long struggle between what they feel like doing and what they should be doing begins by making moral and thoughtful distinctions in childhood that are fostered by loving adults who have a firm grasp of Dick Management.

Our culture has many common expressions and phrases that make this initial moral distinction between what we want to do and what we ought to do. This also reiterates the local and non-local nature of human consciousness. We can make a distinction between good behavior and bad behavior precisely because we have a non-local standard against which to judge it. We all know what the local behavior of an ASS looks like:

* Don't be an ass.
* Stop acting like an idiot.
* Learn to behave.
* Act like a human being and not like an animal.
* Where is the nice boy (or girl) who was here earlier?
* Learn self-control.
* You may not have everything that you want.
* Who do you think you are?

Locally speaking, consciousness is fairly simple and even animalistic but we are never, even as children, just local entities. We are a local/non-local synthesis that requires a constant effort to keep in balance. (Yin and Yang is the symbol of this balance.) Children's non-local awareness can be overwhelmed by local biological impulses. (This is why it is important to maintain latency until the onset of puberty.) The trick to teaching children to behave is to guide them constantly and steadily to a non-local awareness of themselves. You can encourage this kind of interiority through religion, social service, good education, sports, martial arts, drama, benevolent discipline, and also in the way that you interact with your children.

Before I discipline one of my sons (never a pleasant job), I first look into his eyes and gauge both his trepidation and awareness of what he has done. If I sense real contrition and can see that he has already gotten the message, then there is no need for physical punishment. A firm word is all that is required. However, if defiance smolders, be sure that further action is needed. Make sure that your own ASS or FIKI is not invoked in the disciplinary process. You must discipline without rage or anger. Your children must understand that you do not want to punish them but that their actions leave you no choice.

The easiest way to teach children Dick Management is to be a good manager yourself. Your children will generally imitate you. If you make a habit of being patient, thoughtful, kind, courageous and wise, and remain firm on important disciplinary issues, your children will tend to respect you. They may not agree with you but that will come in time if you act consistently and fairly.

The most important thing of all, though, is that children see you in dialog with a realm beyond the senses. They will sense when you are reaching beyond your immediate three and four-dimensional reality and will seek to imitate you. They may not understand what you are doing, but rest assured, their souls will get the message! Beyond good example, it is important to teach children that all their experiences occur on two levels. One is visible and the other isn't.

- **The Visible**: The four-dimensional world that they can see and experience around them at all times.
- **The Invisible**: The non-local world of their souls and its life-long local struggle with the very visible ASS of biology.

The invisible world is part of a larger and subtle multi-dimensional universe, which is on a continuum with the Divinity and their own consciousness. It waits to be accessed but cannot be entered by those enslaved to the ASS.

What are good manners but a shield against the violence of the ASS and FIKI? Notice how all manners create a buffer zone between your ASS and yourself. Have you ever wondered why we say "please" and "thank you" instead of "gimmie" and grunts of ac-

> Studies by the Centers for Disease Control have shown that a violence prevention curriculum for grammar school children can reduce aggressive behavior by as much as thirty percent.

knowledgment? Manners enable us to temper our immediate reactions and keep the ASS in line. This is why we train children to answer us when we call them. "Yes, Mom," or "Yes, Dad," rather than allowing them to ignore us.

The key to developing a child's awareness of the two worlds is to observe the following useful rules for raising children.

- Teach your children to be respectful.
- Help them to control their impulses.
- Do not allow them to use filthy language.
- Do not use foul language in front of your children.
- Monitor their TV watching.
- Punish them lovingly when necessary.
- Insist that they practice good manners.
- Listening to musicians who screech about their balls and who they want to "do" should be discouraged.
- Encourage your children to practice kindness.
- Volunteer at a local soup kitchen or retirement home.
- Make sure that they read for at least half an hour every day.
- Discourage fighting.
- Do not argue in front of your children.
- All discipline should be done in private.

Teach your children that the real enemy is within themselves and that laziness, unkindness, violence, rudeness and thoughtlessness come to those who do only exactly as they please. There is no progress without self-discipline and some suffering. Teach your children this and you will prepare them for life.

For Socrates, knowledge and virtue (acting in accordance with reason) were the same thing. If virtue has to do with "making the soul as good as possible," it is therefore, closely related...When someone commits an evil act, said Socrates, he always does it thinking that it is good in some way...For him, virtue meant fulfilling one's function. As a rational human being, a man's function is to behave rationally. At the same time, every human being has the inescapable desire for happiness or the well-being of his soul. This inner well being, this "Making the soul as good as possible," can only be achieved by certain appropriate modes of behavior...Socrates knew that some forms of behavior appear to produce happiness but in reality do not. For this reason men frequently choose an act that may in itself be questionable but that they, nevertheless, think may bring them happiness. A thief may know that stealing as such is wrong, but he steals in the hope that it will bring him happiness. Similarly, men pursue power, physical pleasure and property, which are the symbols of success and happiness, confusing these with the true ground of happiness.

—Samuel Enoch Stumpf, *Socrates to Sartre*

MANAGEMENT TIPS

• If you are afraid of using fear to manage and motivate a child, you must ask yourself: what state of being is this child in? The art of discipline involves the ability to discern the workings of your child's consciousness and then choosing a course of action that corresponds to the child's state of being. At times, some form of corporeal punishment is necessary, on other occasions the denial of privileges is more appropriate.

• Always be consistent; always follow through on threats to punish but never withhold your love. Children must always know that you love them.

• Make sure that your children understand that they must struggle against themselves in certain instances. Not everything that seems good is actually good. They may want to do things that are both contrary to common sense and detrimental to their long-term development.

• Do not allow children to guzzle as much candy and soda as they want or watch TV whenever they feel like it. You will end up with butthead children instead of human beings.

• Encourage your children to read. This is a terrific way to foster interiority. Many children who can't read or who are poor readers have a greater need to spend more time hanging out on the street than those who can entertain themselves with a good book.

CHAPTER 29

DICK MANAGEMENT OR
SEX EDUCATION?

A new idea does not succeed by convincing the world of its brilliance.
A new idea succeeds by having those who do not believe it dying off
and being replaced by a new group who take it for granted.

—Linus Pauling

THE CURRENT STATE OF SEX EDUCATION IN AMERICA MIGHT BE LIKENED to a house drenched in gasoline with the residents being told to cup their lit matches to avoid a house fire. Sex education has become an ideological tool of those with social and psychological agendas not rooted in even a marginal understanding of traditional morality. Reading the works of many modern sex educators would lead a normal person to conclude that their privates are really only advanced toilet fixtures designed to sustain a flush of orgasmic activity. Pregnancy, giving birth and raising decent families are only accidental to toilet sexuality. The main rule of toilet sex seems to be to get off, and the more often, the better. Drain the lizard!

Beyond a brief description of sexual mechanics, a listing of various birth control methods and basic hygiene, what more does the active dick require? Certainly not dry-humping (having sex with your clothes on) or "outercourse" such as screwing armpits which has been suggested by various sagacious elements of the sex-education community.

"Only you can decide," has become the banner of the "ejaculate first, think later" crowd. Yes, only you can decide, but what do you decide with? Surely you do not allow your genitals to make the decision—do they ever say anything but yes? What moral tools are sex educators giving their charges? "Choice" seems to be their primary moral tool, which suggests that by making a choice regarding sexual activity, the death penalty, or abortion, that choice becomes automatically moral simply because a choice was made. This kind of sloganeering does a disservice to honest people on all sides of these issues. Choices are never good simply by being chosen. Having the option to choose wrongdoing may be important but it is not the same thing as a morally good choice.

> The National Center for Juvenile Justice, a private non-profit agency in Pittsburgh that specializes in crime and delinquency studies, found that rape arrests among teenagers younger than fifteen had more than doubled in ten years over the previous decade's reported statistics. The unreported figures would make this figure frighteningly higher.

Ayn Rand used to speak about *anti-concepts* which obfuscate all discussion by simply being brought up. Racism, for example, can be used as anti-concept. If you are charged with racism, this charge alone may be sufficient to convict you in the forum of public opinion—never mind that you may in fact not be a racist. J. Edgar Hoover and other conservatives used to do the same thing by simply branding liberals "communists," and liberal politicians later played the same game against conservatives, by accusing them of "McCarthyism." These slogans are all examples of anti-concepts employed with a wide brush.

Sex education itself has become somewhat of an anti-concept. If you are for it, you are progressive, but if you are against it, you are regressive, a conservative Neanderthal, someone possibly unconcerned about the well being and future of your children. If you are for sex education, conservatives may accuse you of not having family values (another anti-concept). Anti-concepts are simply no substitute for thinking. Often it is easier to think in terms of slogans, but morality and consciousness do not respond to sloganeering. Slogans are generally a sign of intellectual laziness and moral decline. Choosing between feelings is generally selecting a preference for one or the other. Real choice involves a dialogue of principle which presupposes some kind of moral and intellectual standards.

Feeling is not a standard; it is a condition of energy reception. Feeling or emotion is not differentiated by more emotion. A set of standards, not rooted in emotion, is required to rise above feelings. People constantly argue whether or not how you "feel" about something is more important than how you "think" about it. The confusion arises because one can hardly exist without the other. From an experiential perspective, almost everything we do is first encountered at the level of feeling; however, to remain at the level of feeling is to remain at the level of undifferentiated reception only. There is little interpretation that can be done without mind or intellect. What you feel is much more touched by non-locality than your most abstract thoughts. Your thoughts and beliefs are already concretized in three and four dimensions and represent a distillation of much larger realities. You may or may not believe in God in the abstract but your experience of God at the level of feeling will be much greater than whatever thoughts you may or may not entertain about your experience.

The dance between mind and feeling reflects the dynamic that exists between the potency of non-locality and the actuality of locality. This is the most fundamental of ecologies and the failure to recognize that the energy of your feelings is directly connected to moral sensibilities is at the root of the modern denial of common sense.

ABSTINENCE PROGRAMS

It is the parents' privilege and responsibility to teach their children about sexuality, but unfortunately, many adults feel uncomfortable discussing the "birds and the bees." Some parents are happier to have this uncomfortable situation taken care of by professional educators, but at some point in the well-intentioned process of providing information about sexuality to youngsters, an evil thing happened. Educators decided that how to instruction was required—without a corresponding moral blueprint. Now please, please, who is not going to do homework when those in positions of authority provide detailed instructions?

One of the more influential players in the sex education game, for example, is the Sexuality Information and Education Council of the United States or SIECUS. The SIECUS position statements on sexuality are extraordinary (in my opinion) in both what they claim, and in what they do not say. Nowhere in the position statements is the word "moral" linked to the notion of self-restraint. We are, however, primly informed that it is "important" for religious institutions to promote the activities of those who might be deemed to possess alternative modes of sexuality. We are also informed that no one should feel guilty for choosing to masturbate or choosing not to masturbate! Apparently there is no moral difference between choosing to whack off or not whacking off! We are told however, that it is appropriate that adults should make it clear that masturbation should be done in private and not in public. Why only in private? If masturbation is a morally neutral act, why shouldn't you jerk off in public? Unlike feces which cannot safely be deposited in a garbage can, quick drying semen can be safely deposited in any public receptacle!

Discussing masturbation as a right without a corresponding teaching of self-restraint to go with it is a form of social suicide. One might as well say that no one should be disturbed at either drinking or smoking, or not drinking and not smoking. To say that there is no moral difference between doing something and how much you might do of something is an extraordinary verbal sleight of hand. The issue here is not guilt but rather the implicit denial of the bad consequences that a reasonable person might attribute to excess of any kind. The moral schema in "politically correct" social engineering tends to make sexuality a morally neutral toilet activity with zero energy consequences for the human psyche.

My favorite piece of nonsense along politically correct lines is spouted by various sexual education groups that warn the public about "fear-based" courses of abstinence. What is amazing about these admonitions is the complete inability of the issuers of these warnings to make a connection between the increasing incidence of violence and misbehavior in public high schools, and the appetitive and sexual indulgence that their own programs may promote. You may walk the hallways of your local high school in terror of FIKI-driven adolescents but DO NOT, UNDER ANY CIRCUMSTANCES, ALLOW YOUR CHILD TO BECOME CONTAMINATED BY FEAR-BASED ABSTINENCE PROGRAMS. It is interesting to note, however, that according to statistics[38] compiled by the National Institute of Justice, adolescent offenders are "prevalent" in reported incidents of indecent exposure. This Institute's research also indicates that most sexual assaults are "a sexual expression of aggression." Do you think that any of the young men in this report were attempting to cultivate sexual self-restraint? Does masturbation increase or decrease the incidence of FIKI among young men? Anecdotal evidence would seem to indicate that the learning of sexual self-discipline is a tightrope walk that cannot proceed without a moral teaching to counteract the negative and violence-tending aspects of the sexual impulse in men.

Without a specific moral code or a theory of Dick Management, organizations that provide sexual information may be providing a serious disservice to the moral health of the country. Modern day sex educators who are

> Vice is a monster of so frightful mien,
>
> As to be hated, needs but to be seen;
>
> Yet seen too oft, familiar with her face,
>
> We first endure, then pity, then embrace.
>
> ◆
>
> —Alexander Pope

ethically and morally deformed simply cannot be allowed to run programs that have an enormous impact on the moral future of children. Indeed the argument should be made that sex education should be part of a larger course of moral instruction that focuses on the soul rather than genitals. Given many parents' reluctance to discuss sexuality with their children, some form of instruction at an appropriate age may be necessary—but only if administered in a moral context.

FIKI is a fundamental human problem that is not at all helped by educators cooing over sex fundamentals. It is time that FIKI came out of the intellectual closet and that responsible evolutionary scientists stand up and fight the reptilian holdover from the Jurassic age that is being resurrected by the dick-drained brains of the sex education crowd. We are like a society that uses reconstituted reptilian DNA to bring back Tyrannosaurus Rex. Is anybody in any doubt as to what the big reptile might do? The same may be said for the ASS and FIKI. These evolutionary holdovers are being fattened and grown by unethical sex education programs and value deficient education as a whole into a monster, which will consume us all, if we let the morally confused pedants in charge of social progress continue to have their way. Without Dick Management or at the least, a discussion of moral virtue, sex education can end up becoming a form of pandering. A panderer, such as a pimp, is of course one who caters to the vices of others. An educator who is really a panderer in disguise is doing both himself or herself, and the community, a disservice.

Losing the way of life, men rely first on their fitness;
Losing fitness, they turn to kindness;
Losing kindness, they turn to justice;
Losing justice, they turn to convention.
Conventions are fealty and honesty gone to waste,
They are the entrance of disorder.
False teachers of life use flowery words
And start nonsense.
The man of stamina stays with the root
Below the tapering,
Stays with the fruit beyond the flowering:
He has his no and he has his yes.

—Lao Tzu, *The Way of Life*

MANAGEMENT QUESTIONS

◆ How much self-control does a bully have?

◆ How many car thieves do you think believe that casual sex should be curbed?

◆ How many muggers do you think would agree that "spanking the monkey" should be a matter of concern?

◆ How many impenitent murderers do you think there are that are concerned about whacking off?

◆ How many rapists do not masturbate with great regularity? Do you think there are any?

"Page two, paragraph six: The moral high ground—we're prepared to yield totally on that point."

CHAPTER 30

THE GANDHI-HITLER INDEX

The means of doing hurt to ourselves are always at hand.
—Samuel Johnson

THE GANDHI-HITLER INDEX IS USEFUL FOR PINPOINTING SERIOUS Management problems that may erupt into a totalitarian consciousness. The Hitler entity is a level of ego and ASS-dominated consciousness that is best exemplified, but by no means exhausted by Adolph Hitler. The Hitler entity is best thought of as a metaphor for biological possession of an individual by the appetites. Others may want to call this demonic possession but the results are the same. If thinking of yourself as Hitler makes you uncomfortable, think about how others may experience you. You may want to imagine yourself as Caligula, Stalin, Charles Manson, Idi Amin or Pol Pot—whatever works best for you. The Gandhi aspect of this test measures your Management progress and needs little explanation.

If your answer is yes to any of these questions, circle yes or the number one (1). If your answer is no, circle the zero (0).

This is not a psychological test. Do not confuse the results of this test with any sort of psychological profile. This test is profiling energy levels that professional psychologists are not able to evaluate. Such professionals may wish to test themselves, however, and come to their own conclusions.

Go to the next page and answer the questions on the GANDHI-HITLER INDEX.

THE GANDHI-HITLER INDEX

1. Do you sometimes scream at people?
   Yes (1)   No (0)

2. Do you enjoy beating others?
   Yes (1)   No (0)

3. Is torturing animals fun for you?
   Yes (1)   No (0)

4. Do you enjoy making people squirm?
   Yes (1)   No (0)

5. Do you prefer pornography or masturbation to normal sex?
   Yes (1)   No (0)

6. Is it very difficult for you to apologize?
   Yes (1)   No (0)

7. Do you like anal sex more than regular sex?
   Yes (1)   No (0)

8. Do you ask your girlfriend or wife to use abortion as a form of birth control?
   Yes (1)   No (0)

9. Do you beat off several times a week on a regular basis?
   Yes (1)   No (0)

10. Do you belong to a gang?
    Yes (1)   No (0)

11. Do you make graffiti?
    Yes (1)   No (0)

12. Do you steal cars?
    Yes (1)   No (0)

13. Does rape interest you?
    Yes (1)   No (0)

14. Do you prefer a mess to neatness?

Yes (1)   No (0)

15. Do like to touch corpses?

Yes (1)   No (0)

16. Do you like to watch scenes of rape or violence?

Yes (1)   No (0)

17. Do you enjoy not washing your hands after you go to the bathroom?

Yes (1)   No (0)

18. Does the sight of blood make your dick hard?

Yes (1)   No (0)

19. Are you envious on a daily basis?

Yes (1)   No (0)

20. Do you use drugs and alcohol on a daily basis?

Yes (1)   No (0)

Total your scores by adding the numbers to the right of the answer you circled. If you score five and below, you are no Hitler. A score of six to ten indicates a problem, and a score of eleven to twenty indicates a demonic infestation of consciousness by the appetites.

The PECER Test and the GANDHI-HITLER INDEX are being considered as screening devices for public officials, hospital workers, police, day care workers and social workers. Forms for the test are available at the back of the book. Put one on your boss, colleague's or teacher's desk. You may also want to post this to your favorite Internet site.

Additional test forms are available at www.dickmanagement.com

The idea that biological crimes can be ended by intellect alone, that you can talk crime to death, doesn't work. Intellectual patterns cannot directly control biological patterns. Only social patterns can control biological patterns, and the instrument of conversation between society and biology is not words. The instrument of conversation between society and biology has always been a policeman or a soldier and his gun. All the laws of history, all the arguments, all the Constitutions and the Bills of Rights and Declarations of Independence are nothing more than instructions to the military and police. If the military and police can't or don't follow these instructions properly they might as well have never been written.

—Robert Pirsig, *Lila: An Inquiry into Morals*

MANAGEMENT TIPS

* Remember, your Appetite Survival System acts frequently without thought—it simply lashes out. Watch your tongue in situations of confrontation.

* We all have murderous instincts, even if you think you don't. Beware—you can be blind-sided by them.

* If you discipline your children, do so without anger. It is possible to administer physical punishment dispassionately.

* It is your responsibility to wear a condom and protect others from any microbial filth you may have.

* Pregnancy is not just her responsibility; it is also fifty percent yours.

CHAPTER 31

TEACHING TEENS THE ART OF DICK MANAGEMENT

Education is the soul of a society as it is passed on
from one generation to the next.

—G.K. Chesterton

THOSE OF YOU WHO HAVE TEENAGERS OR HAVE TO WORK WITH THEM MAY have noticed how difficult it is sometimes to get them to help themselves. Many teens refuse to follow in anyone else's footsteps and insist upon making all of their own mistakes and achieving success all on their own. This is admirable in that all human beings wish to make their lives their own, but it becomes difficult when the collective wisdom of adults that is supposed to be taught in school is not taught, and teenagers are left to swim or sink in a sea of emotion with few or no moral guidelines other than an appeal to do what they think feels best.

The purpose of being a teenager is to become an adult. Once you become an adult, you have an obligation to help those younger beings who are seeking to become more mature. If you are operating under a system of education that encourages immoral actions or ignores the notion of morality in general, you are operating at a serious disadvantage.

Many parents choose to send their children to private schools, rather than allow them to become contaminated by the values of value-free education. In many instances parents are concerned about their children's' safety in schools where administrators are forbidden by bureaucratic guidelines to discipline or morally manage the little ASSES that have emerged like wild dogs in their moral free zones. Children can no more be raised in an environment without morals than they can grow healthy and strong without decent nutrition. Feed children educational excrement and you will raise shitheads.

The fundamental question to ask teens is: Are you happy? If you ask most teens if they are happy, they will gladly either tell you that they are and then proceed to tell you why they are not, or they will flat out tell you that they are unhappy. They are usually able to articulate all the reasons that true happiness is not theirs. They are too fat, too short, too clumsy, not smart enough, not pretty or big enough, their parents don't let them do what they want to do, they don't have enough money, their boyfriend or girlfriend left them, they did not make the varsity team, their teachers are morons, the town or city they live in sucks, etc. If you ask them if they feel good inside about themselves, the answer is often that they do not. Teens are often confused by values they think they should have and their inability to measure up to those values. Have you seen all the T-shirts proclaiming NO FEAR? Teens know they should be courageous but since courage is not discussed as a virtue, the best the culture has to offer them is an impossible ideal—NO FEAR. There are many terrified individuals wearing T-shirts bearing this silly slogan.

Teens often don't question the values that they have, they only know that they have them. Teens live in the immediacy of the moment. If they can't have it now, then what is the use? It is precisely for this reason that they must have moral tools for dealing with impulses. The virtues of courage, justice, wisdom and self-restraint are the stepping stones to nonlocality. Differentiating the differences between ASS generated preferences and non-local intuitions is the most serious task facing teenagers. On the one hand they are firmly in the grip of their local appetites, but at the same time they are full of strange yearnings that seem to have nothing to do with their basest desires. For instance, they may have a lofty desire to love someone special and at the same time wish to fuck anything that moves. They may also become intensely idealistic as the non-local consciousness of the core self begins to awaken and penetrate their awareness.

> When you see kids with their asses hanging out of their baggy pants, running their mouths at adults and using the street as wastebaskets, just think what a little Dick Management might do for them.
>
> ◆
>
> —Kaye Ralleigh

More than any other group, teenagers need to understand the difference between locality and nonlocality, to understand that there is more to their consciousness than just what they feel with their bodies. Teens are very aware of a variety of dualities in their thinking. One moment they may feel like being kind, and the next, fighting like cats and dogs with their best friends. Strange impulses move through their hearts and they do their best to understand what is happening, but without Dick Management or a moral code, how do they define the boundaries of what they are experiencing? How do they make some sense of the powerful sexual energies that rip through them daily? How do they deal with the feeling of being invincible one minute and feeling worthless the next? Teens have an intense need for:

- Discovering boundaries and limits for their feelings
- Adults who understand them and who are willing to listen
- A metaphysical system to help them make sense of their deepest philosophical thoughts
- Sexual management
- Regular hours to help them focus their energy
- Adults who will protect them from their worst impulses
- Gang control and security
- The approval of their peers
- Education that challenges them
- Sports or outdoor activities that help them burn off excess energy
- The company of the opposite sex
- Enough nutritious food
- Parents who love them

THE GANG DYNAMIC

One of the most powerful drives that all human beings share is the desire for unity and belonging. We desperately want to belong to something—some of us to someone—but our primary social desire is to belong to a group that supports and helps us make progress in our lives. As adults we look for the perfect company to work for, one that has excellent benefits and a powerful group dynamic, in short, a company that is going somewhere. This same desire is at the root of the negative dynamic of gang membership. Gangs help protect you—they have benefits—you get more girls, more turf and more dope. You are someone if you belong to a gang!

The primary gang dynamic is belonging—brotherhood, sisterhood—in short, homies (homeboys or homegirls). Would gangs still have the same power to attract young people if they belonged to loving supportive families? Research at the University of California indicates that boys who come from families without fathers are twice as likely to engage in acts of juvenile delinquency as boys from families with a father present. Clearly the small dogs behave much better—as much as fifty percent better— when the big dog is about. This is where FIKI is at its most useful. Fathers in general know how to deal with boys. Nothing quite gets the attention of a young man as a father who knows all the tricks and who is prepared to administer unpleasant punishment. The perception of the father as a man serene and confident in all his actions is something a young man can relate to as a model of impulse management, and can have a far greater impact than punishment. If the youth admires his father, he will seek to be like him. This is a two way street, of course. If the father is a poor administrator of his own moral life, then the boy may also be similarly lacking but in general, the presence of a larger FIKI counterweight to the boy's own has a limiting and beneficial affect on a young man's impulses.

A family is not merely a legal arrangement but a planetary community of souls. The binary sun of this community is the parents. Yes, a family will have light with only one parent but it is a half light. Our educational thinkers and social planners have made a terrible blunder. They have bought hook, line and sinker into the notion that Americans are all rugged individualists who have little or no need for family or group support. Sorry, but teens are voting with their feet. They would rather belong to a rugged group than be rugged individualists. If schools and family do not provide teens with a hearty and powerful self image, they will seek it elsewhere!

> A good teacher affects eternity.
>
> ◆
>
> —Chinese Proverb

The growth of gang membership is directly proportional to the failure of our public institutions to provide leadership, guidance and discipline. If schools don't touch children morally and physically, they will seek this toughening elsewhere. Where there are gangs, there are schools and families in a state of moral disintegration. Do not confuse this with economic disintegration. They may be related, but one is not a requirement for the other.

TEACHING DICK MANAGEMENT

Dick Management likewise begins with the notion of belonging. You belong to eternity and any moral code that you adopt must be something that enables you to deal with your own need for acceptance by the

Divinity. A moral code, much like a gang code, tells you what you can and cannot do. It tells you who you should "hang" with and who you shouldn't, how you should act and how you shouldn't. A moral code is the code of God's gang.

Teenagers learn or don't learn the Art of Dick Management from adults. If you or the teachers of your children are not managing their dicks, chances of your children doing so are slight. In order to teach teenagers a moral code, you must:

- First have a code! Do not expect them to automatically become moral with no help.
- Secondly, techniques for mastering the code must be taught.
- Provide disciplinary action for breaking the rules of the code.
- Make teens feel secure in their environment.
- Provide a teacher or leader for the process.

One of the most powerful techniques for teaching Dick Management to teenagers is the concept of the mental diet introduced by Emmett Fox in the 1940s. A mental diet consists of putting your mind and your ASS on a diet. If you want to lose weight, you must do three things: eat better and less, move and breathe. Likewise, if your ASS or your thinking in general is bloated, fearful, lewd or vicious, you must put it on a diet. That means that you must learn to control the kinetic energy of your thoughts by managing the energy that flows to your ASS. For example, if you are overly fearful or paranoid, you must simply stop allowing such thoughts to take up residence in your mind. Easier said than done but the attempt must be made, otherwise you will be ruled by your fears.

This is how such a mental diet works: For seven days you must not allow yourself to entertain any negative thoughts—of any kind. Everything you allow yourself to think about must be positive, constructive and kind. If you succeed for a few hours and then fail, the clock starts all over again! This will probably be the most difficult exercise you will ever practice but the rewards are astonishing. After a week of this exercise, your mind will be supercharged with both positive thinking and abundant energy.

The reason this diet really works is that your mind and your ASS operate on the same principle that computers operate on—GIGO—garbage in, garbage out. The most ancient of all metaphysical laws is that you become what you know or do. In the realm of excellence this is most obvious. If you want to become good at doing anything, you must practice and practice and practice. Likewise, if you entertain negative or violent and shameful thoughts all the time, why should you be surprised if negative, violent and shameful things happen to you? The most powerful effect of this exercise is that it forces you to disconnect from your ASS. For high school students this is probably one of the single most salutary exercises to practice—even for one whole hour! Think of it as a vacation from your ASS.

A NEW PARADIGM FOR PUBLIC EDUCATION

Schools must stand for something. They must make students proud and happy to belong. They must have a value system that is not an expression of the typical "all values are equal" paradigm. A school that does not have strong moral principles and good discipline is busy unraveling education at the same time it is trying to provide it. It is practically impossible to present education as value-free information. Students weigh all the information you give them and assign it a value regardless of how neutral the presentation!

What did the founders of our modern day system of secondary education create? A sanitized education system that few respect and that now functions as a breeding ground for teenage monsters. Boys who seek to impregnate as many girls as possible, and who communicate with knives more readily than with words are the legacy of our present system. Young women who think their bodies are public playgrounds and their children as disposable as condoms are engaging in more violent acts than ever before, if we are to believe the most recent statistics of major news sources. FIKI rules! This situation is unlikely to be remedied anytime soon without a public philosophy or a non-denominational moral code.

The Buddhists have an interesting concept that provides us with some mental leverage to understand the process of transformation that a public moral code could bring to the individual and society. The concept is *dana*, an act of sacrifice that allows the *dayaka*, the giver, to glimpse a higher state which assists in the transformation of consciousness. The sacrifice that a young person can make by doing violence against their own unruly appetites through metacognitional acts of virtue is indeed just such a form of dana. Those who are busy waging war against their own inner animals have little time to be bothering others. The cultivation of metacognition is the first step on the path to both ethical and moral thinking. Metacognition also signifies the awakening of each soul to its universal and yet unique character and mission.

What America's schools desperately need is a public moral philosophy that incorporates concepts such as locality, non-locality, virtue and compassion. Such a moral philosophy must begin in grade school and continue through high school and college. Without such a public moral code there will be little need for any hell created by God. We will have created one here on earth, and far sooner than we think.

A rational society, be it a corporation or a country, can only maintain itself if personal responsibility and accountability are at its core; that is, from top to bottom, every agent or citizen must be empowered to conduct her or his role and to be fully accountable for its performance. To the extent that this is done, there is order, freedom, efficiency and progress, but when personal accountability is diffused, the ultimate result is license, confusion, backbiting, and finally a frightening and destructive anarchy. As Plato wrote in The Republic, in such a society "even the dogs become arrogant."

—James L. Fisher, *The Baltimore Sun*

MANAGEMENT TIPS

• If you have children in a public high school, ask an administrator to explain the difference between morals and religion. The answer may surprise you and help guide you in your choice of schools.

• Sexual harassment is nothing new. In the old days this was known as lewd or immoral conduct. Insist upon discussing harassment issues in terms of a moral code.

• If you suspect your children are using drugs, take them to a drug rehabilitation center and talk to recovering addicts.

• If any of your teens have a proclivity towards excessive violence take them on a tour of your local state penitentiary. A visit can be arranged with the warden's office. It doesn't work for all teenagers but for some it can be an illuminating experience.

• Challenge your kids constantly. Make up mini-programs with teenage boys, for example, to be kind to one person a day that they don't like, or have them quit masturbating for a month. This is very difficult for many teenagers. You will have their attention!

CHAPTER 32

FROM BOYS TO MEN

*It is terrible to see how a single unclear idea, a single formula without
meaning, lurking in a young man's head, will sometimes act like an
obstruction of inert matter in an artery, hindering the nutrition of the brain
and condemning its victim to pine away in the fullness of his intellectual
vigor and in the midst of intellectual plenty.*

—Charles Sanders Peirce, *Chance, Love and Logic*

WHAT IS A MAN? WHAT IS A BOY? HOW DOES A BOY BECOME A MAN? IF
the difference between a man and a boy is limited to job description,
genital activity or body size, then we are in for trouble. If the difference
between a man and a boy is the degree of wisdom which each may have
respectively attained, then perhaps we have a landmark by which a path
of moral development might be outlined.

We are all children at one time, and during this period, a common
experience is running smack dab up against what we feel like doing, and
what our parents will or won't let us do. The parental "No" is a paradigm
in miniature of the larger "No" that according to many psychologists gets
internalized as the super ego. Whether you call this super ego, or wisdom
of the core-self, we must all attempt to regulate our appetites and passions
or, upon dying, return to quantum reality without ever having discovered
who we really are. The ability to say no to some of our desires, and to step
back into the metacognition of our own non-locality is the beginning of
wisdom.

If there is one message that I take from the story of Adam and Eve, it is
that each of must learn to say "no" to something in our lives—and that
something may sometimes be very desirable. Wisdom teaches us how to
deal with this paradox.

Prudence is "the ability to govern oneself by the use of reason." This
means that you govern yourself with your dimensionally interactive
cyber-kinetic mind and not your cyber-kinetic ASS. Prudence in this

respect is a species of wisdom but what does this really mean? Wisdom is always prudent but it is prudent only because it is deeply connected to something else and it is this something else that professors of Ethics and Theology sometimes forget. Only a person can be prudent or wise and the essence of personhood is found in the soul, which abides in the divinity, as an image of something greater than itself. The core self is the most highly advanced consciousness that we have of the soul's superluminal identity. It is for this reason that wisdom in the form of prudence mirrors the knowing and metacognitional character of the core self.

Wisdom is one of the overall goals of all teaching, from parent to child, from educator to student. How can we infuse the education system with the process whereby wisdom is attained? At present, education is founded upon the notion of information transfer, i.e., knowledge is something that is taken out of box A in a teacher's mind, and placed into box B in the student's mind.

Real education involves formation. Forming minds, hearts and wills so that students will acquire and digest information on their own creates psychic independence. No amount of information by itself will create emotional maturity, or lead to reflection and considerate behavior. Some of the difficulty is located in the concepts that we use to describe our psychological landscape. Maturity, for example, is a nebulous term. We all have some sense of what it means to be mature, but the process is socially undefined, and clearly hit or miss.

> Perhaps the most valuable result of all education is the ability to make yourself to do the thing you have to do when it ought to be done whether you like it or not. It is the first lesson that ought to be learned and however early a person's training begins, it is probably the last lesson a person learns thoroughly.
>
> ◆
>
> —Thomas Huxley

There can be a terrible range of social failure for those who never mature. Young people who die early from violence and drugs are on the same continuum with those older citizens who may be psychologically destroyed by continuing to burn their candles out at both ends. Both young and old alike can fail in the most basic human project of all—the acquisition of wisdom. Economic and social enterprises can suffer the same fate. ASS-dominated economic systems that treat human beings as economic production and purchasing units without reference to morals in either the larger or smaller picture are themselves immature and contribute to social decay by being incontinent institutions. This failure to cultivate wisdom is symptomatic of a culture that does not understand the distinction between, and need for, intellectual, moral and spiritual excellence.

The fundamental ability to step back from our desires and impulses and take a position of calm (but not passive) observation is rooted in something greater than our local conception of ourselves. The stepping back is not just stepping "away" from something, as in saying, "No" to incontinent behavior, rather the stepping back is a standing up (the Tibetan kun long) into something that is just beyond our ability to mentally grasp. Call it atman, core-self, dasein, ka, quantum entity, soul, spirit, thetan, cyber or non-locality, but whatever it is, the development or awareness of it is at the root of what we loosely call maturity. What is maturity if not the beginning of prudence, justice, courage, and the self-restraint of continence?

We must develop the psychic technology, of which Dick Management is a precursor, to clearly show young people how important virtue is—some way of initiating psychomaturation or soul development. There is yet another wonderful concept in Buddhism that specifically refers to the awakened heart and mind. The term is *bodhicitta*. The individual with an enlightened heart and mind is radiantly forgiving, thoughtful, kind, fair, brave, intelligent and serene. Do we not seek bodhicitta for our children and ourselves? Do we not all wish to have awakened hearts and minds? Note how very useful it is even to have such a term. There would appear to be no such concept in common use within our western culture and the reasons for this should not surprise us. If there were no being to be awakened or enlightened, then indeed such terms would be useless. The implicit idea of modern culture presupposes enlightenment as a result of freedom. Freedom is one of many conditions for enlightenment, perhaps the most important but to equate freedom with appetitive freedom is a modern day spiritual amnesia.

Western institutions and particularly academic life seems to attract NDMs and spiritual amnesiacs. The situation has grown so intolerable that some of these NDM's and amnesiacs refer to the great intellectual repositories of Aristotle and Plato as products of "dead white men" as if somehow Western culture was being held back from a glorious future of appetitive indulgence by the dead hand of the past. The reality is unfortunately exactly the opposite: the dead hand of the present is the inner reptile that seeks the freedom of FIKI. We see this dead hand all around us from Kosovo to the Congo. There is hardly a country that has not felt its scourge—from the inner cities of the West to houses of government throughout the world—ASSES ride upon the shoulders of men whose ancestors tended at least to be aware that they had ASSES. Welcome to the new world; it may well be ruled by Non-Dick Managers (NDMs) who really won't give a rat's ass about you or anyone else. The time has come for Dick Management. Will the world go the way of the Dick Manager or the NDM? The moral choices that you make will help bring one of these worlds into being. A responsible world full of light and happiness is waiting to be born but in the shadows, the big ASS of Mother Nature lurks.

The answers to life's mysteries require serious thought and reflection. The educational lives of all human beings cannot be relegated to the moral indifference of testicular neo-primitives. A new rite of passage with ceremonies that embody truths of self, sexuality and moral conduct needs to be developed for our young people, so that their true selves might be revealed rather than obscured. Family has to be understood as part of a much larger organic or ecological relationship between all of being, rather than just immediate biological or tribal kinship. We are here to create a work of art, and are called to unity with our fellow men and women as part of a larger cosmic family that goes beyond much of what we can imagine. Elucidating a metaphysics of self-discovery and developing the social structures to accommodate teaching this truth to all of Earth's people is the task of the Third Millennium.

Who are you? You are God stuff. You have tremendous freedom and unbelievable power but you are like a tortoise that is afraid to stick its head out of the shell for fear of what might be outside. Your ego is merely the carapace of the larger reality that you are, and learning to manage your dick is the first of many steps towards discovering who you really are.

The warrior aristocrats of Japan were known as Samurai, and the chivalric code of honor by which they lived was *bushido*. Bushido is martial virtue that by our standards is excessive but the notion of such a code, whereby honor is held sacred is very close to what is required in order for men and women today to obtain and hold fast to wisdom.

The ancient Chinese had a similar but more forgiving system called Li, the Way of Heaven. The Way of Heaven is only open to those who seek wisdom, cultivate decency and manners and accept the good counsel of others. Virtue, as a concept is in itself the Way of Heaven. Similarly and for Aristotle, practical wisdom was a quality of mind concerned with things just and noble for man.

MANAGEMENT TIPS

- Patience is a way of stepping forwards in time.

- Thoughtfulness is a way of consulting non-locality.

- Kindness is a way of stepping into non-locality by being generous.

- Fortitude helps you hold fast to your moral convictions.

- If you desire maturity and wisdom, you must plumb the depths of your soul.

CHAPTER 33

A QUEST PROGRAM FOR
HIGH SCHOOLS

Gravitation cannot be held responsible for people falling in love.

—Albert Einstein

HAVE YOU EVER NOTICED THE FINE LINE BETWEEN DOING NOTHING, AND purposeful activity? What is it that makes someone choose goals rather than choosing to do nothing at all? Sometimes the simplest things make a huge difference. One of these things is to care about what kids do with their lives. Young people know if you care or do not care. What you are serious about they will pay attention to. This does not mean they will immediately change their behavior, but what you are concerned about hangs in their consciousness like a lantern.

Young people have a desperate need to be noticed and to contribute to the needs of society. We must have a rite of passage, some ritual coming of age that would be preferable to gang-fights, graffiti making, casual sex contests and general juvenile delinquency. Why don't we take some of the money that is being spent on a variety of useless or outmoded public school courses, and create character development, or psychomaturation programs? A world-class council made up of the elders of many different cultures and military training officers might design these programs. Although this might seem like an unlikely mix, each group has centuries of cultural experience in developing rites of passage.

An awareness of the five core values of wisdom, justice, courage, self-restraint and compassion might also be developed through a participation in Outward Bound or military boot camp programs. For lack of a better label, let us call this the Quest Program. This program might work as follows:

PHASE ONE: THE QUEST

All high school students would be required to study Aristotelian ethics, the history of religion and quantum psychodynamics (a science that like Dick Management studies the relationship between particle physics and psychology). The First Amendment would not be violated because no religion in particular would be established or favored.

PHASE TWO: THE DELPHI ANALYSIS

The motto of the Oracle at Delphi was: "Know thyself." At the beginning of the junior year, each participant in the program would be required to analyze himself or herself in relation to one's understanding of the moral virtues and pick ways in which each might be more courageous, self-restrained, wise, just, compassionate and more aware of their non-local connection with the universe at large. They might also focus on the obstacles to the attainment of such knowledge. Rather than list all the vices as Aristotle does we might look to Buddha's five obstacles for a simple summation of the obstacles to inner knowledge: craving, ill-will, laziness, restlessness and doubt. Such things leave us wide-open for a full scale ASS infestation of consciousness and do not cater to the development prudence.

A knowledge of personal virtue and the obstacles to higher consciousness can also make civic virtue a possibility—the Greek *sophrosyne*, which was moderation, self-discipline, and self-sacrifice on behalf of the common cause. We tend to forget that a society is composed of individuals and that when more, rather than fewer of those individuals are self-regulating and creative, the better our society will be as a whole.

An outline of a program similar to the Delphi Analysis is found in the Buddhist *Eight-Fold Path*[39] which Lama Surya Das lists as follows:

Wisdom Training
Step 1. Right View
Step 2. Right Intentions

Ethics Training
Step 3. Right Speech
Step 4. Right Action
Step 5. Right Livelihood

Meditation Training
Step 6. Right Effort
Step 7. Right Mindfulness
Step 8. Right Concentration

Clearly and in order to understand the "right" anything we must have a system that outlines moral values—in short a moral schematic of virtue and vice. Without such a schematic or moral code, there will be little grasping of the "right" at all. Your ASS wants freedom without responsibility. Have you ever watched spokespeople for the motion picture industry blandly stating that there is no evidence connecting bad behavior as seen on TV and at the movies, and some of the bad behavior we see on the streets? There is actually plenty of evidence that TV influences behavior. Studies done by Johns Hopkins University conclude that television can and does affect children adversely.[40] One of the most striking examples (unfortunately not cited by this study) is that for years, hold-up artists used to bash people over the heads with guns and clubs in an attempt to knock them out.[41] In reality it is much harder to knock someone out than it is on TV, but where do you think the hold-up artists got this idea? Can you imagine asking a coyote if it might pose a danger to the chickens? Students know that there is a connection between what they see and what they want. If bad behavior is glamorized by the motion picture industry, you can be sure that there will be some young people who will want such glamour. This is why it is terribly important that students have a moral system to evaluate what they see and hear. Ignorance limits choices and obscures the dimensions of moral responsibility.

Most students thoroughly enjoy discussing moral and social issues, and questions regarding the nature of virtue are excellent points for discussion. Even though this might seem a bit simple, the mere raising of moral issues *as if they mattered* can be beneficial. Asking the right question can be half the distance to an answer. If moral issues are not brought up in school when or where might they be brought up? Under a program like the Delphi Analysis, each student might be required to help develop his or her own one-year program for self-improvement in conjunction with an established program structure. This might involve community service, boot camps or even participation in athletics, drama or the martial arts for those who would not ordinarily play sports.

PHASE THREE: THE RITE OF PASSAGE

At the end of their junior year, participants would be required to declare and defend their moral or religious beliefs. They would also be free not to have any beliefs or to profess their ongoing confusion. A student could just as easily profess atheism or agnosticism, as well as profess belief in various Buddhist, Christian, Hindu, Jewish, Moslem or other sects. The point is that they would have *the opportunity to declare an affiliation,* to choose a moral or religious code after three years of study, and publicly defend their position. This rite of passage would be a more formal way of joining the adult community than by simply graduating from high school.

An alternative and probably more acceptable rite of passage—given our cultural and historic disinclination for public religious instruction—might be to construct a learning program around the discovery of the inner self, with emphasis being placed on describing non-local experiences, including those of athletes "in the zone," as they relate to the discovery of the dimensionally interactive core-self. (The Twelve Steps of Dick Management could be integrated into such a program.) The guides and teachers for these courses would be responsible for allowing students to pass or fail in much the same way that a Zen master observes that a student has attained or not attained enlightenment.

PHASE FOUR: AWAKENING AND GUIDANCE

Seniors would be responsible for conducting the Quest Program as associate guides in conjunction with teachers. This would give them valuable teaching experience and be an excellent example to the younger students.

The most extraordinary result of such a program would be astonishingly simple. By giving students a moral framework from which to conduct their thinking, the overall tonality of consciousness would be changed from simple moral floundering to at least a level of intelligent inquiry and boundary making. By giving young people a moral map, the moral and metacognitional equivalent of literacy might be achieved.

A life of virtue, it should be pointed out, is one with many ups and downs, lapses, "left trips," and mistakes. A life with virtue as a goal is a life tending to virtue.

—B.A. Boone

MANAGEMENT TIPS

• Politeness and manners are a way of limiting eruptions from the ASS.

• Boys who make graffiti are probably not the kind of friends you would like your daughter to go out with.

• Get boys to manage their dicks and they will be better able to manage destructive impulses.

• Are guns another way of expressing the intentions of your genitals?

• "Road Rage" and short temper in general indicate poor Dick Management.

CHAPTER 34

EVERY WOMAN IS
A DICK MANAGER

In our approaches to woman, and when we come into contact with her,
we are enveloped in a sort of indistinct glow if illumination—the instinctive
feeling that a new world awaits us and is about to develop in the depths of
matter—if only we fold the wings of spirit, and surrender ourselves to it.

—Pierre Teilhard de Chardin

THE IMPORTANCE OF WOMEN IN THE DICK MANAGEMENT PROCESS cannot be overstated but not for the obvious reasons. Women are psychologically closer to non-locality than men. What we call women's intuition and that mysterious depth that many of them possess are signs of something very different from male consciousness. For this reason, women are able to inspire many a man to reach beyond the limitations of the focused three and four-dimensional consciousness that is characteristic of male thinking. Every woman is a front-line Dick Manager, and it is time that we honor this truth with the appropriate social structures. Women need to take an ever larger role in the ethical formation of men. Indeed, men are desperately in need of this instruction.

We take it for granted, for example, that we all have mothers. It is one of those things, like breathing, that is a given. What is not appreciated is that for most of us, our mothers are part of the first line of defense against FIKI. Don't mothers first teach young toddlers the rudiments of self-control by teaching them not to be selfish and to share? Haven't many mothers saved younger siblings from beatings and even death at the hands of out-of-control fathers and brothers?

The managerial capacity of women regarding the containment of male sexuality is the sine qua non of civilization. A society that does not respect women as the first mentors of human beings and revere young girls as potential mothers is rotten to the core. The present social insanity that equates motherhood with the lowest elements of the job ladder is symptomatic of a dick infestation of social consciousness. Those who have dicks always assume that the truly important work of life can only be done by them—as if bearing cocks conferred the right to sit endlessly in front of the television or abdicate help with important household tasks. Only a dishonest man can assume that staying home with children is easier than whatever job it is that he might have.

It is essential that marriage be seen as more than simply a contractual genital exchange. It is a pledging of souls whereby a man must turn violence into vigilant self-defense, and surrender his hunting and sexual instincts to the service of wife and family—in short, to the glorification of Being. A man who cannot understand the danger that the ASS presents to a marriage has no business getting married. Ninety-nine percent of all spousal abuse is rooted in an inability to grasp the danger of an unregulated cathection to FIKI.

Remember, wisdom is the ability to perceive inner states and energy links that are either appropriate or inappropriate. Prudence is required to deal with inappropriate cathections to drinking, smoking, violence and excessive sex.

Everyone is more or less aware of the vast influence that female spouses have on their male counterparts. Everything from common household management to finances, to education and advice (both social and political) is dispensed by a man's "better half." Unfortunately, this contribution is looked upon as somehow secondary to the male's contribution! This is of course a male bias but it is rooted in a common devaluation of the woman as a Dick Manager. Even as coarse a fellow as Larry Flynt, publisher of *Hustler* magazine, recognizes the innate power of women: "It's not money," he said, "it's not politics—it's who controls the pussy that controls the world." It goes without saying that this control should be in the hands of women, and not in the hands of men who would snatch it away from them.

Women are Dick Managers of the first order, and the failure to recognize and honor this fact only results in an impoverishment of the status of females everywhere. The No or Yes of a woman to sex should be rooted in an understanding of what it is she in fact wants from a man. If sex is all she wants, then that is probably all she will get. If she wants more, it is imperative that the sifting and sorting process be applied as soon as possible, without excessive sexual involvement, in order to find the best mate.

Many of the differences between the sexes are based on differing perceptions of the meaning of sexuality. Female emotions regarding sexuality are more closely aligned to the true meaning of sexuality. For example, a common experience of casual lovers everywhere is a certain boredom with partners to whom we have no intention of committing ourselves. There is a deep instinct on the part of both sexes to absolutize relationships i.e., to make them take on the characteristics of permanence—even if they are not in fact relationships that will or can endure.

Every sexual relationship involves a compromise between what we are seeking for our future in a life-partner and what we want as far as short-term pleasure is concerned. This is the *love ratio*, a formula written in the heart. The recognition of this proportionality, or ratio of deep future-oriented desire, to short term fulfillment is one of the enduring conundrums of human existence. We constantly find ourselves accepting less than we deeply want—whether it's out of insecurity, or for the sake of something more temporary, and perhaps more immediately gratifying. The aversion many individuals experience after a one-night stand is an almost universal characteristic of the love ratio—even if we are in a gloating mood over conquest or the excellence of the sex. We know what feels right, and what feels funkily out of proportion. In this way, we all pay homage to what we may not even believe on a conscious level.

> **P**erhaps the profoundest liberation achieved by a happy and lasting love-affair is the liberation from wandering lust.
>
> ◆
>
> —John Cowper Powys, *The Meaning of Culture* (1929)

Women are perhaps, in a deeper way than the male, more non-locally or intuitively cognizant of the love ratio, and are not as quickly swayed by their hormones as the FIKI-driven males. Nonetheless, the female equivalent of Dick Management is required for the ladies. Let us call this delicately, Y Management. The principles of Y Management are parallel to those of Dick Management, with the differences related more to energy processing and style, rather than substantial differences. Women's role in the aggravation of FIKI needs to be considerably examined. A resident scholar at the American Enterprise Institute, quoting a federal judge, raises this issue rather elegantly: "Every woman has a right to assume that the workplace is not a brothel and that, when she enters it, she will meet nothing, see nothing, hear nothing, to wound her delicacy or insult her womanhood."

He goes on to say, "But suppose working women were to wear deliberately enticing clothing, the sort of stuff that men might expect to encounter in a brothel? Asking men to restrain themselves in this situation

might be asking too much. Would it not be fairer to ask women to restrain themselves?"

It is extraordinarily difficult to raise this issue in an egalitarian sexual
culture that assumes that sexual differences between men and women are
purely volitional or patterned after some sort of malleable social contract.
The specter of FIKI as a condition that haunts male sexuality is one that
prudent women everywhere would be wise to take into account when
making their selection of wardrobe. It is the combination of male and
female self-restraint in this regard that makes for civil relations between
the sexes. One might wish that it were otherwise, that there were some
other explanation for male violence and incivility other than FIKI, but
the preponderance of everyone's common experience is entirely to the
contrary. By taking into account the biological differences between men
and women and employing the judicious moral perspective afforded by
Dick Management, a very different and beneficial understanding of the
relations between the sexes might be arrived at.

The single greatest difference between men and women is that
women are paradoxically much closer to the force side of the consciousness-force paradigm than are men. It is a bit of a joke in all cultures how
hard women must work, and how much work and energy they must put
into maintaining the level of organization that family life requires to pros-
per. Women have access to enormous force, and the Women's Movement
is emblematic of women everywhere seeking to recover their ancient
cosmic birthright. Beyond all the high charged rhetoric of "equal rights"
is the primordial equality of the sexes as exemplified by the dynamics of
Yin and Yang. There is no ultimate inequality in the overall energy
dynamics between men and women—they are, as most sensible people
will observe, just different.

Men are noisy consumers of energy. We might call this the Shiva aspect
of male consciousness. Shiva is the second God of the Hindu trinity, also
known as the Destroyer. (Brahma is the Creator and Vishnu is the Pre-
server.) The best example of energy broadcasting and "destroyer" energy is
to be found when men get together in groups to play sports, go to war or
to "party." Men collectively produce waves of energy that can give the
group a high, in addition to tearing things apart. You may have heard of
the joy of battle, pack behavior or even of crowd energy in sports. This is
Shiva energy, although a perceptive observer might simply want to think
of this as the energy of a group of assholes.

Conversely, when women get together, the energy can be collectively telepathic or empathic in a very powerful way. In both cases a kind of group mind is produced. Unfortunately, group mind can be extremely negative for both sexes when it results in mob political gatherings, character assassination, gang rape and armed conflict, but it can also be extremely positive. Collective enterprises such as corporations or businesses can also emerge from such energy pools. Dick Management can be a powerful tool to manage group consciousness by limiting the violent potential of group mind. A crowd of Dick Managers is a well-behaved crowd. A visit to a monastery, for example, can bear powerful witness to the management of destructive impulses by cyber-kinetic knowledge under religious auspices.

A very serious problem for society to consider is the Non Dick Manager. Take a stroll down any city street and observe Dick Managers and NDMs, and then catalog their behavior. DMs are usually polite or at the very least, considerate. NDMs, on the other hand, can be as violent as packs of hungry dogs, or as obtuse and noisy as hogs rooting in garbage.

Families also represent an energy collective. The energy of mother, father and children creates its own group identity. This is also a way of understanding the dynamics between the negative earth energy, Yin and the positive energy of Yang. Which is the more powerful? Electrons are negatively charged—uh oh. The battle between the sexes is far from over!

The dynamics of sexual management for both sexes revolve around the way energy is processed, and even though men and women have similar sexual management issues, both sexes are required by circumstance to deal with the process differently. For instance, the female capacity for multiple orgasm indicates that a different energy storage and release mechanism is at work in women than men, but this is a topic for another book.

Despite sexual management differences, the proper and balanced relationship between a man and a woman is the basis of hearth, home, community and the proper functioning of civilization in general. The importance of parents' roles in society-building is only now being reflected upon by responsible social scientists. Dick Management is a vital tool in this process.

"My name is Laura Kate, and I am a slut. Pardon me, I am a recovering slut."
That's how Laura Kate Van Hollebeke began her titillating missive last July to
Dr. Laura Schlessinger, the nationally syndicated, moral-preaching radio shrink.
The blond-haired, blue-eyed 26-year-old Bremerton landscape gardener went
on to tell the good doctor that she'd simply had it with sex. She would never
again climb into bed with a man until the prerequisite "I do's" had been
pronounced before a priest. To make a long story short, Schlessinger, laughing
delightedly, read the letter to her faithful millions over the air, and everyone
went gangbusters. Now a militantly chaste Van Hollebeke is hop scotching
about extolling the virtues of her new Born-Again Virgins of America club, all
the while pedaling a line of "Sexless in Seattle" T-shirts. Talk-show hosts are
eating it up. The other day, Van Hollebeke, the animated and highly theatrical
product of a large Catholic family, talked about her conversion to celibacy... It
came after a long series of unfruitful sexual adventures. "Oh I loved the sex, and
I was pretty promiscuous, a really bad girl," she said, her face scrunching from
frown to smile, smile to frown. "I really enjoyed it, yeah. It was great for about
10 minutes, anyway. But I'd wake up the next day and I'd have this feeling of
emptiness. I felt I wasn't getting anywhere, that it was stunting my growth."

—Ellis E. Conklin, "Born-Again Virgins..."

MANAGEMENT TIPS

- If you like to sleep after sex, what does that tell you about energy usage?

- Sleep in separate beds occasionally so that your energy is not always commingled with your partner. You will probably sleep better, have better sex, and appreciate your beloved even more.

- Feeling like beating off? Clean your closet, wax your car. If the urge persists take a cold shower.

- When all else fails, beat it.

- Put down that toilet seat. It is a small but powerful sign of respect for women.

CHAPTER 35

MARRIAGE

If the sign of life is in your face. He who responds to it will feel secure and fit. As when, in a friendly place, sure of hearty care, a traveler gladly waits. Though it may not taste like food and he may not see the fare or hear a sound of plates, how endless it is and how good!

—Lao Tzu, *The Way of Life*

ONE OF THE MOST FEARSOME AND USEFUL SOCIAL INVENTIONS OF ALL time is marriage. Many men routinely tremble at the prospect of limiting their love horizons to just one woman. Marriage represents a serious form of deprivation to your ASS and it will usually try to avoid this unpleasant obligation. Marriage is the non-local tutor that many men fear the most, and even though some of us have a sense that we need to get married at some point in our lives, we are frequently not sure what to do with this knowledge. Now it is not true to say that all men fear marriage, but it is one of those things that in our culture is almost universally attributed more to men than to women. Women seem to intuitively understand the utility of marriage and usually work diligently on the man of their choice, until all opposition is broken.

Marriage is commonly thought of as a ceremony performed by a minister or civic functionary, but this is an incomplete view. The minister, priest or rabbi is only a witness to a non-local oath that is engendered by the couple itself. What is unique about marriage is that it is a public sharing of a private bond. But what does this bond consist of? Promises and covenants are only part of something much larger. If we think of men and women in terms of the positive and negative charges of a magnet, then we begin to understand how the two sexes create energy just by being in each other's company. Electrons flow when the positive and negative pole of a magnet or a battery are brought into proximity with one another or linked. Marriage is taking this positive and negative energy exchange and subsequent flow to a higher level. Couples who simply choose to live together enjoy some of the benefits of this DICK exchange but not all. Marriage brings an extra set of benefits that living together does not.

THE WAY OF THE TAO

The Tao, in its ultimate sense, is the Way of God; to be connected to the Tao is to be connected to God in a higher dimensional way. Rationally speaking, it can be argued that if God exists then it would be inconceivable for He, She or It not to wish the highest good for humankind. This highest good, described from a Confucian perspective, is the *Way of Li* (the moral duties of the individual to society which are rooted in the Tao) and would be described as moral and spiritual virtue from the Western perspective of Natural Law.

The Way of the Tao is easier to understand, if we bear in mind Aristotle's notion that all things seek to imitate the perfection of the Unmoved Mover. This perfection causes all things to want to be like God. This desire to imitate what is better is at the root of all personal transformation and is the lodestone of the soul. Concepts such as the Tibetan *Kun Long* (the standing up of the soul in its own moral consciousness) or Heidegger's *Dasein,* which is non-existent Existence (doesn't exist out of any matrix) reflecting on its own derived existence as soul and signification in time and eternity, are ultimately reflections of a profound desire on the part of all things to imitate their Source. We can change for the better because we are called from all eternity to imitate that which is perfect and free of all suffering and strife.

The way of the Superluminal Tao, Unmoved Mover (if you prefer that term) or Divine and Eternal Entity is the royal road to consciousness, and it is completely free. There are no hidden charges but you must discover what it is you must imitate before you can actually imitate. This discovery of what is imitable in Divine Law is the basis of all Natural Law. The codified aspect of the law, or as William Blake describes it, the religion of Caiaphas, is not the Way, it is merely a reflection of the Way. Despite their imperfections, natural law constructs such as the Ten Commandments and religious codes of conduct, other than direct revelation, point in the right direction!

> **M**arriage draws a man and woman into the current of eternity.
>
> ◆
>
> —Fr. Tony X

MARRIAGE CONNECTS YOU TO THE WAY OF THE TAO

A proper marriage is one in which a couple finds themselves in the presence of an invitation from the Way. It is nonverbal and many couples find themselves truly surprised at what the Way offers them. How many times have you heard that: "He or she was not what I expected but it has been wonderful none the less." One individual described his experience of this invitation as a dream about an enormous green wave. He knew implicitly that he had the choice to take a ride or not to. He chose to surf the wave and married a woman who completely changed his life and the lives of many others in the process.

The true meaning of marriage is found in the non-local sharing of the life energy of another, and in the acceptance and forging of a different future as a new entity open to the non-locality of the Tao. Marriage is the public declaration of this sharing. This is why some marriages are such a headache. If the life energy of Yin and Yang cannot be properly shared then there can be no real marriage. Given the generative powers of the soul, marriage without children may involve a restriction of its capabilities and may be destructive, if its life energy has no other outlets—such as commitment to political, religious, and social causes, adoption and volunteerism in general.

Marriage is really a form of channeling —you literally allow the future to come through you. Marriage is not just about companionship and who pays the bills or who makes the meals. We get so focused on the biology and the social mechanics that we forget that each child connects us non-locally to thousands of generations and events in both the past and the future. That future has an impact in the here and now as the core-self will make adjustments in the present for futures you cannot imagine.

> For God mingles not with humanity; but through Love all the intercourse and converse of God with humanity, whether awake or asleep, is carried on. The wisdom that understands this is spiritual.
>
> ◆
>
> —Diotima of Mantineia, one of Socrates' female instructors

Marriage should also not be viewed as only a license to have socially acceptable sex. Marriages of this sort are really not much better than arrangements made to live together. Remember that the life force is constantly seeking its own balance and truth. Permissive sex, poor marriage choices and casual habits of masturbation will derail your efforts in this regard.

WHAT HAPPENS WHEN TWO PEOPLE MAKE LOVE

The exchange of Chi in sex involves far more than just screwing. Have you ever noticed how sex frequently depletes men and seems to enliven women? Imagine this: you have just finished having wildly satisfying sex and you are ready to pass out and—your wife or girlfriend is eager for energetic conversation and afterplay! Where do you think she gets this sudden burst of energy? She gets it from you—she just received your Yang energy! Women transform a man's local Yang Chi energy and give some of it back to him in the form of non-local Yin Chi. The ego boosting, moral support and character influencing that women are rightly famous for comes from this most elemental of energy exchanges. This is why copulation is ecologically superior to masturbation. You get some of your energy back!

The real reason that marriage is one excellent form of Dick Management is that Chi requires channels to transmit itself properly. Your life energy and that of your spouse creates an interlocking directory of psychic channels. Your life energy flows into her and she takes some of that energy and gives it back to you non-locally. Practitioners of yoga refer to this female/male energy conversion principle as *shakti*.

Shakti is the female aspect of Dimensionally Interactive Cyber-Kinetics. Shakti creates binding energy in relationships. This is why if a woman gives up on a relationship it is really over. If you create shakti bonds without marriage, both partners can give away more of themselves than they may be aware of. This is one reason that break-ups with long-standing sexual partners are problematic—you have already created non-local bonds and channels that are not so easily dissolved. Dividing the furniture and deciding who gets the cat is the tip of a huge iceberg. This may be a source of much pain, and certainly may distract you from your life path.

Two persons joined in marriage or sex become an entity that alters the future fabric of quantum reality. The ankle bone is connected to the leg bone up and down the time-lines of past, present and future. Additional energy is created by the merging of Yin and Yang through the Dimensionally Interactive Cyber-Kinetics of love. The commitment of marriage involves an act of will from both parties that enables them to merge. Without the commitment, there is no merging, and no real energy for personal transformation.

One of the core tasks of all human beings is to find an appropriate marriage partner and to have an improved moral, spiritual and intellectual package to bring to that relationship. The failure to do this, or to abuse this core task, will result in many deviations from the future that is calling to you. Remember, your soul knows the future as part of the quantum continuum. Discipline and self-reflection are required to know and discover consciously those things that the core-self already knows implicitly.

For some people, cohabitation works; but it is not the same as marriage. Research suggests that cohabiting women are more than twice as likely as married women to be victims of domestic violence, and more than three times as likely to suffer depression; cohabiting partners tend to be less sexually faithful and less likely to invest together. Partnership is less durable than marriage, which shouldn't be surprising. Marriage, after all, is much more than a legal certification of a pre-existing relationship; it uses a thousand subtle social mechanisms—like rings, weddings and joint invitations—to help bind couples together.

—Jonathan Rauch, National Journal for *The Wall Street Journal*

MANAGEMENT TIPS

- Apologize for past transgressions sexual or otherwise. Don't worry about how much time has passed. Ask for forgiveness.

- Be quick to apologize for present transgressions. Don't let the sun go down on your anger, as they say.

- Tell your spouse or lover that you love them because you or they may not wake up in the morning. Life is a gift.

- Get married and say yes to children. They are a gift.

- Buy yourself some new underwear.

CHAPTER 36

BEATING SPEARS INTO WANDS

*Living, said Plato, is likewise an art, and the soul's unique function
is the art of living. Comparing the art of music with the art of living,
Plato saw a close parallel, for in both cases the art consists of recognizing
and obeying the requirements of limit and measure.*

—Samuel Enoch Stumpf, *Socrates to Sartre*

YOU HAVE COME A LONG WAY. YOU HAVE DISCOVERED YOUR ASS, LOOKED at your dick from a metaphysical angle and you have taken the PECER Test. You have learned a different way of thinking about energy and morals and you may have become aware of the Dick Manager. You are delighted that much of your energy comes from your balls and that continence can provide you with a bracing moral tonic. Your mind is brisk with a new confidence instead of crouching like a confused armadillo in your trousers, but occasionally, you wonder, "When am I supposed to use this thing?" "Surely," you think, "I can't be required to sit on all this energy until I explode."

There are several ways of looking at the problem of excess energy accumulation. Sublimation is one way of channeling excess energy into productive pursuits but your ducts won't be satisfied with this for long. Your dong wants to be about its business! Masturbation is one way of keeping your spear comfortably balanced but as we have seen, masturbation is a dead end—all output and little input—too much of it and your navigational skills are impaired!

Aside from a periodic self-service adjustment, your love spear is looking for a target. In this respect your dick functions as a homing device and notifies your ASS when you have achieved the proper coordinates. For example, you have discovered a woman who is receptive to your advances. The lady is clearly in your sights, your ASS is confirming "crotch lock" and—what is that warning buzzer that is going off? You have just discovered what happens when your dick moves from spearing mode in four dimensions to magic wand rotation in five dimensions and above. Your dick has intersected with another level of reality and you have to deal with this or ignore it. Sadly, once most of us have achieved "crotch lock" we are unable to pay much attention to our conscience, which, in this example, is simply our own higher dimensional awareness (metacognition) of both our relationship with our bodies and the bodies of others.

You are the spear balancer and you must disarm your ASS driven dick whenever warning signals are present. This is of course much easier said than done but it points to a fundamental dichotomy in the will. Your will goes out to all things that appear as "good" (it looks good doesn't it?) in three or four dimensions but it simultaneously sees and apprehends higher goods in a metacognition of five dimensions and above.

This is why you must cultivate the metacognition of your higher self. What strengthens this self or soul are choices and subsequent modes of action that are dimensionally higher based than those of your body. This is very difficult to do because what you want in three and four dimensions does not automatically go away simply because you are merely aware of a higher dimensional choice.

Many people have difficulty with the concept of higher dimensional beings but when it comes to managing yourself in higher dimensions, you need a dimensional partner—an angel or a deity—someone who knows the territory. When we find ourselves in a higher dimensional state where we feel that we are losing our grip on what we need to do, or find that the ASS is taking us for a ride, we need help! The natural reaction is to call out for help but the answer does not come in three or four dimensions— the answer comes in a higher dimensional form. So you must pay keen attention to what you are instructed to do. Whatever the Superluminal or your higher self instructs you to do, or not to do, you will know the instruction in your heart.

This is where the art of living cannot be fully circumscribed by a moral code. This is not to say that your ethics will become situational but that your ethics will be a function of who you are and who you are seeking to become. Your higher self is by its nature an ethical entity but it is not a fool either. It knows its own reality in the blinding light of the Superluminal and what it sometimes wants may be puzzling—even to you. Your higher self, as the master of Cyber-Kinetic Knowledge, knows what to do. You must however:

• Pay attention

- Be honest
- Keep trying
- Don't give up
- Exercise patience

Your soul ultimately know where to go and how. For example, when the right person for marriage is located, a wonderful synchronicity occurs. Your Yang meets her Yin and your higher self tells you that this is your new home. Your Appetite Survival System suddenly finds that it has a new set of priorities and something that satisfies its requirements for food, sex and defense. Welcome to marriage, a time-honored practice that allows your Appetite Survival System and your dick to make peace with one another.

Your ASS as an instinctive entity and tireless advocate of **Non Dick Management** seeks to propagate itself indiscriminately. Your Cyber-Kinetic self, on the other hand, is much pickier. It seeks the ripeness and fullness of a spouse and children that are well-loved. That is what it does best and that is what you want on the deepest level of your being. An associate described lovemaking where children were produced as the most satisfying sex he has ever had—indeed, part of the excitement of fathering illegitimate children is that your dick is hungry for its piece of the future! See that you do it right. Future generations depend on you.

There is a God. It is more than an ultimate reality. God is an ultimate reality that makes moral demands of us. To me, the essence of God is the sense of moral obligation. I am disappointed in what I see as the consensus of New Age religion, which depicts God as a source of energy that we can tap into. This moral concept—this sense of the Covenant, that God will hold up his end of things and keep the world running smoothly only if we will hold up our end of things and behave like human beings instead of animals—that whole dimension is missing from it.

—Rabbi Harold Kushner, from *Tying Rocks to Clouds* by William Elliott

MANAGEMENT TIPS

- You may catch yourself thinking about some future event, only to notice after several minutes that what you were thinking just happened. You just had a mental shift into non-locality.

- The experience of Deja Vu is frequently a non-local shift of consciousness.

- If you are really disturbed about something and can't figure it out—watch out for a continuum shift! Sometimes the continuum shits on you.

- Simply by listening to someone—and without injecting your own thinking into the situation—may enable you to receive all manner of non-local information about that person.

- With practice, shifting your awareness can become as simple as shifting gears in a standard transmission.

CHAPTER 37

SURFERS OF THE TAO

Man is a god in ruins.

—Emerson

IS IT POSSIBLE TO LIVE YOUR LIFE AS IF IT WERE A WORK OF ART INSTEAD of a glorified assembly line towards economic or spiritual salvation? Are we not, each one of us, larger than any system of thought, belief or religion that we may belong to? Sri Aurobindo Ghose, the great Indian philosopher and mystic of the mid-twentieth century, once said that all experience—no matter how terrible or wonderful, feeds the development of the higher self. It is almost as if there were someone else watching and observing us—someone unafraid, calm and intensely interested in our reactions to things. This detached, multi-dimensional observer is the soul, the atman, the quantum entity, the Buddha nature—in short, the spiritual self that has been waiting for you from the beginning of time. Is this not who you really are? Your ultimate identity can only be found in the Superluminal who made your soul out of its own generous and eternal self-knowledge. You are at your core, an information and energy construct based on the Superluminal's own knowledge of Itself as Existence, Consciousness and Bliss. You are like Them and They want you to be ever more like Themselves. This is a tremendous gift that is worth frequent reflection.

Go to the beach on a sunny day

From a three and four-dimensional perspective God appears to be singular but from a higher dimensional perspective, God is multiple—higher still and God is singular again—a great mystery. So don't be confused by my use of God as They or God as Him—I am simply trying to get at the enormous richness of the Divinity.

and gaze upon the ocean. Let your thoughts dwell on the Mother of this earth. Look into your heart. There is someone there beside you. Who do you think that is? Do not be afraid. It is you and the Father of this you. Walk together and do not pretend that either of you does not exist.

If there is anything that religion and ethics in general can be accused of it is of being perhaps too slow to enable human beings to recognize who they are. The metacognition of the soul is hardly adverted to except by way of the bogeyman of conscience. Almost by default, the religious or ethical person comes to know himself or herself accidentally in the process of living, and then their real identities are constantly filtered through a system of thinking that may or may not allow them to discover inner riches. This is not to say that your religion or your beliefs should be automatically discarded, but you are not your religion or your beliefs— these are all things that *you* are engaging. Your only real identity is found in the Divine and if your religion or your beliefs take you into a real relationship with this entity, then they are good for you. If they don't bring you closer to the Divine, then try something new!

God doesn't care about your faults as much as you do. He sees the bigger picture, sees where you are and the direction you are taking. This is what God is concerned about. Do you think that God does not enjoy Himself? He/She/It wants the same for you, but you have to be very aware that when you are called to do something that is other than fun, you must be prepared to give up your pre-conceptions of how life should proceed and follow the dimensional pathways laid down for you. The Buddhist *Law of Dharma* is the embodiment of this truth. Dharma is not the blind acceptance of either Gods or doctrine; it is rather an acknowledgement that the right way to live one's life will help lead to the enlightenment of other human beings, and is a declaration that each individual has a unique opportunity to discover this essential truth. Dharma is the road of the gods and ultimately, when enough human beings get on this road together, the world will be transformed forever. Those on the dharma way can help build a superluminal bridge between Heaven and Earth. Whatever your dharma or life's purpose is; only you can discover it, and only you can live it. No one else can live it for you and ultimately, no one else can make it happen for you—except by way of the living example and grace of his or her own dharma.

The Divinity doesn't need you to live your life for the sake of any rule external to Itself. You may need rules to keep yourself in line but if the Divine wanted mindless followers, such could be had with a snap of the fingers. What God wants is the one thing that you can give back—your free allegiance to your own dharma. This is not to say that moral relativism is God's calling card, but rather, that the Divinity wants sons and daughters who are partners in the great Dharma of God's own Existence, not slaves. Your participation in any religious or ethical system of belief must always bear this in mind, otherwise

> What is freedom for? To know eternity.
>
> ◆
>
> —Theodore Rothke

you can end up chasing phantoms or worse, persecuting those who don't share your beliefs. You have the power of the infinite within you. Be careful of what you allow yourself to believe. You have the power to believe in falsehood but you also have the Eternal's desire for truth.

Remember that morality is the language of your soul's dharma. Learn to speak this language. Above all, listen to the voice that will speak in the heart of your being. This metacognitional voice stands only in the truth. It cannot be anywhere else and neither should you. The truth really will set you free but as someone once observed with great accuracy; it will first piss you off. There is only one person you can really be angry with on an on-going basis and that person is yourself. Nobody but you can ruin your life and you can do this in as many imaginative ways as there are to blame others, rather than yourself. No more excuses. You have the tools you need now to chase down your life force's ASS and not take any more nonsense from it. Your ASS at its worst is lazy and at its best it awaits further instruction from its master—you. The words of Marcus Aurelius are good to recall here:

As surgeons keep their lancets and scalpels always at hand for the sudden demands of their craft, so keep your principles constantly in readiness for the understanding of things both human and divine; never in the most trivial action forgetting how intimately the two are related.

How can we model the idea of cultivating virtue as an art, so that we have a more useful idea of how wisdom really operates and how we may or may not behave? I like the metaphor of surfing. Surfers always try to ride waves that are much more powerful than themselves. They practice their timing and balance carefully, so that when the big one comes they can hop on board and go for a great ride. Listening to God, practicing virtue and managing your dick are like surfing. There are a lot of forces in your life that you will never be able to fully control but with the right balance, management and timing they can be your ticket to destiny. You need a long stiff board to ride those waves. Keep in mind that an undeveloped and weak DICK won't get you anywhere! Surfing the Tao requires that you be a human being with great moral and spiritual qualities. With God, the surf is always up and the waves are wonderful! This is the Way of Heaven.

The purpose of human life has been revealed. The vastness created these human circuitries in order to have an experience of itself that it couldn't have without them. Through this humanness, the substance we are all made of has an opportunity to love itself—and the love of the infinite for itself is awesome. The words "love," "bliss," and "ecstasy" only begin to describe the hugeness of the infinite's appreciation of itself that occurs through these circuitries.

We are all in this together. We are all made of the same infinite substance, and when a number of circuitries are consciously participating in the infinite simultaneously, there is a substantial increase in the volume of the love the infinite experiences for itself. This is the power of what has been called community. The wondrousness, the love, the ecstasy, the bliss of the infinite is constantly increasing as it surges within itself and amplifies the ecstatic love it has for itself out of itself.

—Suzanne Segal, *Collision with the Infinite*

MANAGEMENT TIPS

+ Behave as if you had only one day to live.

+ Have you ever seen or touched love? Belief, like love, cannot be touched or weighed.

+ Fantasizing can create nets in your soul. Don't allow yourself to get trapped in them.

+ The next time you feel like yelling at someone, remember that there are many ways to disgrace yourself.

+ You only have a partial idea of who you are. Who you are to become is part of the great mystery and adventure that is life. Treat yourself with reverence.

THE MILLENNIUM CODE

*Wherefore my counsel is that we hold fast to the heavenly way
and follow after justice and virtue always, considering that the soul is
immortal and able to endure every sort of good and every sort of evil.
Thus we shall live dear to one another and dear to the gods, both while
remaining here and when, like conquerors in the games who go around
to gather gifts, we shall receive our reward.*

—Plato, *The Republic*

THE WORLD NEEDS A MORAL CODE THAT IS APPLICABLE TO ALL PEOPLES
and that will serve as a basis for cultural development. The Millennium
Code, like the Code of Hammurabi or the Ten Commandments, is a simple statement of principles now and for the next millennium.

1. Existence is the non-local origin of all that is.
2. All things return to the superluminal reality of Existence.
3. Your ego will die. This is the basis for the mystery of life.
4. Moral law is based on the Divine's eternal knowledge of who
   you are.
5. The family is the first school of the soul.
6. Responsibility and accountability are based on a hierarchy of
   moral and intellectual values. These are the values of your soul.
7. There are eleven moral values that defend against the excesses
   of the Appetite Survival System: Courage, Self-Restraint
   (Continence), Liberality, Magnificence, Magnanimity, Honor,
   Compassion, Friendship, Temperance (with respect to pleasure),
   Truthfulness and Justice.
8. There are five intellectual values that help us to access and grasp
   truth: Science, Wisdom, Understanding, Prudence and Art.
9. Vice is the doorway to entropy and to evil.

10. Truthfulness, honor, happiness, and respect for life are the hall-
marks of the awakened soul.

We must not be afraid of the future. We must not be afraid of man. It is no
accident that we are here. Each and every human person has been created in
the image and likeness of the One who is the origin of all that is. We have
within us the capacities for wisdom and virtue. With these gifts, and with the
help of God's grace, we can build in the next century and the next millennium
a civilization worthy of the human person, a true culture of freedom. We can
and must do so! And in doing so, we shall see that the tears of this century have
prepared the ground for a new springtime of the human spirit.

—John Paul II, Speech to the United Nations

AUTHOR'S POSTSCRIPT

For thirty years I have been fascinated with the idea that God, if He exists (and I believe He does) must know about each and every one of us from all eternity. Clearly this does not mean that we exist from all eternity, for to exist means to "come into being" and if we aren't alive, well we really haven't come into being—at least not in the ordinary sense of the word. God's Being however, is a different story. If we are to believe two very influential philosophers, Aristotle and Aquinas, then we must say that an idea in the mind of God *is* God. God, you may recall, has no moving parts or any kind of time affecting his Being. Therefore, an idea in God's mind isn't something that floats about waiting to be grabbed as ideas tend to in our minds. The mystery is how God can know anything and not make it be in some relation to Himself. We might say that un-created is as good a relation as any but is it really? The dignity and value of our personhood can only reside in an eternity that is from all time. Otherwise, we will have no firm footing on which to establish the moral and spiritual values of the human person. Without the objective value of eternity, your values are no better than those of a cannibal, or for that matter, a pederast. The whole hideous carapace of politically correct and equivalent values collapses under the eye of eternity and enduring values.

Let us not pay lip service to eternity or to God. You are special because you have sprung from no less a mind than God's. He has known you from before the beginning of time and certainly before being in the womb. Let us honor God as the great giver of life from all eternity and not merely as a Deity who spits out beings into time as the whim presents itself. Being, no matter how small, takes on the force of Divine origin in a metaphysic that recognizes our pre-existence in the splendid fabric of God's own Being. The medieval philosopher Duns Scotus refers to this as the *ens diminutum* or "little being." This little being, I argue (without referring to it as such) in *How to Manage Your DICK: Destructive Impulses with Cyber*

Kinetics is the ka of the Egyptians, the atman of the Hindus, the Buddha nature of the Buddhists, the soul of the Christians and the higher self of the New Age movement.

Recent developments in multi-dimensional theory make it possible to consider for the first time that God's foreknowledge of His creation makes it possible for the higher self of beings to pre-exist in a multi-dimensional universe in a way that earlier philosophies could only barely conceive. Why should anyone be concerned about this? It is my belief that our own unique identities and values are intimately bound up in God's knowledge of Himself, and that if we can understand this unusual relation between creator and created in a non-sectarian fashion, we might end centuries of moral, philosophical, theological and even political confusion.

A number of closely related metaphysical questions have played in the background of my life over the years like some sort of strange and persistent music: does God enjoy His, Her or Its Being and if so, how would this concept of an indulgent God affect the development of moral ideas? What does God's energy have to do with our life force energy, and vice versa? How does the perception of God and self relate to how you treat others and what you do with your sexuality? What does it really mean to be immortal? *How to Manage Your DICK* is an attempt to begin to deal with these speculations in a fresh way. These are not old questions, as they have been raised by philosophers and religious founders as diverse as Lao Tzu, Buddha, Socrates, Plato, Aristotle, Jesus, Avicenna, Aquinas, Duns Scotus, Aurobindo, Heidegger and Wilhelmson. They are, however, at their root revolving around metaphysical and moral realities that do not admit pat answers no matter how clever or learned the source of those answers. How you chose to investigate such questions are part of the art of living and will determine how poorly or how well you live your life.

As a child of the nineteen-fifties and the first son of an immigrant Irish physician, I was raised in a strict Catholic family. Pleasure was viewed as a form of self-indulgence and often times as an obstacle to the salvation promised by the Catholic Church. Growing up in the nineteen-sixties I, like many others, had some difficulty in understanding how happiness in a future life after death could be solely contingent on a set of moral actions achieved or not achieved in the here and now. The link seemed to me to be purely one of faith. As I grew older, I desperately wanted to understand how moral actions were rooted in the now, and how they affected me in the present and not tomorrow.

The truth that kept presenting itself to me over and over again, in daily experience was that morality was a life and death issue: that what I did or did not do in the here and now had an immediate impact on how I felt about myself and behaved towards others. There was no escaping the fact that the content of my character rested squarely on whatever moral and spiritual values I adhered to. Looking for some sort of universal rule to apply to traditional religious ideas, I began to feel that a morality and religion that did not address the issue of how moral actions affect us in the present was deficient, and any religion so disposed was on its way to the graveyard of history.

One of the most extraordinary experiences of my life occurred while I was in Rome, as an undergraduate for a semester abroad. I rediscovered the sacrament of Confession in St. Peters one day, while wrangling with myself as to whether or not it was worth doing. I decided that if I was having an internal dispute about its validity that the best way to solve this dispute was to go in and try it. I did and never felt better. I had the feeling that some highly unusual spiritual technology was at work that didn't conform to the normal parameters of modern theological interpretation. What I discovered was that Confession made me feel better and gave me a tremendous energy focus. How was I to explain this in terms of modern psychology, which I was studying at the time? There was no explanation that did not involve reducing the experience to the realm of self-deception and psychic manipulation. The experience was real from my perspective and only a fool would deny the obvious benefits.

The theological explanation of God's forgiveness being extended through space and time in the person of the priest made perfect religious and mystical sense, but there was no scientific mechanism to explain how this happened. I was convinced that there was a mechanism. There may ultimately be a conflict between faith and reason but what I found was that ever ascending levels of explanation, while they do not exhaust faith, certainly go a long way towards providing intellectual comfort and rational parameters for belief. (In this belief, I take vast comfort in Thomas Aquinas' own assertion that there is no conflict between faith and reason.)

I felt at the time that the Catholic Church was not exploiting the richness of its own sacramental system, which operates on the supposition that the sacraments are modalities of Christ's presence. How present? The extraordinary failure of Catholic theologians, as a group, to properly dialog with the discoveries of modern physics struck me as being somehow lacking in creativity and intellectual curiosity. I had some loose ideas about how the sacraments might work from my childhood studies of Hatha Yoga but nothing that was coherent, aside from the suspicion that I was not being properly served by the hide-bound intellectual custodians of my religion.

I found myself frequently going to Confession over the years that followed—not only because I felt I had to but because I really felt better and more focused when I did. If I felt good doing it, why weren't more people taking advantage of the sacrament and indeed, why were so few priests "gung ho" on Confession? I came to the sad conclusion that either I was out of my mind or that Confession had fallen into disrespect because so many priests and members of the laity were either unrepentant meat beaters or sexually active in other ways. If one doesn't have to go to Confession for sins of the flesh, then why indeed go at all?

I remain astonished to this day that the practice of hearing Confessions on Sunday which was fairly common up the mid nineteen sixties was largely abolished by self-serving administrative fiat on the part of the clergy. The rationale was that it was somehow liturgically improper to be conducting several sacraments at once and that one should not be distracted from the glories of the Mass. This unspeakable piece of liturgical nonsense has been responsible in no small part in its own way for the decline of Confession and ultimately, of the Church itself. The reality that prompted the change is that declining membership in the priesthood has made the offering of Confession on Sunday more difficult. The other side of this admittedly difficult situation, however, is the sheer laziness of some clergymen who can't be bothered to take the time required to hear confessions or to be hearing sins that they themselves may be guilty of.

I had an extraordinary experience of priestly negligence, in this regard, one day many years ago in Washington D.C. I was last in line for Confession when the priest suddenly came bustling out. Where are you going? I asked after the wind of his cassock. "I have an appointment," he hurriedly replied. Indeed. Where might he have been going? Did he need to take a dump, attend a theology or sociology class, or visit his mother? "I have an appointment." "As if," as they say today. As if such a response was sufficient for his lack of spiritual courtesy. For all he knew this might have been my first Confession in twenty years but he had an appointment. Might he not have referred me to the rectory and hence to another priest? "When the Son of Man comes again will he still find faith?" I think not.

Sometime during the late nineteen-seventies while bored with a job that gave me some free time to read, I started to reread some of my old

290 How to Manage Your DICK

college philosophy texts and rediscovered for myself, the morality of Socrates and Aristotle. I was astonished to find that some of the basic concepts regarding virtue and self-restraint made immediate and intuitive sense to me at just that particular moment in time—something that had eluded me while I was in school. I had however been blessed with some extraordinary teachers at the University of Dallas in Texas where I spent my undergraduate and later, my postgraduate years in a Catholic seminary. One of them, Dr. Frederick Wilhelmsen, was so extraordinary in the range of his thinking, and particularly in the application of his metaphysical insights to human history that I shall be forever grateful to him. For whatever reason, the ideas he planted were to lie dormant in my soul for nearly ten years until I could grow into them.

As I continued to read books on metaphysics, I began to feel the need to go to some of the original sources and grasp meanings, which I suspected had been overlooked in Christianity's rush to destroy paganism. Once I started reading the original, albeit translated, texts of Aristotle without the utterly brilliant, yet sometimes obfuscating presence of Thomas Aquinas, I began to discover the outline of a common-sense moral philosophy with metaphysical implications that appeared to have been overlooked by both religion and science. Here, I thought was a calculus of morality, and indeed spirituality that made sense, rooted as it was in the concept of excellence as a mean to be discovered, relative to the individual and contingent on the limitation of pleasure and impulse. Here was my old Catholic morality but with an earthly twist!

To make a very long story short, I had rediscovered what generations of scholars have known for centuries, namely that the morality of Christianity (despite its own original and powerful achievements) is based on the far older morality and philosophy of ancient Greece. The critical difference between the morality of the ancient Greeks and the morality of Christians, in the most global sense, was that Christians took morality to be useful in the service of a post-life achievement award called heaven, whereas the Greeks, being practical fellows, only thought how to improve their lives in the here and now. The reality is, of course, not quite so simple but in practical terms. As Christian theology and ethics tended to move further away from its core belief in the metaphysical and spiritual power of Christ, the more it moved away from the raw nexus where the human heart engages spirit. Cold theologies that bordered on mathematical complexity of argument soon fell prey to those who would dismiss reason altogether. Faith without reason is as empty as reason masquerading as faith. One cannot filter God through the intellect like some sort of psychic teabag. One must expose oneself to the raw power of God as it falls upon us without respect for our personal belief systems.

I digress. Getting back to my little story... As time went on, I took metaphysics and theology as my intellectual starting point, and re-engaged a long-held interest in Eastern Philosophy. I found that ancient Greek morality in service of God and self brought me to an understanding of Catholic Christianity and morality that was very familiar but also very different. I found myself in two metaphysical camps at once. On the one hand, my metaphysical speculations were very New Age, on the other, my moral understanding found itself rooted in something much more traditional, yet tempered by the discoveries of modern science.

A lot of people reject Western spirituality for Eastern or New Age beliefs, but what I found was that the information contained in both systems enabled me to have a larger view of all the issues, and particularly, of the shortcomings of both Eastern and Western belief systems. Just as two legs give better balance than one, and having two language skills provides useful contrast for nuances of meaning, by having two separate metaphysical points of view, I was able to take a very different stand than one or the other would have afforded.

What was most extraordinary (and in hindsight) was the intuition that kept me coming back again and again to the same insights until I got them right, until the speaking of them engaged the greater reality of their origin. My own soul had been speaking to me all along under the guise of intuition, and the more deeply I dug, the louder was the voice of my spirit. I had begun to discover the living reality of my own spiritual presence and higher self.

One might intuit, for example, from the perspective of this higher self that if God is a very serious fellow, then morality will also be very serious business, but on the other hand, if God has a sense of humor and enjoys a good joke at both his own and our expense, then the moral terrain looks a bit different. If our God is a laughing God, then our morality will also be more playful, less focused on what we have done and more focused with good humor on what we should be doing. If this new moral vision were true, how could we possibly know it for sure? The answer can only lie in the direction and discovery of our unique cosmic and divine identity.

Jesus states that we are God's children. I believe this to be true. We are but what does this really mean in concrete terms? It means that we share our identity with an eternal Identity that has no beginning and no end. It means that we are known from before time began, and it means that we are related to God's own knowledge of Himself.

God's knowledge of Himself, as outside Himself, and the return of the all to the All is known in general, as the *Law of the Return.* The moral implications of this Law have never been properly examined from the perspective of energy management. The rules governing Dimensionally Interactive Cyber-Kinetics enable us to reconsider what morality, the Christian sacraments, and the spiritual practices of other religions mean in the larger scheme of things, as opposed to our evaluation of them in terms of our private prejudices.

Dimensionally Interactive Cyber-Kinetics allow us to consider God's grace from a scientific perspective. The Divine can and does affect our souls through spiritual forms of cyber-kinetics. If this affect and the subsequent effect within our souls is not real, or cannot be accounted for through some rationally postulated system of energy dynamics, then it is simply a theological metaphor accessible only by faith. Dimensionally Interactive Cyber-Kinetics allow us to look at God's existence and interpret our own existence in the light of His. We might surmise, for example, that if the Divine enjoys Existence, then we are probably here to do the same, although we, like the Deity Himself, may suffer in the process of honoring our life's task. Discovering life's meaning and participating in our identity in the Divine is the root meaning of Christianity and of all religion.

We are the immortal offspring of eternity. Immortality is not some sort of Indian giving that comes with religious strings attached—it is the utterly free gift of a Divine genius so far above and beyond our own comprehension that our attempts to link it to quasi-judicial accounting systems will always fail. I love the story in the New Testament about the vineyard harvest master who pays the latecomers as much as the ones who have been working all day, or the forgiveness and kindness to be extended even to one's enemies. This is so far removed from how we think things should be done as to be utterly laughable. God's justice is not our own and neither are His ideas for us concerning immortality and eternal fellowship with Him. God does not necessarily play by our rules and it is up to us to go with whatever Divine game plan is given us. Each one of us has a different stone to contribute to the mansions of eternity. The master builder delights in the diversity of His creation and the lines of His handiwork are multi-dimensional and beyond counting.

Zeus and the other Olympians never had it so good. Your identity in God is so startling and so original that if you encountered it on the street, you would probably fall down and worship yourself. This true self, immortalized by Shakespeare ("To thine own self be true.") and countless others, literary and religious is the source of both our strength and happiness. Discovering yourself is discovering a paradox. *When you truly discover yourself, you also discover God, but you are not God.* How can this be? An indirect answer is that God is both creative and playful. You are God knowing Himself as you, and that is part of a much bigger picture than your four-dimensional ego can handle. This does not mean, however, that you lift yourself up by your own hair in this life—far from it. You must encounter the Master of Entropy on His terms, not yours. Once you get that, you will be lifted out of the vast darkness of your own subjectivity into a light that has no end.

I'll give you a special clue to the mystery of life, although it is in the form of a question. Do you think God is waiting for you in eternity? If you do, think again.

The encounter with your true self and its peculiar relationship with God's eternal nature is part of the purpose of life, the source of all real happiness, and the denial or forsaking of it, the road to all unhappiness. One may not necessarily buy into the destination theologies of Heaven and Hell as promulgated by many religions, but the Dimensionally Interactive Cyber-Kinetics of spirituality are sound to the core. Your dick is part of a vast theological ecology. Let it render to God what is God's and render to ourselves what is ours.

Hopefully, the moral tools outlined in *How to Manage Your DICK* will help you to understand your own personal psychology and help you to deal with that part of you which does not want to be awake but prefers to sleep or sit on its ass. So saddle up and put on your mental spurs. The adventure is only just beginning.

SEAN O'REILLY
Peoria, Arizona

GLOSSARY

Appetite—Derived from the Latin *appetere* which means "to strive after."

Approbation—To approve or to sanction, and when used in relation to God's foreknowledge of things indicates that His knowledge of them precipitates their reality.

Apotemnophilia—An attraction to the idea of amputating a limb

Aristotle—(382–324 B.C.) sometimes called the father of metaphysics. He was a student of Plato and is considered the first truly encyclopedic mind of the ancient Greek world.

ASS—Appetite Survival System; an aggregate of evolved impulses and hormonal systems linked to the most primitive elements of the brain stem.

Atman—The indwelling divinity of the soul as described by the Vedas

Cathection—A concept developed by Sigmund Freud to explain the mechanism whereby the instinctual energy of the Id could be converted into psychic and other forms of energy.

Cathexis—The action of cathection in verb form

Chakra—A non-physical interface between higher dimensions and ourselves. There are seven chakras or centers of consciousness and energy that in Yoga theory and other eastern disciplines are linked analogously to major internal organs and human body structures. The heart chakra for instance governs the heart and emotions, while the third eye or the center between the eyes controls the thinking mind and higher functions. These connections are manifestations of the subtle soul or astral body.

Chi—Multidimensional energy

Cicero—Marcus Tullus (106–43 BC) Roman statesman, orator and moral philosopher

Compassion—This is the moral virtue that Aristotle refers to as gentleness but I believe that this is only a partial translation of Aristotle's original meaning. Compassion comes closer to what gentleness would mean inside the overall context of his thinking.

Continent—Exercising self-control in respect to impulses and desire. Distinguished from the virtue of temperance only by its focus. Temperance is self-control in respect to pleasure alone. Where continence ends and temperance begins is really only determined by the attention that the soul brings to bear on any cathection that it may be engaged in.

Core-self—A new age description of the inner being or higher consciousness

Dana—An act of self-giving that enables the giver to glimpse a higher reality

Dasein—The German philosopher Heidegger's word for Existence knowing itself as finite

Dharma— "Dharma means to be yourself as fully as you can, acknowledging that each human consciousness is a unique precious experiment in finding the way to the essential truth. It can also mean, as it does in the Buddhist tradition, the teachings and practices that can lead to self-realization...The dharma does not mean blind acceptance of this god or that doctrine; it is, rather, an acknowledgement that the right way to live one's life will lead to the enlightenment of all sentient beings and a declaration that each human being has a unique opportunity to discover that essential truth." Dharma is your life's purpose.

Divine—Of or pertaining to God

Ecology—A branch of science concerned with the interrelationship of organisms with their environment.

Ego—The sense of "I-ness." In Freudian psychology an identity derived from an instinctual source of energy known as the Id.

Eight-Fold Path—Buddha's steps to enlightenment have three levels of excellence and eight steps: *Wisdom Training*: Step 1. Right View, Step 2. Right Intentions *Ethics Training*: Step 3. Right Speech, Step 4. Right Action, Step 5. Right Livelihood *Meditation Training*: Step 6. Right Effort, Step 7. Right Mindfulness, Step 8. Right Concentration

Entelechy—The actuality or "end" which is the goal of all potential; that which potential is ultimately aiming at

Entropy—The Second Law of Thermodynamics; the *tendency* of all things towards a lower energy equilibrium, rather than a higher state of energy and order. All atoms and molecules tend towards randomness rather than order, and this randomness increases over time. This is commonly known as the Law of Entropy.

Envy—A vice defined as: painful or resentful awareness of an advantage enjoyed by another

EP—Energy Permission—Allowing life force energy to flow in any given direction

Essence—The ultimate or real nature of a thing as opposed to its existence; that which existence posits in the realm of reality

Existence—That which exists in and of itself. Possessing existence through no other thing or essence other than itself

FIKI—Fuck It Kill It, a concept developed by philosopher Ken Wilber

Form—See the definition above of essence. Form is a synonym for essence.

Honor—A state of soul that accrues to those who practice virtue.

Hyperspace—Multi-dimensional space; the dimensions above four

Hyperspace Exchange—see ZPEX

Id—In Freudian Psychology, the source of instinctual energy in human beings

Incontinent—Unable to restrain or hold in

Ka—Ancient Egyptian concept of the soul or double

Kundalini—Serpent energy—In Hindu metaphysics, a source of life force energy located at the base of the spine; analogous to the Freudian Id

Kun Long—A Tibetan word which in English is like a participle (an "ing" word) that means to thoroughly awaken or to make stand up from the depths, a person's whole heart and mind. This is what the higher self does when it engages locality from the perspective of higher knowledge.

Leptons—A category or family of subatomic particles of which electrons are members

Life energy—The energy of the soul as it manifests in life

Local—A description of four dimensional space time (height, length, width and time)

Memes—Social viruses, snippets of information and feeling that seek to reproduce in your mind; positively speaking, a meme can reinforce good habits. On the negative side memes can cater to vice.

Mindfulness—A state of mind characterized by a focus in the present and multiple levels of awareness.

Natural Law—A body of law or specific principle held to be derived from nature and deemed to be binding upon human society.

Negentropy—The "winding up" principle of the universe as opposed to the "winding down" principle of negentropy.

Non-Local—A synonym or description of hyperspace

Ontological—Pertaining to being and its attributes. Being as opposed to non-being or actuality which is not-yet-being.

Plato—(427–347 BC) Considered to be the father of Western political science; the teacher of Aristotle.

Practical Wisdom—Practical wisdom is the quality of mind concerned with things just and noble and good for man

Prime Matter—The kind of matter that Aristotle referred to as potentiality

Psychomaturation—The wisdom of the soul

Qi—Variant spelling of Chi favored by the government of China

Quantum—One of the many small increments or parcels that many forms of energy are subdivided into

Quantum Psychodynamics—A psychology of human consciousness based on quantum physics and the theory of hyperspace. See Endnote 31 for a further elaboration.

Quarks—A hypothetical particle that carries a fractional electric charge and is held to be a constituent of all subatomic particles

REC—Reverse Energy Conversion

Self—The union of elements (thought, emotion, physicality, etc) that constitute an individual's total identity

Shakti—The dynamic energy of a Hindu God personified as his female consort.

Shiva—The god of destruction and regeneration in the Hindu Trinity of Brahma, Vishnu and Shiva

Sin—An offense against God and man

Sine Qua Non—That without which

Singularity—Usually associated with black holes. A point in space-time at which space-time curvature becomes infinite

Sloth—The disinclination towards action or labor; in theology, the neglect of spiritual duties

SM—Soul Memory

Sophrosyne—Moderation, self-discipline, and self-sacrifice on behalf of the common cause

Soul—The immaterial essence, animating principle or actuating cause of individual human life, sometimes referred to as the oversoul in New Age literature

St. Augustine—(354–430 AD) Bishop of Hippo, author of The City of God and considered to be one of the theological Fathers of the Catholic Church

St. Thomas Aquinas—1225–1274 AD. Author of the Summa Theologica. Known as the Angelic Doctor of the Catholic Church due to the profundity of his teachings

Standard Model—A theoretical construct that governs a set of axioms regarding modern physics. It states that all matter is composed of six leptons and six quarks. These particles are thought to be 100 million times smaller than the atom. The best known of these particles is the electron.

Stoics—A member of a school of philosophy founded by Zino of Citeum around 300 BC. Maintained that the wise man should be free of passion, unmoved by pleasure or pain and be obedient to natural law.

Strong Force—One of the four elemental forces of physics: The others are: 1. Electromagnetic energy (electricity, light, radio waves, etc.) 2. Gravity (this particle remains elusive) 3. Weak Force (exchanges between electrons and other particles) 4. Strong Force (exchanges between quarks) The strong force might be thought of metaphorically as Chi or Qi.

Sublimation—The psychic process whereby the energy of instinctual desire or impulse is converted into other forms of satisfaction

Substance—In Aristotelian metaphysics, the combination of matter and form

Super ego—In Freudian Psychology, the internalized precepts of parents and society

Superluminal—Faster than light

Superluminal Negentropic Energy Transfers—Energy transferred from non-local space into local space at faster than light speed. Chi may be one manifestation of such transfers and evolution another.

Supermind—According to Indian Philosopher Sri Aurobindo, Supermind is the consciousness of the Divine making itself manifest in human affairs and in the individual enlightened mind.

Superstring Theory—According to this theory, all matter is a manifestation of the activity of superstrings or vibrations of energy from the fifth to the twenty-sixth dimension. Superstrings that are theoretically *hundreds of billions of times smaller* than subatomic particles are caused by nearly incomprehensible movements in these dimensions.

Tachyons—Mass-less particles that theoretically can travel faster than light

Tao—Anglicized variation of Ta-Hua. Ta-Hua makes every modality of being in the universe a dynamic change rather than a static structure. A piece of stone, a blade of grass, a horse, a human being, a spirit and Heaven all form a continuum. They are all integrated by the pervasive Chi (vital force and material force which constitutes both matter and energy) that penetrates every dimension of existence and functions as the constitutive element for each modality of being. (Mircea Eliade, *The Encyclopedia of Religion*)

The Law of the Return—All things return to the All, i.e., all things come from God and then return to God.

The Way—A metaphor referring to the Tao or Ta-Hua

The Way of Li—In Confucian teaching, the moral duties of the individual to society as understood from the metaphysical perspective of the Tao

Trans-quantum—Beyond or above the quantum order of physics

Trans-Quantum Entity—God or gods

Urge energy—The Chi of appetite or urges. This is energy with quantum and kinetic values.

Venus Paradigm—Love of truth brings us closer to love itself

Vice—Habitual bad actions that bring us bad results

Virtue—Habitual good actions that bring us good results

Wave-Form—A way of describing energy

Weak Force—See definition of strong force

Wisdom—Ability to discern inner qualities and relationships; insight and good sense

YY Ratio—Yin to Yang ratio; a metaphorical measure of actual energy to potential energy. Imbalances can create physical and mental problems.

Zero Point Entity—God

Zero Point Exchange or ZPEX—The dimensional nexus between four dimensions and the twenty two higher dimensions of hyperspace. Some of the energy from the collapse of quantum waves passes through this point into our four dimensional universe

ACKNOWLEDGMENTS

THANKS TO: MY WIFE BRENDA FOR BEING ONE OF MY BEST CRITICS, AND TIRE-lessly putting up with the many hours and obligations that this book indirectly dumped on her, James O'Reilly for his numerous creative and scurrilous con-tributions to the text, Tim O'Reilly for critical evaluation, Wenda Brewster O'Reilly for jump starting the cover, Frederick D. Wilhelmsen for his startling vision of reality and fabulous teaching style, George Simon for being George and Etienne Gilson for mapping the scholastic territory; Jo Ann Deck and Phil Wood for catching the vision, Larry Habegger for wrestling with the manu-script, Tara Weaver for the permissions work, and Diana Howard for her crea-tivity; Fr. Edward Berbusse, SJ, Peg Balka and Amy Greimann Carlson, Steve Gagnier, and Michael Ghiglieri for vetting the text in its early stages, Raj Khadka, George Wright, David Yeadon, Dennis Helming, Hans King, Andi Beckham, Sean O'Reilly, MD, Mrs. Anne O'Reilly, Frank, Maggie, Kate, Anne Mary, Clement, Seumas, and Reverend Seumas O'Reilly, Father David O'Reilly, Liam, Tobias, Declan, and Joan Marie Shenandoah O'Reilly, Edward Vieira, Peter Ginelli, Jennifer Leo, Cynthia Lamb, Kathleen Meengs, Fred and Kathy Phelps, Wayne and Dee Hendricks, the University of Dallas Department of Psy-chology, Haviv Schieber, Bert and Beatrice Hernady, Tracy Baumgardner, Alicia Robertson, Susan Conlin, Mike Reilly, and Mark Schwartz for the great T-shirt. I would also like to thank the Lorton Penitentiary, Luke Air Force Base, Arizona State University West, the Sleeping Lady Retreat and Conference Center, Thun-derbird University, and Estrella College for the use of their facilities. A special thanks to the staff at Ten Speed Press. There are also many authors whose think-ing vastly increased the range of my own. I've listed some of them and their works in the section at the back of the book entitled, Recommended Reading.

Speed Bump by Dave Coverly copyright © 2000 by Creators Syndicate, Inc. Reprinted by permission of Creators Syndicate, Inc. www.creators.com

Selection from *Courtesans and Fishcakes: The Consuming Passions of Classical Athens* by James N. Davidson copyright © 1997 by James Davidson. Published by St. Martin's Press, New York, and HarperCollins Publishers, Ltd., London.

Selection from *Life and Death*, by Andrea Dworkin. Copyright © 1999 by Andrea Dworkin. Reprinted by permission of The Free Press, a division of Simon & Schuster.

Selections from *Tying Rocks to Clouds: Meetings and Conversations with Wise and Spiritual People*, by WIlliam Elliott. Copyright © 1995 by William Elliott. Reprinted by permission of Quest Books, a division of Theosophical Publishing House.

Selection from *An Outline of Psycho-Analysis*, by Sigmund Freud. Copyright © 1949 by W.W. Norton & Company. Reprinted by permission.

Illustration by J.B. Handelsman from The New Yorker. Copyright @ 1998 The New Yorker Collection from cartoonbank.com. All Rights Reserved.

Selection from *Selected Non-Fictions* by Jorge Luis Borges. Copyright © 1999 by Maria Kodama. Reprinted by permission of Penguin Putman.

Selection from *Among Warriors: A Woman Martial Artist in Tibet*, by Pamela Logan. Copyright © 1996 by Pamela Logan. Reprinted by permission of The Overlook Press.

Illustration by Lopez from the Oct 11, 1999 issue of The New Yorker. Copyright @ 1998 The New Yorker Collection from cartoonbank.com. All Rights Reserved.

Selection from *On Aggression*, by Conrad Lorenz. Copyright © 1963 by Dr. G. Bortha-Schoeler Verag, Wein, English translation by Majorie Kerr Wilson copyright © 1966 by Konrad Lorenz. Reprinted by permission of Harcourt Trade Publishers.

Selection from *The Way We Lived: California Reminiscences & Songs*, by Malcolm Margolin. Copyright © 1993 by Malcolm Margolin. Reprinted by permission of Heyday Books.

Selection from *The Biology of Violence: How Understanding the Brain, Behavior, and Environment Can Break the Vicious Circle of Aggression*, by Debra Niehoff, Ph.D. copyright © 1997 by Debra Niehoff. Reprinted by permission of The Free Press, a division of Simon & Schuster, Inc.

Selections from *Lila: An Inquiry into Morals*, by Robert M. Pirsig. Copyright © 1991 by Robert M. Pirsig. Reprinted by permission of Bantam Doubleday Dell, a division of Random House, Inc.

Selection from *The Meaning of Culture*, by John Cowper Powys. Copyright © 1929 by John Cowper Powys. Published by W.W. Norton & Company, Inc.

Excerpt from *Scepticism and Animal Faith* by George Santayana copyright © 1979 by George Santayana. Reprinted by permission of MIT Press.

Selection from *Integral Yoga: The Yoga Sutras of Patanjali*, by Sri Swami Satchidananda. Copyright © 1985 by Satchidananda Ashram. Reprinted by permission.

Illustration by H.L. Schwandron reprinted from the July 3, 2000 issue of Barron's. Copyright © 2000 by H.L. Schwandron. Reprinted by permission.

Selections from *Collision with the Infinite: A Life Beyond the Personal Self*, by Suzanne Segal. Copyright © 1996 by Suzanne Segal. Reprinted by permission of Blue Dove Press.

Selection from *How to Argue and Win Every Time*, by Gerry Spence. Copyright © 1995 by Gerry Spence. Reprinted by permission of St. Martin's Press, LLC.

Selections from *Socrates to Sartre* by Samuel Enoch Stumpf copyright © 2000 by Samuel Enoch Stumpf. Published by McGraw-Hill Book Company.

Selection from *Fear and Loathing in Las Vegas* by Hunter S. Thompson copyright ©1971 by Hunter S. Thompson. Published by Random House, Inc.

Ballard Street by Jerry Van Amerongen copyright © 2000 by Creators Syndicate, Inc. Reprinted by permission of Creators Syndicate, Inc. www.creators.com

Reality Check by Dave Whammond copyright © 1999 UFS, Inc. Reprinted by permission of United Feature Syndicate. www.comiczone.com

Illustration by David Williams reprinted from the June 12, 2000 issue of Barron's. Copyright © 2000 by David Williams. Reprinted by permission.

Selection from *Star Wave* by Fred Allen Wolf copyright © 1984 by Youinverse Seminars, Inc. Published by Macmillian Publishing Company.

RECOMMENDED READING

Aquinas, Thomas, (1948), The Summa Theologica, Benziger Brothers Inc., New York, Chicago

Aristotle, (1941), The Basic Works of Aristotle, translated by Richard McKeon, Random House, N.Y.

Aristotle, (1941), The Ethics of Aristotle, Carlton House, N.Y.

Aristotle, De Anima

Atwater, PMH (1996), Future Memory, Birch Lane Press, Secaucus, N.J.

Augustine, Saint, The City of God,

Bach, Richard, (1984), The Bridge Across Forever, Dell Publishing, N.Y.

Berlinski, David, (1995), A Tour of the Calculus, Pantheon Books, NY

Bloom, Howard, (1995), The Lucifer Principle, The Atlantic Monthly Press, New York

Bly, Robert (1990), Iron John, Addison–Weslely Publishing Company, Reading, Massachusetts

Brown, Tom, (1979), The Tracker, Berkley Books, New York, NY

Capra Fritjof, (1975), The Tao of Physics, Shambhala, Berkeley

Chia Mantak & Winn Michael, (1984), Taoist Secrets of Love, Cultivating Male Sexual Energy Aurora Press, New York, NY

Cicero, all of his books make for fascinating and informative reading

Das, Surya Lama, (1997) Awakening the Buddha Within, Broadway Books, a Division of Bantam Doubleday Dell Publishing Group, Inc. New York, NY

De Becker, Gavin (1997), The Gift of Fear, Dell Publishing, New York

Freud, Sigmund, (1960), The Ego and the Id, W.W. Norton and Company

Friedman, Norman, The Hidden Domain, 1997, The Woodbridge Group, Eugene Oregon

Gilson, Etienne (1949), Being and Some Philosophers, Medieval Studies Toronto, The Hague

Hall, James (1994), Sangoma, Touchstone Books, Simon and Schuster, New York, NY

Herbert, Frank, (1982), Dune, A Berkley Book, New York, NY

Kaku, Michio (1994), Hyperspace, Oxford University Press, N.Y., Oxford

Lama, Dalai, (1999) Ethics for the New Millennium, Riverhead Books, A member of Penguin Putnam Inc., New York, NY

MacIntyre, Alasdair (1984), After Virtue, Notre Dame Press, Indiana

Niehoff, Debra, Ph.D., (1999) The Biology of Violence: How Understanding the Brain, Behavior, and Environment Can Break the Vicious Circle of Aggression, The Free Press, A Division of Simon and Schuster Inc, New York, NY

O'Reilly, Sean, O'Reilly, James, O'Reilly, Tim (1997), The Road Within, Travelers' Tales Inc., San Francisco, California

Paglia, Camille, (1991) Sexual Personae: Art and Decadence from Nefertiti to Emily Dickenson, Vintage Books A Division of Random House, Inc., New York

Peck, M. Scott (1983), People of the Lie, A Touchstone Book, Simon and Shuster, New York

Peck, M. Scott, (1978), The Road Less Traveled, A Touchstone Book, Simon and Shuster, New York

Pieper Joseph, (1966), The Four Cardinal Virtues, University of Notre Dame Press, Notre Dame, Indiana

Plato, (1950), The Dialogs of Plato, selected by J.D. Kaplan, Pocket Books Inc., USA

Prabhupada, Bhaktivedanta, A.C., (1972), The Bhagavad Gita As It Is, Bhaktivedanta Book Trust, USA

Raymond Panikkar, (1968), The Unknown Christ of Hinduism, Darton, Longman and Todd, London, England

Rheingold, Howard, (1988) They Have a Word for It: A Lighthearted Lexicon of Untranslatable Words and Phrases, Sarabande books, Louisville, Kentucky

Rhodes, Richard, (1999) Why They Kill: The Discoveries of a Maverick Criminologist, Alfred Knopf, New York, NY

Solara, (1996), How to Live Large on a Small Planet, Star-Borne Unimited, Whitefish, Montana

Stumpf, Samuel Enoch, Socrates to Sartre: A History of Philosophy, 1966 and 1975, McGraw-Hill Book Company, New York, NY

Talbot, Michael, (1992), The Holographic Universe, Harper Perennial, N.Y.

Tipler, Frank, (1994), The Physics of Immortality, Anchor Books/Doubleday, N.Y

US Department of Justice, (1996), Crime in the United States 1996, US Government Printing Office, Washington DC

Vogelin, Eric, (1968), Science, Politics and Gnosticism, Henry Regnery Company, USA

Watts, Allan, (1957), The Way of Zen, Pantheon Books, New York, NY

Weinandy, Thomas, (1985), Does God Change? St. Bede's Publications, Still River, Massachusetts

Wilbur, Ken (1996), A Brief History of Everything, Shambhala, Boston

Wilhelmsen, Frederick, (1970) The Paradoxical Structure of Existence, University of Dallas Press, Irving Texas

Wilhelmson, Frederich D., (1970), The Paradoxical Structure of Existence, University of Dallas Press, Irving, Texas

Wilson, James, Q., (1995), The Moral Sense, The Free Press, N.Y., London

Wolf, Alan Fred (1984), Star Wave, Macmillan Publishing Company, New York

Wrangham, Richard and Peterson, Dale (1996), Demonic Males, Mariner Books, New York

Zukav, Gary (1989), The Seat of the Soul, Fireside Books, N.Y.

JUMP STARTING THE
INFINITE IN YOU

Now I'm going to speak directly to your higher nature. Your mind and your ASS may jibber with indignation but we are going to by-pass these filters and speak directly to *you*. Let's make a metaphysical and inferential jump and say that the non-local actions and thoughts of a Superluminal Being must have one nature, since there is no potential of any kind in the Superluminal. Let's also speculate that God's thoughts/ actions cause quantum waves to collapse into particles in our space-time. If this is the case, we would say that this God's thoughts about anything outside Himself would necessarily involve reflecting on something that *is not identically commensurate with His own non-local Being*. God, thinking His Eternal thoughts about us, cannot but help think about us in terms of the space-time that we are to inhabit. God thinks about us in context. Such Divine thoughts might be said to precipitate the very reality they consider! (Scholastic theologians knew this as *creation by approbation*.) Furthermore, such thoughts/actions would indelibly stamp something of their essence on everything, from the smallest particle to the farthest star. All actions would ultimately be linked to one monumental Act of Self-Knowledge, which you are metaphorically speaking, part of.

All of this is very hairy thinking but let us consider an analogy from computer software. An oblique but useful example of the incompatibility between God's thoughts and three and four-dimensional space might be the experience you may have had of trying to read a document that was formatted in the latest word processing software with software that was released three years ago—it usually can't be done. The higher release can read the lower release but not vice versa. Actions in a higher dimension can come down to the lower dimension but actions from a lower dimension cannot access the higher dimension without some sort of superluminal intervention.

What we have here is the vast and peculiar chasm that seems to separate the Divine from humanity. God can't communicate with us unless He mocks up some sort of intermediate software to bridge the gap between higher and lower dimensional space. In my opinion, miracles and religion are a product of just such dimensionally intermediate software. We need to be constantly aware that God has new releases of His software for us at all times but that we have to make an effort to subscribe to the new releases. This is what genuine spirituality is all about. The only reason that the Divine seems so remote is that we keep trying to communicate with Him using all the wrong technology. God is not only behind us, in terms of a superluminal and cognitive transformation of matter, time and space, He is ahead of us as part of that same superluminal cognition and transformation of all that can ever be. The future belongs to the Divine. This *Law of the Return*—of the all back to the All (or of God understanding Himself outside of Himself, as presented by the nineteenth century, German philosopher Hegel) is as old as human history but it makes sense as never before when considered in the light of the discoveries of modern physics.

GOD, THE ULTIMATE GENDER BENDER

There is nothing intrinsically wrong with old spiritual software—some of it is the foundation of the new but trying to use old software with the latest hardware is just not the way to go. One is reminded of Jesus' admonition to not put new wine into old wineskins. The teachings of Christianity on the Trinity, likewise, are given extraordinary new meaning when considered in the light of superluminal energy dynamics. The Christian teaching that the Son of Man shares the same One Divine nature as the Father, and *assumed* a human nature is simply another way of saying that the Divine knows Himself in different multi-dimensional ways. He knows himself, in all the ways that He might be imitated, as both Son and creation. This is one entire order of dimensionality. He also knows Himself, as He is in Himself as Father, and He knows Himself in eternal fecundity as *Herself*. The perpetual attraction of man to woman and vice versa is mirrored, from a Christian perspective, in the love that the Trinity has for itself. This attraction might also be thought of from an Eastern perspective, as participating in the original Yin and Yang that originates from a formless source of origin.

We might also want to ask ourselves how there could be a Divine Son without both a Divine Father and a Divine Mother. The increasing role of Mary in Catholic theology and in visions worldwide suggests that the Mother of God may herself have a superluminal relationship with the Divinity that we do not yet fully understand and that has not yet been revealed. I am not suggesting that Mary is an incarnation of the Holy Spirit, as we presently understand incarnation. The Incarnation is not, as we might think, the end of the line in the relationship between God and humanity; what Mary may be is probably something entirely outside the realm of anything that is theologically familiar to us. I suspect that she is a multi-dimensional bearer of the Holy Spirit in some way that is analogously commensurate with the significance of the Incarnation but yet completely different. Here words fail me. There may also be some way in which God knows Himself as an *Itself* and this would play to an entirely different spiritual tradition.

Nonetheless, the "let *us* make man in *our* image, in the likeness of *ourselves*" of Genesis (Chapter I, verse 26) can only mean by derivation that man and woman are made in the likeness of God. If only man and not woman is made in the likeness of God, then we would have to ask ourselves in whose image is woman made? Clearly woman is not made derivatively in the likeness of man, despite the rather obvious and patronizing cultural attempt to deliberately attribute a lower female lineage with the image of her being made from the rib of Adam while he slept. A more enlightened interpretation of Genesis would indicate that both sexes are made in *Their* image. One can almost imagine the author(s) of Genesis saying to themselves, "but they can't be the same as us, let's clarify Yahweh's teaching because that can't possibly be right." You see the same mentality at work on the teachings of Jesus in the New Testament—"he can't possibly have meant what he just said, I think it means…"

On the basis of equivalent origin and only on this basis can we reconstruct the equality of the sexes and assign human and social duties based on ontological characteristics, rather than on psychosocial and wishful thinking. The fecundity of woman is rooted in God's own knowledge of Himself, *as Herself* and the respect that we must have for women is rooted in the same respect that we must have for ourselves. We are of Divine origin and both religion and scientific materialism, each masquerading as the one true science of Being, have done an extraordinary dance around their own fundaments, when it comes to honestly reflecting on the meaning of the data they have in hand.

BIG ASSES ARE A PROBLEM

Hegel described human history as an evolutionary relationship with the peculiar sounding trinity of the *In-Itself* of Being, the *For-Itself* of Being and the new synthesis of Itself, through the *dialectic* of history, in *Being In and For Itself*. Hegel, unfortunately, never had the advantage of modern physics or a scholastic religious tradition, to fully critique and develop his own intuitions in a more enlightened context. One senses in Hegel a vast darkness, a God who is more akin to the process of cosmic digestion, than a Being of radiant consciousness.

There have been many other philosophers and physicists who have tried to grasp the idea of energy and God by the ears, and attempted to account for the entire process of creation in terms of a cosmology that is not dependent on a conscious God. It is no accident that the Marxist disciples of Hegel took the road to an unconscious God. The vast human ruin and concomitant destruction and violence attributed to Communism, itself an Hegelian derived philosophy, show the danger of considering the Superluminal as lacking consciousness. If God is in this sense dead, then indeed, whatever surgery[42] is performed on the body of history—no matter how violent or shameful, can be justified.

No matter how noble the appearance of a philosophical enterprise, human beings must be constantly vigilant for the intrusions of the ASS into their thinking patterns. When the Appetite Survival System gets a hold of philosophy, philosophy ceases to be philosophy and becomes a mouthpiece for the unspeakable. Who could have listened to Stalin, Chairman Mao or Hitler at the height of their power and not have felt revulsion for who and what they had allowed themselves to become? They were, in fact, supreme ASSES.

THE PECER TEST

YOUR PERSONAL ENERGY CONSCIOUSNESS EQUIVALENCY RATIO (PECER) measures the Chi available to your psyche, i.e., energy that has either not been cathected or used up by other activity. The higher the score, the harder your virtue. Scoring is based on the hypothesis that there are four basic levels of Chi: (4) High, (3) Medium, (2) Low and (1) Running on Empty. Scoring is calculated using this four point system with four being the highest score and one being the lowest. Immoral activity in general consumes large quantities of Chi and will usually result in low scores. Higher scores reflect conservation of Chi and generally are indicative of virtuous activity. The PECER Test is a kind of rough measuring instrument that gives you an overall idea of how your Chi is being apportioned. (A sophisticated dong-o-meter to measure the Chi that is actually used by your dick would be most helpful but unfortunately such an instrument does not yet exist.)

This is not a psychological test. Do not confuse the results of this test with any sort of psychological profile. This test is profiling energy levels that professional psychologists are not able to evaluate. Such professionals may wish to test themselves, however, and come to their own conclusions.

Now, turn to the next page and begin The PECER Test!

BEGIN THE PECER TEST HERE

Circle the number to the right of the answer that most clearly applies to you. Positive questions (e.g. question 1) earn points from high (4) to low (1); negative questions (e.g. question 5) earn points from low (1) to high (4). Positive actions earn more points than negative actions. High scores indicate energy well used and low scores indicate energy misuse.

1. How often do you feel creative?
   Frequently (4)   Sometimes (3)   Rarely (2)   Never (1)

2. How often do you perform acts of kindness or courtesy?
   Frequently (4)   Sometimes (3)   Rarely (2)   Never (1)

3. How often do you masturbate?
   Frequently (1)   Sometimes (2)   Rarely (3)   Never (4)

4. How often are you happy?
   Frequently (4)   Sometimes (3)   Rarely (2)   Never (1)

5. How often do you overeat?
   Frequently (1)   Sometimes (2)   Rarely (3)   Never (4)

6. How often do you talk about people behind their backs?
   Frequently (1)   Sometimes (2)   Rarely (3)   Never (4)

7. How often do you feel hatred towards anyone? (To be distinguished from hating how someone behaves.)
   Frequently (1)   Sometimes (2)   Rarely (3)   Never (4)

8. How often do you get into fights just for the fun of it?
   Frequently (1)   Sometimes (2)   Rarely (3)   Never (4)

9. How often do you get into fights to help a stranger or to stop an act of vandalism or rude behavior?
   Frequently (4)   Sometimes (3)   Rarely (2)   Never (1)

10. How often do you curse?
    Frequently (1)   Sometimes (2)   Rarely (3)   Never (4)

11. How often do you lie?
    Frequently (1)   Sometimes (2)   Rarely (3)   Never (4)

12. How often do you take credit for other peoples' work?
    Frequently (1)   Sometimes (2)   Rarely (3)   Never (4)

13. How often do you steal?
    Frequently (1)   Sometimes (2)   Rarely (3)   Never (4)

14. If you have murdered, raped, or tortured an innocent person, and are not ashamed of your actions YOUR SCORE IS 26. Disregard your cumulative score. Write your score in the margin next to this question. This is your final score. Pray for help or seek assistance.

15. How often do you smoke?
    Frequently (1)   Sometimes (2)   Rarely (3)   Never (4)

16. How often do you exercise?
    Frequently (4)   Sometimes (3)   Rarely (2)   Never (1)

17. How often do you have sex outside of marriage?
    Frequently (1)   Sometimes (2)   Rarely (3)   Never (4)

18. How often do you honor your appointments, commitments, promises and contractual obligations?
    Frequently (4)   Sometimes (3)   Rarely (2)   Never (1)

19. How often do you take care of relatives and friends including your parents?
    Frequently (4)   Sometimes (3)   Rarely (2)   Never (1)

20. How often are you courteous to those who are physically challenged or old?
    Frequently (4)   Sometimes (3)   Rarely (2)   Never (1)

21. How often are you intolerant of other's beliefs or customs?
    Frequently (1)   Sometimes (2)   Rarely (3)   Never (4)

22. How often do you apologize when you make a mistake?
    Frequently (4)   Sometimes (3)   Rarely (2)   Never (1)

23. How often do you take illegal drugs?
    Frequently (1)   Sometimes (2)   Rarely (3)   Never (4)

24. How often do you give money to those in need?
    Frequently (4)   Sometimes (3)   Rarely (2)   Never (1)

25. How often do you get intoxicated with alcoholic beverages?
    Frequently (1)   Sometimes (2)   Rarely (3)   Never (4)

26. How often do you seriously think about having sex with someone
    besides your significant other? (Having a passing fantasy that you
    do not engage does not affect your score.)
    Frequently (1)   Sometimes (2)   Rarely (3)   Never (4)

The PECER Test is based on a series of twenty-six carefully formulated
questions. Add your scores by totaling the numbers that you circled.

1. If your score is twenty-six to fifty-one, you have a serious
   Management problem. Your soul may be running on empty!

2. If your score is fifty-two to sixty-seven you are in need of
   Management.

3. A score of sixty-eight to seventy-eight qualifies you as a
   practitioner of Management.

4. A score of seventy-eight and above indicates a very high level of
   Management.

The following descriptive analysis may be more helpful in evaluating your
score:

1. If your score was twenty-six to fifty-one your soul is running on
   empty and there is a good chance that you may be an ASSHOLE.

2. If your score was fifty-two to sixty seven your Management skills
   need serious work. You may be a LOSER.

3. If your score was sixty-eight to seventy-eight you are working within acceptable moral parameters and are probably a GENTLE-MAN or a GENTLEWOMAN.

4. A score of seventy-eight and above indicates a high level of virtue. You may be a PRINCE OR A QUEEN.

Remember, on this test, a score below sixty-eight indicates energy deficits. You may be surprised by your total. The Psychic Energy Consciousness Equivalency Ratio or PECER shows how much of your allotted psychic energy (think Chi!) has been converted to consciousness, and how much to drive or appetite. Energy converted towards consciousness is useful and tends to produce a feeling of well being. Build up your PECER strength with virtue! Energy connected to drive is quickly consumed.

On-line test forms are available at www.dickmanagement.com and additional copies of *How to Manage Your DICK* may be ordered by calling 1-800-841-2665.

THE GANDHI-HITLER INDEX

THE GANDHI-HITLER INDEX IS USEFUL FOR PINPOINTING SERIOUS Management problems that may erupt into a totalitarian consciousness. The Hitler entity is a level of ego and ASS-dominated consciousness that is best exemplified, but by no means exhausted, by Adolph Hitler. The Hitler entity is best thought of as a metaphor for biological possession of an individual by the appetites. Others may want to call this demonic possession but the results are the same. If thinking of yourself as Hitler makes you uncomfortable, think about how others may experience you. You may want to imagine yourself as Caligula, Stalin, Charles Manson or Pol Pot—whatever works best for you. The Gandhi aspect of this test measures your movement in the positive direction of Dick Management.

If your answer is yes to any of these questions, circle yes or the number one (1). If your answer is no, circle the zero (0).

This is not a psychological test. Do not confuse the results of this test with any sort of psychological profile. This test is profiling energy levels that professional psychologists are not able to evaluate. Such professionals may wish to test themselves, however, and come to their own conclusions.

Go to the next page and answer the questions on the GANDHI-HITLER INDEX.

Begin Answering The Questions on the GANDHI-HITLER INDEX

1. Do you sometimes scream at people?
   Yes (1)   No (0)

2. Do you enjoy beating others?
   Yes (1)   No (0)

3. Is torturing animals fun for you?
   Yes (1)   No (0)

4. Do you enjoy making people squirm?
   Yes (1)   No (0)

5. Do you prefer pornography or masturbation to normal sex?
   Yes (1)   No (0)

6. Is it very difficult for you to apologize?
   Yes (1)   No (0)

7. Do you like anal sex more than regular sex?
   Yes (1)   No (0)

8. Do you ask your girlfriend or wife to use abortion as a form of birth control?
   Yes (1)   No (0)

9. Do you beat off more than several times a week on a regular basis?
   Yes (1)   No (0)

10. Do you belong to a gang?
    Yes (1)   No (0)

11. Do you make graffiti?
    Yes (1)   No (0)

12. Do you steal cars?
    Yes (1)   No (0)

13. Does rape interest you?
    Yes (1)   No (0)

14. Do you prefer a mess to neatness?
    Yes (1)   No (0)

15. Do like to touch corpses?
    Yes (1)   No (0)

16. Do you like to watch scenes of rape or violence?
    Yes (1)   No (0)

17. Do you enjoy not washing your hands after you go to the bathroom?
    Yes (1)   No (0)

18. Does the sight of blood make your Dick hard?
    Yes (1)   No (0)

19. Are you envious on a daily basis?
    Yes (1)   No (0)

20. Do you use drugs and alcohol on a daily basis?
    Yes (1)   No (0)

Total your scores by adding the numbers to the right of the answer you circled. If you score five and below, you are no Hitler. A score of six to ten indicates a problem, and a score of eleven to twenty indicates a demonic infestation of consciousness by the appetites.

The PECER Test and the GANDHI-HITLER INDEX might be considered as screening devices for public officials, hospital workers, police, day care workers and social workers. Forms for the test are available at the back of the book. Put one on your boss, colleague's or teacher's desk.

• Feel free to copy these test forms and place them on the desks of those who may be libidinally challenged.

• On-line test forms are available at www.dickmanagement.com and additional copies of *How to Manage Your DICK* may be ordered by calling 1-800-841-2665.

END NOTES

[1] Wrangham, Richard and Peterson, Dale (1996), *Demonic Males*, Mariner Books, New York

[2] Those males who get to mate with more females by killing other competing males and successfully defending territories against predators (while producing progeny) are the ones whose genes and secondary sexual characteristics survive in their descendents. If this form of Natural Selection is true, and as Wrangham and Peterson note, we may have millions of years of violent behavior backing up our genes. (Wrangham, Richard and Peterson, Dale (1996), *Demonic Males*, Mariner Books, New York)

[3] Wetherill, Richard (1906-1989), Alpha Publishing House, Wetherill Enterprises

[4] Wilbur, Ken (1996), *A Brief History of Everything*, Shambhala, Boston

[5] Reuters News based on a ten year experiment of 54 international scientists at Fermilab's Tevatron accelerator in Chicago.

[6] This experiment has been duplicated in research labs around the world.

[7] Howard Bloom discusses vitalism and the determinism exercised by the selfish gene in his excellent book, *Global Brain: The Evolution of Mass Mind from the Big Bang to the 21st Century.*

[8] Cytowic, Richard, MD, 1993, *The Man Who Tasted Shapes*, page 146, Warner Books, Los Angeles, California

[9] L. Ron Hubbard refers to this as *reactive mind* in his well-known book *Dianetics* (1992, Bridge Publications, Los Angeles). Reactive mind produces what he calls Engrams, which sometimes function as mental blocks that inhibit clarity of thought and action.

[10] Freud, Sigmund, 1949, *An Outline of Psycho-Analysis*, page 12, The Norton Library, New York

[11] Aristotle defines virtue as, "a state apt to exercise deliberate choice, being in the relative mean, determined by reason, and as the man of practical wisdom would determine." He has been criticized by Christian apologists for not getting at the heroic aspect of virtue. If every choice were based on a mean,

then those men of virtue would be able to enjoy a modest level of vice. Indeed, Augustine and others labeled the virtues of the pagans as "splendid vices." There is certainly some truth to this view but would you rather have men and women with splendid vices or grotesque vices? A more complete definition of virtue might be " a state apt to exercise deliberate choice being in a mean relative to both God and man, determined by reason, and as the man or woman of practical wisdom would determine."

[12] Wilhelmsen, Frederick, 1970-1974, Lectures at the University of Dallas, Irving Texas

[13] O'Reilly, Sean MD, *Discourses and Notes*

[14] Epistemology is the metaphysical science of how human beings can know reality.

[15] The Atlantic Monthly, December 2000, *A New Way to Be Mad*, Carl Elliott, pgs. 73-83

[16] This concept was popularly developed in a book called *Flatland: A Romance in Many Dimensions* by Edwin A. Abbott

[17] Kaku, Michio (1994), *Hyperspace*, Oxford University Press, N.Y., Oxford

[18] Ibid

[19] *Webster's New Collegiate Dictionary*, 1975, G&C Merriam Co., page 944, Philippines copyright

[20] Ibid

[21] Mitchell, Edgar, Dr., 1996, *The Way of the Explorer*, page 109, G.P. Putnam & Sons, New York, NY

[22] For an excellent discussion of carrier waves see Fred Alan Wolfe's complex, but rewarding book, *Star Wave*. (Wolf, Alan Fred (1984), Star Wave, Macmillan Publishing Company, New York)

[23] It is my understanding that physicist Jack Sarfatti has also developed this concept. As of this writing, I have not yet had the privilege of reading any of his books.

[24] Friedman, Norman, *The Hidden Domain,* 1997, The Woodbridge Group, Eugene Oregon

[25] Ibid, Endnote twenty-one

[26] Aquinas, Thomas, *Summa Theologica*

[27] Aurobindo, Sri, *The Life Divine*

[28] Wilhelmsen, Frederick, (1970) *The Paradoxical Structure of Existence*, University of Dallas Press, Irving Texas. Pg. 150

[29] Candace Pert discusses cyber studies in medicine in her groundbreaking book, *The Molecules of Emotion: Why You Feel The Way You Feel*, (1997) Scribner, New York, N.Y.

[30] Kaku, Michio (1994), *Hyperspace*, Oxford University Press, N.Y., Oxford

[31] Wolf, Alan Fred (1984) *Star Wave,* page 272, Macmillan Publishing Company, New York. Fred Alan Wolf appears to have invented this term or coined its usage in this book. Quantum Psychodynamics for Wolfe is related to another concept that he calls the *morpheme*, or smallest unit of speech. Wolfe takes the notion of quantum psychodynamics and applies it to the parallel universe theory in vogue in some scientific circles. Both the idea of dimensionally interactive cyber-kinesis and the idea of parallel universes are scratching at a new metaphysic or quantum model to account for human consciousness. The former goes the way of metaphysics and theology, the latter in the direction of materialism and further scientific reductionism.

[32] Cytowic, Richard, MD, 1993, *The Man Who Tasted Shapes*, page 146, Warner Books, Los Angeles, California

[33] Freud, Sigmund, 1962, *The Ego and the Id*, page 20, The Norton Library, New York

[34] Rhodes, Richard 1999, *Why They Kill: The Discoveries of a Maverick Criminologist*, Alfred Knopf New York, NY. Page 79

[35] Reingold, Howard, (1988) *They Have a Word for It: A Lighthearted Lexicon of Untranslatable Words and Phrases*, Sarabande books, Louisville, Kentucky. Page 200

[36] Rhodes, Richard 1999, *Why They Kill: The Discoveries of a Maverick Criminologist*, Alfred Knopf, NY

[37] Targ Russell and Katra Jane, 1998, *Miracles of Mind*, New World Library, Novato California

[38] National Institute of Justice, ACCN: 105053

[39] Das, Surya Lama, 1997, *Awakening the Buddha Within*, Broadway Books, a division of Bantam Doubleday Dell Publishing Group, Inc. New York, NY

[40] The Boston Globe, Richard Saltus, *Children Mimic TV Sex and Violence*...March 26, 2001

[41] As reported in academic circles in the 1970's at George Washington University, Washington, D.C.

[42] I believe this phrase originated with the philosopher Eric Voegelin who wrote *Science, Politics and Gnosticism*